W9-AWA-835

# A Six-Month Bestseller

This is the complete text of Walter Stewart's superb critique of the Trudeau regime, the most important book on Canadian politics since *Renegade in Power*.

Stewart probes every area of the government's performance and analyzes the uniqueness of the Trudeau style, with which the Prime Minister exercises mastery over his party and the media.

Taking us into the inner circles of power, Stewart identifies the "Supergroup", the hand-picked advisers who help Trudeau run the country. With a wealth of anecdote he describes how these men have taken over the reins of government, insulating the Prime Minister from public opinion and wresting decision-making power from Parliament and Cabinet.

One of Canada's outstanding journalists, Walter Stewart has worked for *Star Weekly, Maclean's* and *The Toronto Star*. For the critics' reaction to *Shrug*, see back cover.

# SHRUG
# Trudeau
# in Power

WALTER STEWART

*new press*

TORONTO

Copyright © 1971 by Walter Stewart. All
rights reserved. The reproduction or
transmission of all or part of this book by
any means whatsoever, including
photocopying or any other means of
electronic or mechanical process, or
storage or retrieval by information
systems, is forbidden without permission
of the author, except for brief quotations
for review purposes only.

DESIGN / PETER MAHER

Paperback edition published 1972

ISBN 0-88770-081-0

*new press*
Order Department
553 Richmond Street West
Toronto 133, Ontario

Manufactured in Canada
Typeset by Bookprint-Rapide, Kingston
Printed by Web Offset Publications, Toronto

*For my wife, Joan*

# Acknowledgments

Much of the material in this book was researched in preparation for articles that appeared in the *Star Weekly* and *Maclean's* Magazine. (In some cases I have used wording parallel to that which appeared in *Maclean's* articles.) I here acknowledge with gratitude the aid of the editors of those publications. Chapter 10, which concerns the resignation of Eric Kierans from the federal cabinet, appears in a form very similar to an article published in the July 1971 issue of *Maclean's*, and I am grateful to the magazine's editor, Peter C. Newman, for permission to use it here.

W.S.
*Sturgeon Point, Ontario*
*August 1971*

# Contents

# 1

## The Man and the Leader: The Single-handed Catapult

*It was as if Canada had come of age, as if he himself singlehandedly would catapult the country into the brilliant sunshine of the late 20th century from the stagnant swamp of traditionalism and mediocrity in which Canadian politics had been bogged down for years.*
The London *Spectator*, June 1968

It hasn't worked out quite the way the London *Spectator* saw it. Prime Minister Pierre Trudeau has not, in fact, hurled us into sunshine and, in fairness, he never said he would. It was always the acolytes, the hangers-on, the supposedly impartial observers who promised miracles from Canada's fifteenth Prime Minister. He himself promised little in concrete terms, which is just what he has delivered. His administration has been more conservative, in light of the problems it faces, than any since that of William Lyon Mackenzie King, and less successful, in terms of the mandate it received, than its much-harried, much-abused predecessor, led by Lester B. Pearson. From the day Trudeau bounced into power (he came, in Gordon Donaldson's graphic phrase, "like a stone through a stained-glass window"), this nation has known that it is in the hands of a strong and resolute man: but not in the hands of an effective leader. We cried out for an end to the evasions, the temporising, and the time- and energy-wasting scuffles of the Pearson and Diefenbaker eras. The evasions and scuffles have been ended; in their place we have had confrontation, division, autocracy and the beginnings of the end of parliamentary democracy.

Trudeau promised — and this he *did* promise — a way out, a new politics, a Just Society. He promised "the creative use of the law", "an attack on the problem of regional disparities", "the pursuit of a prosperous economy as well as the fair distribution of its proceeds", "reform of Parliament", a "politics of participation" and "the maintenance of the integrity of Canada".[1]

With a new election in the offing, the time has come to measure Trudeau's performance against those general promises. I believe that when Canadians go to the polls, they will re-elect him and his Liberals with nearly as strong a majority as was bestowed in the 1968 election (155 Liberals were returned, seventy-two Conservatives, twenty-two New Democrats, fourteen Creditistes, and one Independent). That new victory will not be won because Trudeau has done well in office, but because of other factors, including his own strong image in an age that clamours for strong men, the lack of a viable alternative, and a general and lamentable ignorance about exactly what has happened to government in Canada since June 1968. I can do nothing about either of the first two phenomena. The nation as a whole is in the grip of personality politics, and the opposition parties are in the grip of internal convulsions that will not quiet for some time to come. But I can try to assess the Trudeau record by measuring it, not only against what was promised when the Prime Minister asked for his first mandate, but against the problems he faced and the opportunities he encountered in his first term of office.

I will argue that, under Trudeau, we are more than ever distant from anything that could be called a Just Society. The law has certainly been used creatively — to slam political malcontents into jail for actions that were not criminal when committed, and became so only retroactively. Regional disparities persist, and continue to grow; the economy is neither prosperous nor fairly distributed; Parliament has not been so much reformed as emasculated; the politics of participation has turned out to be, not to put too fine a point on the matter, a fraud; and Canada's unity has been maintained only at rifle point, while our economy and national integrity are still on the auction block to the United States.

Beyond these negative points is a positive evil. The Prime Minister has torn most of the decision-making power out of its normal resting places and lodged it with a small coterie of loyalists connected directly to himself — the Supergroup. This is a body made up of members of the Prime Minister's Office, some of the Privy Council secretariat, a selection of cabinet ministers, a scattering of senior bureaucrats, and a handful of outsiders. They are the advisors to the Prime Minister, the men who sit at the foot of the throne, and the links that bind them are toughness, discretion, loyalty and a zest for power. Canada has never known anything quite like the Supergroup, although the United States has, in the claques that always circle a president. Trudeau did not invent the instrument, not even in Canada; the complexity of modern government has brought more and more experts into the East Block office of the Prime Minister ever since the days of Louis St. Laurent. But he has speeded up its development, strengthened its membership, and flattened all opposition to its fiat across the land. With the aid of the Supergroup, the Prime Minister is well on the way to becoming what he has always said he never wanted to be — the President of Canada. Worse, he is permanently distorting the decision-making process within this nation, so that whoever comes after him, philosopher or fool, skilled politician or dangerous demagogue, will inherit an administrative machine of awesome power. That machine will free him from all those "countervailing forces" of which Trudeau speaks so highly, in the party, the cabinet, the civil service and the House of Commons. With the Supergroup, Trudeau has created an administration aiming for efficiency, but it is a kind of government that has little to do with parliamentary democracy as we have known it.

Well, I am not a slave of the past, but I prefer parliamentary democracy, with all its sloppiness, its tedium, even its name-calling, to the single-minded rule of an overbearing man, and that is the path down which we are being cake-walked today. Unless some of the power is wrested away from the Supergroup, the Prime Minister will soon live in that happiest of all political worlds, the one without an opposition. He will be more powerful than any American president. An American ruler, however strong his mandate, may be balked by Congress, and see his legislative programme dismantled. A Canadian prime minister, because he is theoretically responsible to the legislature, must be able to get his programmes enacted, or fall from power by a want-of-confidence vote in the House. He lives every day under the distant but real possibility of instant dismissal, which exerts a marvellously humbling influence. He must satisfy the legislature, as no American president must do;

he must answer its questions, soothe its fears and carry its members with him, as no American president must do. He is accountable, and it is that accountability, rather than any native Canadian sweetness imbibed with the mother's milk, that explains the saneness of Canadian administrations compared to their U.S. counterparts. An American leader may regret his Vietnams in the fullness of time, but a Canadian leader's judgments may be rubbed in his face any week-day afternoon at two o'clock, when the Question Period opens. Second thoughts are built right into the system.

Or at least they were: by his point-blank refusal to answer questions, by the iron discipline he has imposed on his cabinet and party, by a series of rule changes that have drastically weakened the opposition, Trudeau has made the legislature his tool, and not his master; he has by-passed the traditional day-to-day accountability and substituted an accountability that occurs only once in any four- or five-year period, at election time.

Government in Canada has been in the past a splintered and inefficient process, made up of a number of parts that fit together only rarely, and only after some jamming. Power has been divided half a dozen ways, among the professional politicians, the bureaucrats, the party workers and, yes, among the opposition parties, whose united rage could bring Parliament to a halt. It was always a sloppy way to do business, and the questions the Canadian people were called upon to decide were often ill-defined. If a truly bad bill came into Parliament, the parties to the left of Mr. Speaker could, by attacking a supply vote, blockade the government long enough to mobilize public support, and if that support was forthcoming, pressure on the government backbenchers mounted to the point where the administration was faced with a bleak choice — to recant, or quit — and almost inevitably recanted. That is what happened to Finance Minister Walter Gordon's budget in 1963. We have a long history of sloppy, raucous and successful dissent. And we had, however imperfectly, a form of participatory democracy that worked, by and large, marvellously well.

Trudeau has swept all that sloppiness aside. Supply can no longer be blockaded, and every piece of legislation, good or bad, is subject to a timetable. The general public has been given only one question to ponder, and that only once, and for the length of time it takes to mark a ballot at election time: do you like Me or Them?

Trudeau *is* the government; he is no longer the head of an administration, but its head, body and soul. When you mark an X beside the name of a Liberal MP, you are not voting for him at all, but for Trudeau. You must give him blanket authority or blanket condemnation. If you admire his foreign policy approach, but detest his economics, you cannot say so; he has removed all the channels of communication but one: the ballot.

It is all very neat, and neater still is the way in which the Prime Minister has turned the process into an exercise in "participatory democracy". If he will not answer the questions of the opposition, he will answer those of the television camera; he has gone over the head of Parliament, an institution for which he shows open contempt, to appeal directly to the people, snug in their living rooms. And they cannot talk back. He can tell them that the opposition is obstructionist, the bureaucracy backward, the cabinet united and the country marching ever onward and upward, and they can only shake their heads or nod. The cabinet has been muted by executive fiat — Trudeau has said in so many words that he would fire any minister who spoke out of turn; the opposition is invisible, by virtue of the fact that television, the crucial observer, is absent from Parliament (this is not Trudeau's fault, of course; he appears to lean towards television coverage of the House of Commons; but it is a key factor in the way we have been ruled by him); and the bureaucracy has been shattered, demoralized and superseded in the decision-making area by that counter-bureaucracy, the Supergroup.

What is more and what is worse, the new system of government is not even efficient. This administration's major moves have simply been implementations of decisions taken in the Pearson years, from the much-delayed Canada Development Corporation to the Regional Development Incentives Act. A review of foreign policy, which came to no discernible conclusions, took eighteen months to complete; so did a study of the Willard Report on Social Programmes, the main effect of which was to exorcise Deputy Health Minister Joseph Willard's key recommendation, for a guaranteed income. The tax reform bill that limped into Parliament this June was the badly mauled result of a proposal made by a royal commission appointed nearly a decade ago. The Indian Act, an urgent priority in Pearson's time, has yet to see the light of day, and Revenue Minister Herb Gray's review of foreign ownership of the economy was bogged down somewhere in the cabinet for more than six months. It is not even easy to get a letter out of this government, as I know from personal experience. I wrote the Prime Minister in February 1969, on behalf of a charitable organization, asking for an early reply to a request. Thirty months later I had received no reply, although I know the letter arrived, because I delivered it by hand.

Anyone who has come this far without clapping shut the book will know that I do not like the Trudeau government, and that my judgment of its performance is opinionated. (I do not hold with the myth of the impartial observer; you cannot watch government as closely as I have over the past eight years and remain a detached outsider unless you are a political eunuch, and no eunuch is a trustworthy guide to the ultimate mysteries.) You are entitled to know my bias.

The only political party I have ever belonged to is the New Democratic Party, which I joined when it was formed. For a brief time in 1962 I was the editor of the *New Democrat*, the Ontario party organ. My parents were supporters of the Co-operative Commonwealth Federation (predecessor of the NDP), and my mother was the Ontario secretary for the CCF and later the NDP, while my father was once national president of the CCF. I don't know whether I am NDP today or not. Probably so. Like many members of that party, I am much confused by arguments over democratic socialism, and having studied that phrase for about thirty years, I still don't know what it means. I suppose it means the strong and planned intervention of the government in the economy, and I am, theoretically, in favour of that. I say "theoretically" because my observation of the strong and planned intervention of the state in some areas of Canada — particularly in the far north — has not convinced me that government, by definition, knows better or does better than private enterprise. Anyone who has watched the operation of government departments in small settlements across the north can testify that, from a standing start, the average bureaucrat can do as effective a job of sapping initiative, crushing enterprise and destroying dignity as any tycoon who ever spat a cigar.

My uncertain loyalties are compounded by the fact that many of my favourite politicians are Tories. I prefer Robert Stanfield to Pierre Trudeau, Jed Baldwin to Stanley Knowles, Dalton Camp to Ed Broadbent, and if I had to pick the best MP in Canada, I would name Gordon Fairweather, the Conservative member for Fundy-Royal, New Brunswick. I have never been fond of the Liberals, who always seemed to combine wishy-washy policies with arrogant attitudes, yet two of the politicians of whom I have written my most extravagant praise have been Liberals — Guy Favreau and Eric Kierans, both of whom, incidentally, were badly treated by their party.

That is all you need to know about my bias. It is not so much pro- as anti-; in that I am a typical Canadian.

You are also entitled to know how I viewed Trudeau when he came onto the political scene, and whether I was looking for fault to find. I always found him arrogant and snide; I thought, and wrote, that the Divorce Bill which won him such acclaim as Justice Minister was a weak and cynical piece of legislation, which by-passed the chance to make real reforms and clung to the archaic and pointless adversary theory of marriage, which assigns, for each divorce, a villain and a victim. I found him personally attractive, as everyone does, but I mistrusted the personality cult, which he assiduously disowned and just as assiduously cultivated during 1967 and 1968. (Trudeau's capers, from the girls he kissed to the clothes he wore, were always calculated for effect. He was always careful of the reporters to whom he gave interviews. One of the first experts he consulted when he ran for the leadership was communication specialist Marshall McLuhan.) I approved his strong federalism, but I was made uneasy by the fact that every French-Canadian commentator whose judgment I valued argued that it was simply not acceptable in Quebec. In my writings before and during the Trudeau rush to power, I said he would involve more people in politics, and I was wrong about that — the new involvement scarcely survived the leadership race, the new concern of youth was a global, not a Canadian, phenomenon; I thought he would bring new life to Ottawa as a capital city — Camelot North was the phrase in vogue — and I was wrong about that; I thought he would make government more responsive to the people, and I was off the mark there; but I did see him, as did some others, as essentially autocratic and conservative, and he has made me a prophet today. And I was sure he would never marry.

What made me uneasy about Trudeau in 1967 and 1968 was his background, which seemed to shape him superbly for the contest for power, and disqualify him uniquely from its successful exercise. Consider that background.[2]

Joseph Pierre Yves Elliote Trudeau was born on October 18, 1919, to Grace Elliott, of Scots United-Empire-Loyalist descent, and Charles-Emile Trudeau, a Montreal lawyer and businessman whose roots were firmly French-Canadian. Our Prime Minister was born rich. Charles-Emile Trudeau had developed a chain of gas stations on Montreal Island, which he sold to Imperial Oil for $1,400,000. The proceeds were invested shrewdly in stocks and real estate, and built a fortune estimated today at $16 million. The Prime Minister-to-be never knew want or poverty or failure. Every morning he was sped to school from his home on McCulloch Avenue in Outremont, above the city and the slums, in a chauffeur-driven limousine, and every evening he was sped home again. He ran with a crowd known as Les Snobs.

Pierre, the elder son (he has an older sister, Suzette, who ratted on him when he gave his age as forty-seven instead of forty-nine during the Liberal leadership race, and a younger brother, Charles) became a strong figure in the family with the death of his father when he was fifteen-and-a-half. He became used, early in life, to getting his way. He attended an exclusive private school, the Jesuit-run Brébeuf College, where he was known for his brilliance and intractability, and where he learned the debating techniques and ordered logic that cut so swiftly through theoretical arguments and blunt themselves so swiftly on the soft, sloppy mass of real life. Brébeuf was divided into boarders and day-boys; Trudeau was in the second group along with most of the children of the wealthy families of Outremont. As remembered by his classmates, he was clever, clannish, arrogant and unpopular at school, a superb athlete who refused to join any team sports, an outstanding scholar who never had to work hard to succeed.

After graduating from Brébeuf, he went to the University of Montreal, from 1940 until 1943. He divided his attention among the study of law, zipping around Montreal on his Harley-Davidson motorbike, and campaigning against conscription. He worked for Jean Drapeau, now Mayor of Montreal and then an anti-conscriptionist candidate, in an Outremont by-election, and made a speech foreshadowing the exaggeration and hyperbole that have since become typical of him: "If we are no longer in a democracy," he shouted, "then let us begin the revolution without delay. The people are being asked to commit suicide. Citizens of Quebec, do not be content to complain. Enough of patchwork solutions, now is the time for cataclysms.''

Trudeau did not serve in the army during the war; he shared a disinclination widely held among French Canadians to fight yet another war for the sake of the English, and in fact was expelled from the Reserve Officer Training Corps (membership in which, plus his university enrolment, saved him from being conscripted) for insubordination. His anti-military stance took the form of riding around in a German uniform and wearing a fake Iron Cross, practical jokes of dubious taste.

After graduation in 1943 Trudeau articled with the Montreal law firm of Hyde and Ahern. (Not only was *its* name safely Anglo-Saxon, so was his own by now; he had taken to spelling ''Elliote'' as ''Elliott''.) He was called to the bar in 1944, but within the year was back at school, studying politics and economics at Harvard. From Harvard he went to Paris and l'Ecole des Sciences Politiques, where he decided he knew as much as most of the professors anyway, so he spent much of his time reading on his own and roaming the city. There, he renewed his acquaintance with an old friend from the University of Montreal, Gérard Pelletier, and the two of them discussed the idea of putting out an intellectual magazine together. In 1947 Trudeau switched schools again, entering the London School of Economics, where he took lectures from socialist Harold Laski, whose ideas, he said, influenced him greatly, although there is little trace of that today. Trudeau left school, theoretically to gather material for a Ph.D. that never got written, and went on a world tour that was to lead to many of the stories and many of the legends that later sprang up around his name. He went alone, travelling with a knapsack, shorts and an untidy beard. He wandered through Germany, using papers he had faked himself, and flew to Belgrade, in an attempt to get into Yugoslavia without a visa. He was jailed, then deported to Bulgaria, where he joined a group of Spanish-speaking Jewish refugees, with whom he rambled through Greece and Turkey. By later accounts he also swam the Bosphorus, which he remembers as cold, with ''a bloody strong current''. He wandered into Palestine and was arrested as an Israeli spy; he was released and began wandering again, only to be picked up by desert bandits, whom he frightened off by feigning madness. He wandered further, to India, where he was attacked by pirates while travelling in a sampan, and escaped in a providential fog. He visited the Khyber Pass during the India—Pakistan conflict, crossed Burma during a civil war, and, after visiting Vietnam, managed to get into China during the final throes of civil war there.

What he brought back from his world tour, besides a roll of anecdotes that continues to unwind, was self-sufficiency, highly-developed physical courage, and a profound distrust of the nationalist movements that seemed to be at the heart of the violence he had seen.

Back in Canada at the age of thirty, he was still far from ready to settle down. When his friend Gérard Pelletier went to cover a brutal strike at Asbestos, Quebec, for his newspaper *Le Devoir*, Trudeau went along, made stirring speeches to the workers, and met Jean Marchand, the strike leader. When the strike had been won, Trudeau drifted down to Ottawa, where he joined the Privy Council Office in a junior capacity. He worked at that from 1949 to 1951. At the same time, in 1950, he and Pelletier founded their much-contemplated intellectual magazine, *Cité Libre*, which pronounced in shrill tones and with awesome certainty on the issues of the day. *Cité Libre*, like Trudeau, reflected a strongly anti-nationalist bias. (In those days, as Claude Ryan, present editor of *Le Devoir*, has pointed out, Quebec nationalism was a technique by which the upper middle class kept firm control on the reins of government, and kept the autocratic Premier Maurice Duplessis firmly in power in the province. When a new, popular nationalism centred in the lower and lower middle classes sprang up under the leadership of men like René Lévesque, Trudeau reacted with exactly the same scorn and fury. He has never, apparently, apprehended the difference between the two.) But Trudeau was not a central figure in the battle against Duplessis; during most of the 1950s and early 60s he was, in his friend Jean Marchand's polite phrase, "underemployed". He travelled a good deal, taught some, wrote and dabbled in politics. He toured China twice, visited Russia and once set out, in 1961, to row to Cuba.

Back in Canada once more, he was invited, with Marchand and Pelletier (who had become considerable political figures, plugging away while Trudeau flitted), to join the Liberal party. The three men spurned the offer. They were supporting the NDP and, in the pages of *Cité Libre*, Trudeau poured terrible scorn on Prime Minister Pearson for accepting nuclear weapons for Canada, weapons that still nestle today where Pearson put them, atop Bomarc missiles at Canadian sites. (Trudeau's article in the April 1963 edition of *Cité Libre* was called "The Abdication of the Spirit", and contained this passage: "I would have to point out in strongest terms the autocracy of the Liberal structure and the cowardice of its members. I have never seen in all my examination of politics so degrading a spectacle as that of all these Liberals turning their coats in unison with their Chief, when they saw a chance to take power. . . . The head of the troupe having shown the way, the rest followed with the elegance of animals heading for the trough.")

But in 1965 the Three Wise Men (as they came to be called) changed their minds and joined the Liberals after all. Nationalism, that dread disease, was sweeping Quebec, and there was no one in the federal Liberal party strong enough to turn it aside. It was Marchand, by then the province's dominant labour leader, whom the Liberals wanted, but Marchand would not come without his friends. Trudeau, the least known and least popular of the trio, was parachuted into a Montreal riding and began his spectacular ascent to power.

Immediately after the November 1965 election, he became parliamentary secretary to the Prime Minister so lately reviled; he performed adequately and, on April 4, 1967, moved up to become Minister of Justice. In that role he left most of the departmental work to the bureaucrats and did not even take much of a hand in the drafting of the new Divorce Reform Bill, introduced on December 5, 1967, a bill that ignored the broad recommendations of a Parliamentary committee and settled for a complicated system under which it still takes years to get a divorce on any grounds other than the traditional one of adultery, real or faked. (Consequently most divorces are still granted on those grounds.)

In this period Trudeau concentrated his concern on two subjects — battling with fellow Quebeckers over federalism, and reforming the antiquated Criminal Code. Beginning with a speech to the Canadian Bar Association in September 1967, Trudeau made himself the champion of a strong federalism and the enemy of any kind of special constitutional status for Quebec. He contended not only with provincial politicians like Quebec Premier Daniel Johnson and Quebec Liberal leader Jean Lesage, but with federal Liberals like Senator Maurice

Lamontagne. Immediately he was seen and embraced by English Canada as a hero. His Criminal Code reforms, like the Divorce Bill, were designed merely as timid forward steps in the reform of the law, but became illuminated by a single phrase thrown out at a press conference: "There's no place for the state in the bedrooms of the nation." It didn't mean much, but it did indicate a more modern attitude than that displayed by almost any other current politician. Afloat on a sea of favourable press clippings generated by his activities in these two limited areas, Trudeau was borne on, inevitably, it later seemed, to leadership of the Liberal party and the Prime Minister's post.

He owed much of his swift rise to two factors — a hunger among English Canadians for a strong man to "put Quebec in its place" and his discovery by the one medium to which he is perfectly suited — television.

TV is at once the most powerful and most deceptive of media, because it depends so much on the accident of appearances. It can make a wise man appear a fool, a bumpkin appear weighty; it may unmask one liar and transmit another as the very heart and soul of integrity. The results may have nothing to do with the real qualities of the man, only with his apparent qualities. Trudeau was quick, cool, detached, articulate, shrewd, a man whose drifting past seemed romantic, whose lack of involvement suited a nation sick to death of the screams and whines of its politicians. Above all, he *looked* superb; whatever quality it is that makes TV work for one man and not another, Trudeau had it. Gordon Donaldson, a television commentator and producer, described the phenomenon perfectly in his book, *Fifteen Men*:

I first met Trudeau in May, 1967, shortly after he became Minister of Justice. It was early in the morning in the West Block office with the secret stairway built by Mackenzie. I was producing a CBC *Newsmagazine* documentary on the new minister, with Norman DePoe as interviewer. We seldom devoted so much time to a fledgling cabinet minister, but this was said to be something special. Trudeau was brittle and uncomfortable — he admits he is not at his best in the mornings. I don't remember what he said because I was fascinated by the film possibilities of his face — the oriental serenity as he listened, fingertips together as in prayer; the graven elegance of the high cheekbones and the big nose; the

sudden animation, the deprecating smile and the depth of the
huge eyes. It should have been an ugly face — it was fur-
rowed and pockmarked — but the parts are masterfully assembled for the lens. From any angle it was alive and com-
pelling.

Graven elegance may not seem an essential quality for high
office but, combined with toughness and wit, it proved enough.
Trudeau's television appearance during the constitutional conference in early 1968, when he debated with Daniel Johnson
and made all the put-downs English Canada was longing to
hear, catapulted him into the first rank of contenders for Pearson's uncertain crown.

Then came the media build-up, the awestruck stories of his
judo prowess, his world travels, the time he threw a snowball at
a statue of Lenin in Moscow's Red Square (an endearing, if
dim-witted, feat), his reputation as a ladies' man, his uncon-
ventional dress. (One episode in July 1967, when he wore sandals and an ascot into the House of Commons and was rebuked
by John Diefenbaker, blossomed into a whole wardrobe of
anecdotes.) Trudeaumania, fanned by the press, inflamed by
the famous kissing episodes (as George Bain of the Toronto
*Globe and Mail* was later to write, "If it puckers, he's there")
spread across the land.

In retrospect, Trudeau's victory at the Liberal leadership convention in April 1968 seems pre-ordained, and so does his victory at the polls that June. It is carping, I know, to note that he
promised not to call a snap election and promptly did so. But
when it was all over, Canada had chosen as its prime minister
a man who, when you think about it, had never really held a
job.

His understanding of the political process was incomplete;
he had not so much run for office as had it thrust upon him,
both in the safe Montreal riding he represented and in the
leadership race. His work habits were uncertain, his stamina
small and his ego large. There had never been anything, ever,
that he really wanted that he couldn't get — or if there was, he
simply walked away and got something else. He had never been
seriously balked, had never had to explain himself, had never
had to suffer fools. He was an intellectual, full of certainty in
the most uncertain of callings, full of arrogance in the most de-

manding of posts, full of quick phrases and handy quotes in a nation that, if words could solve its problems, would have been wafted to Nirvana long ago.

His history shaped him as a single-minded man in a complex nation, an anti-nationalist in a country whose political independence threatens to crumble, an aloof and detached ruler in an age demanding involvement. He has never needed patience and, for want of it, he has turned to confrontation as his chief political technique, and confrontation is what his people can least afford.

Given his background, the wonder is not that Trudeau has done as badly as he has, but that he has not done worse. He is not, after all, a politician hammered into shape by the bruising and educating scramble up the rungs of power; he is a Montreal snob slung into governance of a nation that many other men have decided was ungovernable. I give him full marks, in the circumstances, for doing his best.

But measured against the goals Trudeau set himself, and against the normal standards of political judgment in Canada — his handling of legislation, the economy, politics, unity and national integrity — I think he has done a bad job, and should be replaced.

The rest of this book is devoted to explaining why.

## Notes

Because this does not attempt to be a scholarly work, I will not burden you much with footnotes. They are irritating, for one thing. For another, so much of this book is drawn from my own observations that the air of scholarly detachment imparted by footnotes would be misleading. In most cases, the references will be evident from the text; in some, the sources are confidential, and you will have to decide for yourself whether I am full of hay; in a few, where the source material is readily available for readers to check for themselves, I will give it.

1. *Towards a Just Society*, *1968-69* (Ottawa: Liberal Federation of Canada).

2. I have drawn biographical material on the Prime Minister from the *Parliamentary Guide*, my own observations, and five of the numerous books about him, all published in Toronto in 1968. The most complete account, if you can stand the awestruck tone, is Martin Sullivan's *Mandate '68* (Doubleday Canada). The others are *Journey to Power* by Donald Peacock (Ryerson), *This is Trudeau* by John D. Harbron (Longmans Canada), *Trudeau, A Man for Tomor-*

*row* by Douglas Stuebing, with John Marshall and Gary Oakes   15
(Clarke, Irwin) and Peter C. Newman's *The Distemper of Our
Times* (McClelland and Stewart).

# 2

# Legislation:
# Nobody Knows the Trouble
# I've Ducked

*The attainment of a just society is the cherished hope
of civilized men. While perhaps more difficult to
formulate for groups than for individuals, even the
members of majorities — political, religious,
linguistic or economic — must know what it is to
suffer injustice. My government is deeply concerned
to provide and to ensure increased justice, dignity and
recognition to the individual, particularly in an age
which is characterized by large governments,
industrial automation, social regimentation and old-
fashioned laws.*
Speech from the Throne, September 12, 1968

There is a man who lives, with his wife and three small children, in a car outside a small town in New Brunswick. Or he
did when I last saw him; God knows where he has gotten to
now. He works hard, when he can, but he is an ignorant man,
and sickly, and work is hard to find. He cannot get welfare because he cannot establish residence anywhere, living in a car as
he does. And he cannot afford a residence because he cannot
get welfare. It's kind of neat, when you think of it. His kids are
rather dirty, and pale, and cry a lot. His wife cries a lot too, and
complains. The man lifts his shoulders and shakes his head
when she complains; he doesn't know what to do; there is nothing he can do. He is about forty, but looks sixty. He does

not know that the Trudeau government is deeply concerned to provide him with increased justice, dignity and recognition.
He thinks he has a hell of a life, and it isn't going to get any bet-
ter, and he is right.

There is a woman who lives in Winnipeg, in a crumbling
slum, in a house that must hide, between its dank walls, at least
thirty people within five rooms. She has several children — I
couldn't make out how many in the hubbub — one of whom is
retarded, a drooling vegetable. The woman is on welfare. Her
husband worked; he had quite a good job as a mechanic, but
then Air Canada closed its overhaul base in Winnipeg, and he
was bumped out of his position by an Air Canada mechanic
with better qualifications and then, because of the anti-
inflation fight, jobs were hard to get. There was no point in going to the Department of Manpower for re-training; he *was*
trained, only he couldn't find work. They lost their house, the
one they were buying, and moved. They moved several times,
each time a little closer to the slums. Finally the man said to
hell with it, and took off. The woman knows where he is, but
that doesn't matter, because he is in another province where no
court order for support can reach him. So the woman is on welfare; she would not tell me to what extent. She is a thin woman,
and mostly beaten down, but when I asked her how much
money she had to live on every month, she told me it was none
of my goddamn business. She works, sometimes, as a pros-
titute, at $10 a trick in a motel nearby, though why anyone
would want that poor, frail, beaten woman I cannot guess. She
told me about the prostitution quite readily. Her increased dignity works only spasmodically, I guess.

There is a man, an Indian, who lives in a filthy shack not far
from the town of Whitehorse, in the Yukon. He has not held a
job as long as he can remember, not a steady one, and he is in
his forties. His father has not held a job either since he was a
young man, nor has his brother. His wife works, sometimes, as
a cleaning woman, but the work is hard, the pay poor, and she
is not a very good cleaning woman. She drinks a lot, for one
thing. For another, everything she earns is simply taken away
from the welfare. This Indian couple have children without
number: children who swarm through their fetid little hovel,
toddlers who grin and run to hide when they see a stranger;
children of six or seven or eight who ignore a visitor and sit
staring bug-eyed at a stove, where a nauseous mess that seems

to have a lot of rice in it, and some bits of bread, is boiling; teen-age children whose eyes contain a tough wariness, a sullen distemper that reminds me of a caged animal. On the back of the stove, leaning against the stove-pipe, stands a toilet seat. It is being kept warm. In the Yukon, the winter weather often gets to fifty below zero, and at that temperature squatting in an outhouse can be agony. So the toilet seat is heated and, when the time comes, whoever has to use the outhouse runs, with the warm toilet seat under his arm, and bangs it down, and squats and runs back to the shack again.

When I think of these people, and all the others I have seen, whose stories I have teased out of them in my line of work, when I think of the hundreds of thousands of Canadians mired in poverty, brutality, squalor and despair, I find it hard to accept the claim that the Trudeau government has hurled itself at the task of creating a Just Society, for I can find no trace in its legislative record of anything that touches the lives of these people in a meaningful way. Their numbers have, in fact, been swollen, first by the anti-inflation drive that froze new housing construction, then by the tight-money policies that threw more and more people from the submerged third of society out of work. We have had welfare legislation that tinkers and fiddles and adjusts old, out-moded legislation so as to turn it into new, out-moded legislation, we have had amendments and sub-amendments, and regulations and directives, but we have not had, not once, not anywhere, any impatience or urgency or thrust towards social or economic reform. We have not had any sign, ever, that the members of the Trudeau government have ever visited a slum, or been out of work, or know what it is to squat in an outhouse at fifty below waiting for the propitious moment, the right economic auguries and proper arrangement of stars that will permit the federal government to consider a proposal to undertake a study to put forward a plan to outline a possible future action to improve the lot of the poor.

No one expected the Trudeau government to solve poverty in Canada — not with a fifth of our people and nearly half our farm families below the poverty line laid down by the Economic Council of Canada. What we did expect, what we had a right to expect, what we were led to expect, was a real, concerted, concerned attack on poverty and inequality. We have not had that. An examination of this government's legislative record shows it to be almost barren of meaningful social legislation.

You needn't take my word for it. The Liberal party, always well organized, puts out a mimeographed memorandum called "Liberal Government Achievements", which includes a list of all the legislation passed since the brave words of the first Trudeau Throne Speech rolled into the somnolent hush of the Senate chamber in September 1968. It is, to the casual reader, an impressive list, all the way from C-2, An Act to Amend the Judges Act, through such nuggets as the Dominion Coal Board Dissolution Act (C-161), the Saltfish Act (C-175), down to that stand-out Senate bill, An Act to Repeal the Leprosy Act (S-7). There have been some sensible, worthwhile measures, which I'll discuss in a moment, but despite all the fanfare for a Just Society that preceded the Trudeau climb to the throne, despite the dashing to and fro of phalanxes of Trudeau aides, despite the disciplined muscularity of the Trudeau machine in the House of Commons, there has been precious little in the way of real government achievement. It is as if the Prime Minister embraced Michael Oakeshott's description of the ruling role, which is "to restrain, to deflate, to pacify and reconcile, not to stoke the fires of desire, but to damp them down".[1] It isn't so much that the Liberals since 1968 have succeeded in damping down the fires of desire, as that they have tried earnestly to do that, and apparently to do little else.

In the bad old days of the Pearson era, when we were, according to the mythology of the time, crippled by an inept minority government, when Parliament was wracked by dissension, name-calling and back-biting, and when the Prime Minister could be seen clinging to the lip of power by his fingernails, we witnessed the passage of more meaningful legislation in a two-and-a-half-year period than we have in the entire Trudeau era to date. The first, battered Pearson government passed a number of laws which, for better or worse, will shape this nation for decades to come. There was the adoption of a Canadian flag, creation of the Canada Pension Plan, establishment of the Economic Council of Canada, establishment (and the first report) of the Royal Commission on Bilingualism and Biculturalism, the Columbia River Treaty, armed forces unification, the Auto Trade Pact, legislation (forced through by that soon-disgraced nationalist, Walter Gordon) to protect Canadian financial institutions from foreign take-over, and a major break-through on the division of tax funds between the federal and provincial governments (what the French call *"l'op-ting-out"*).[2]

All of that was pushed through a Parliament which, we were told with some justice, was long-winded, contentious, antiquated and stupid, by a Prime Minister who seemed hesitant, indecisive and chronically disorganized, and whose major efforts were devoted to quieting down the scandals that rocked his regime. But the Trudeau government, with the majority Pearson only panted after, with layers of efficiency experts and a brutal, thrusting approach to Parliament, has given us little that is comparable in terms of fundamental impact on our lives. In fact, the most significant legislation passed has been the Public Order Act, an authoritarian law that had nothing to do with individual justice or dignity, much to do with repression.

Pearson, with all his weakness, gave us Medicare and a pension plan; Trudeau, with all his strength, has given us submachine guns and bread lines.

The positive legislation of the Trudeau years to date can be ticked off on six fingers: the Official Languages Act, regional development incentives, the bills enacting government re-organization, establishment of the Canada Development Corporation, new unemployment insurance legislation, and amendments to the Tax Act embodying the White Paper proposals.

Of these, the Official Languages Act is new, although an outgrowth of policies enunciated years ago; the Canada Development Corporation is a watered-down version of a Walter Gordon plan from the early 1960s; and the tax amendments are a betrayal of even the modest progress towards economic justice hinted at in the White Paper. (They are discussed more fully in Chapter 6.) The government re-organization acts — and there have been a number of them — are designed to improve, and do improve, the functioning of government, if not of Parliament. Only the unemployment insurance changes and the regional development acts can be called innovative and they are, with some minor criticisms, laws that any government should be proud to have on its record. (There have also been electoral reforms, reducing the voting age to eighteen, adding the party name to ballots and extending the system of advance polls. But they were so long overdue, and so woefully weak in attacking electioneering abuses through the disclosure of funds, that they cannot be compared with, say, the re-drawing of the electoral map during the Pearson era.)

The Official Languages Act was one of the early achievements of the new government, a long-overdue recognition, at
the federal level, of the dual nature of this country. The law de-
clares that English and French are the official languages of Canada and for all purposes of the Parliament and government of
Canada, and that they enjoy equal status. (The British North
America Act does not protect French language rights outside
Quebec, only the rights of religious groups.) Although it has
been represented, particularly in western Canada, as an act to
ram French down unwilling English and New-Canadian
throats, the Official Languages Act is nothing of the sort. It
provides that Canadians may approach their federal government in either French or English in a number of specific places:
in the new capital region of Ottawa and Hull, in federal head
offices and federal bilingual districts (a bilingual district is
defined as an area where the people who form the official-lan-
guage minority comprise at least 10 per cent of the total population) and, "to the extent feasible", in major centres outside
the bilingual districts where there is a significant demand.

The act brushes aside sensibilities in the west, where there
are few Canadians whose mother tongue is French, but many
who speak some other first language than English. "What
bloody sense does it make," complained a Ukrainian-Canadian
lawyer in Winnipeg, "if you have a community with a 12 per
cent French language group, 70 per cent Ukrainians, and the
rest English, and you tell them the two official languages are
French and English? They've got to learn English to get along,
and they've got to learn French, but they can't learn Ukrainian.
What bloody sense does that make?" In some parts of Canada,
perhaps it doesn't make too much sense, but in others it does.
The act does not provide, as this man, among others, insists,
that anyone has "got to" learn French; it simply raises French,
on the official level, to a higher status than any other language
except English: a minimal concession, in terms of Canada's history and traditions, which, had it been made a few decades ago,
might have eased some of the problems that haunt us today.

It is one of the ironies of our time that, when English Canada
finally got around to approving a bilingual policy, French Canada was losing its interest in the subject. "Every time I hear talk
about bilingualism," said a senior French-Canadian civil servant, "I know it's just another way to screw the French-Canadian."

Just the same, the act does make belated acknowledgment of the French fact in Canada, and is therefore worthwhile, although the way in which it has been interpreted leaves much to be desired. An Official Languages Commissioner was created, to whom complaints could be relayed. His staff have not always exercised discretion, or even common sense. There was, for instance, the case of the languages snoopers who approached Air Canada ticket salesmen, asking to be misinformed in the language of their choice, and who carried concealed tape-recorders to catch out unwary, non-bilingual clerks. The Languages Commissioner apologized when the facts of this incident came out.

The civil service interpretation of the act has been bizarre. Instead of striking out for equality, the act has been made the excuse for pro-French bigotry in the hiring and promoting of civil servants, which is not much superior to the pro-English bigotry of former years. The merit system, the alleged underpinning of the bureaucracy, has taken a battering in the scramble to promote bilingualism. And it has become apparent that in official Ottawa, bilingualism is an attribute of French Canadians who speak passable English. English Canadians whose working knowledge of French includes a bad accent are still subject to criticism and embarrassment which, if offered to a French Canadian, would lead to a nasty incident. They accept it meekly, perhaps in atonement for their years of putting down French Canadians, and take their revenge in circulating stories attacking the new policy. (Two examples follow, one true, one false. The true story concerns an inter-departmental meeting which dealt with Indian Affairs, and which began with the chairman announcing pontifically that "the language of this meeting will be the mother-tongue of your choice", at which a delighted Indian civil servant broke into a long string of Cree. The false story concerns a lifeguard at a national park who was called upon to save a drowning girl. "I'm sorry," he said, "but I can't swim." "Can't swim! My god, how did you get the job?" The lifeguard grinned. "Oh, that's easy. I'm bilingual.")

But these are complaints about the implementation of the act; its principle is a sound one, and this may, in the long run, prove to be the most important piece of legislation to the Trudeau government's name.

The legislation to encourage regional development — the second in my short list of positive achievements — was also long overdue, but has already had a significant impact. The first step was the establishment of a Department of Regional Economic Expansion, and the installation as its minister of Jean Marchand, whose appointment ensured a steady flow of funds. The department's first major act, the Regional Development Incentives Act, provides up to $12 million to private companies willing to set up new enterprises in designated areas — mainly in eastern Quebec and the Maritimes. Manufacturers can receive up to $30,000 for each new job created under the legislation, or one half the capital required, whichever is less. This legislation, introduced in May 1969, was followed by a more ambitious programme a year later, in which the department earmarked $200 million for spending over a two-year period in twenty-two special areas across eight provinces. (British Columbia and Prince Edward Island were left out, but PEI already had a $225 million agreement for special assistance from Ottawa.) The programme covers aid to the provinces for utilities and services in key areas, to make them more attractive to industry, and includes incentives to industry and special adjustment programmes, such as manpower retraining.

Provincial politicians argue that the same ends might have been met by returning a larger share of the tax take to the poorer provinces. In fact, that argument is put forward at every federal-provincial conference, but it is hard to see how a responsible federal government could pass out grants without retaining some control over the spending. When Ottawa undertakes to redistribute wealth among the provinces, it asks in effect that the richer areas — Ontario, British Columbia and Alberta — contribute to the poorer areas out of tax funds. However the scheme is worked out, whatever it is called, that is the net effect, whether it is done by giving New Brunswick a higher tax rebate or boosting Newfoundland's special payments. To turn a programme like the regional development scheme into a straight cash-payment plan, with no strings attached, would not only deprive the federal politicians of the kudos and votes they reap today, it would suggest that the have provinces make unconditional payments to the have-nots without the intervening authority or central control of the federal government. That is not likely, or feasible.

So the principle of the new legislation is a sound one, although its implementation has led to some anomalies. One is the curious way in which the cry for new industry and aid has met more positive response when it comes from areas inhabited by Liberals, particularly Liberal cabinet ministers, than elsewhere. In the single Newfoundland riding occupied by Transport Minister Donald Jamieson, for example, more than $14 million out of a $20 million grant found a happy home. The province's other, lamentably Tory, ridings shared the rest.[3]

Another anomaly arises from the fact that there is no provision that the new industries should be mainly, or even partially, Canadian-owned. The act puts us in the curious — though familiar — position of financing our own sell-out with cash gifts to the outsiders, particularly Americans, who will wind up siphoning off all the profits, and much of the resources. Thus, when an American firm was invited to set up a pulp and paper mill in northern Saskatchewan, it automatically became eligible for up to $12 million in federal grants, even though there was no perceptible need for the mill in light of declining world prices and markets for pulp. The president of a Canadian company, whose own mills were built without any government grants, waxed eloquent on the subject. "Already," he said, "the market is being flooded by pulp dumped there by mills that can't sell their product. Now we are going to have another one. What's more, I'm going to help pay for it through my taxes. It's going to create jobs in northern Saskatchewan, and unemployment in Hull. It's going to give millions of dollars away to somebody who doesn't even live here, doesn't give a sweet damn what happens to us."

The regional development programme, for all its failings, has created jobs, has poured money into economically depressed areas of the nation, and has established clearly the federal responsibility to treat regional disparities through the federal treasury — and for that, the Trudeau regime is entitled to take credit. But the gains laid down by this legislation have been more than wiped out by the anti-inflation war carried on doggedly since 1968, the chief effect of which has been to promote unemployment in the deprived regions of the country. (This war of attrition will be dealt with more fully in Chapter 5.) The jobless form 25 per cent of the working force in some Maritime towns, and along the Gaspé in Quebec there are villages where literally no one has a job. Layoffs always come first in the deprived regions, and they are the last to feel returning prosperity. The net effect of the government's action has been to promote a few thousand jobs through regional incentives,

and to destroy many thousands more through its economic policies.

The improvement in unemployment insurance benefits wrestled through Parliament by Labour Minister Bryce Mac-kasey also comes under the heading of What-the-right-hand-giveth-the-left-hand-taketh-away. The need for such benefits might have been perceptibly lessened by a more intelligent and flexible approach to economic questions, but the improvements are, nonetheless, real. The main elements of the new scheme [4] were to extend the coverage of the insurance (formerly, only hourly-rated workers and those on salaries of less than $7,800 a year were covered, about 80 per cent of the labour force; now all but self-employed workers must join the scheme, which covers 96 per cent of the labour force); to improve the benefits (from a maximum $53 a week to a maximum $100 a week); and to ease eligibility requirements (formerly, workers had to be employed for thirty weeks in the previous two years to claim benefits; now a record of twenty weeks' work in the past year is sufficient). The financial underpinnings of the plan were also altered. Under the old law, the cost, about $700 million a year, was split 40-40-20 among employees, employers and Ottawa; under the new law, employees and employers share the entire burden until the national unemployment rate hits 4 per cent. Then Ottawa takes over the extra costs.

The scheme is a poor substitute for a guaranteed annual wage, but a good substitute for the old legislation.

I will come back to the other major legislative enactments— government re-organization, the Canada Development Corpo-ration, and the new tax measures — in later chapters. The point to be made here, briefly, is that none of them represents any threat to the *status quo*, although all of them were adver-tised as such. The Canada Development Corporation may prove to be a fundamental departure — it is really too early to tell — but its early development suggests that it will turn out to be the disappointment of the decade. The CDC will attempt to provide a pool of capital for private investment, but it will not help to buy back Canadian industry or even protect the in-dustries now falling into American hands at a rate of about 170 a year.[5] Profit is the key; industries that make money, however pointless their product or looney their motive, will be kept Ca-nadian by the CDC; those that fail the black-ink test, however well they serve Canadian needs, will be let go. Americans who interfere with deodorant factories will find they have roused a tiger, but if they want our textiles, our hand-crafted furniture factories, our woollen mills, even our burial grounds, so be it. (One of the saddest lines I have ever heard came from *Financial Post* columnist Alexander Ross on his return from a trip to his native Vancouver. "The Americans," he said, "just bought my father's grave.")

The other legislation we have had since 1968 has been of the house-keeping or tidying-up variety. A number of badly out-of-date laws have been advanced at least part-way to modernity, but nothing has happened likely to aggravate the Benchers' Society, perturb the Chamber of Commerce, or roil the smooth, still waters of the Canadian establishment. Take, for instance, the Omnibus Bill to amend the Criminal Code, the first major legislation of the Trudeau era. The changes brought our Criminal Code up to date— the date being about 1950. The principal amendments, to legalize abortions under certain circumstances, and to remove the criminal label from homosexual acts between consenting adults, stamped the Prime Minister as a rogue in some eyes, but in fact these highly touted changes amounted to little. Under the old Criminal Code, abortion for any reason was illegal. (That was under one section of the code; another permitted abortion to save the life of the mother, and doctors never knew which section applied.) It is still illegal except under a set of strictly defined circumstances: it must be performed by a qualified medical practitioner in an approved hospital; the practitioner must first receive a certificate in writing from the therapeutic abortion committee of the hospital; the committee must be composed of at least three doctors; and it must be convinced that continuation of the patient's pregnancy "would or would be likely to endanger her life or health".

   The law does not work. It does not work because, in the first place, Canada's 275 Catholic hospitals, which still regard abortion as murder, have simply refused to set up the necessary committees (which are not mandatory in any case), and a great many non-denominational hospitals have followed suit.[6] It does not work because the hospitals that have accepted the change are swamped, and often must turn away patients whose right to a legal abortion is established beyond doubt, but who simply cannot be accommodated. It does not work, finally, because the built-in bureaucracy means that some hospitals with active, concerned committees work faster and better than others. A survey conducted by the Toronto *Star* showed that the Hamilton, Ontario, General Hospital performed 511 abortions in the first eight months of 1970 while, in the entire province of Saskatchewan, there were fewer than 100.

In her excellent study, *Abortion In Canada*, Eleanor Wright Pelrine puts the number of illegal abortions performed in this country at about 100,000 per year, and the number of deaths caused by those abortions at a probable 300 to 400. In the first full year after the law changed, there were 4,375 abortions performed in 143 hospitals in Canada. Clearly, illegal abortions still outnumber legal ones by a ratio of about twenty to one; clearly, rich, lucky and well-situated women can obtain what amounts to abortion on demand, either through their own hospitals or by flying abroad to more enlightened lands, while the poor, unlucky and poorly placed must take their chances with the back-alley operators or bear unwanted children. Clearly, to call the changes forward-looking is a monstrous fraud.

The change in the provision regarding homosexuality is not a fraud, just an amusing and unimportant updating of the law. Police are enjoined not to charge people for acts that were never normally prosecuted in any event.

There have been improvements in the administration of justice since 1968; bail has been made almost automatic for minor offences, and that is a long-sought reform; wiretapping has been brought under control; the expropriation of property has been hedged about with safeguards; a Law Reform Committee has been established to keep up the good work. Good changes, all of them, but hardly a wholesale attack on the inequities of our time. On the major issues, we have had little but protracted, calculated and fruitless weaseling worthy of the late Mackenzie King, of whom poet Frank Scott once wrote, "Never do anything by halves that can be done by quarters."

There is a story that Canadian Indians like to tell. It concerns a chief who called his tribe together to put a matter of some urgency before them.

"My people," he said, "I have always spoken to you with a straight tongue. When a thing was so, I have always told you it was so, whether that thing was good or bad. Today I have two things to tell you, one good, and one bad. I will tell you the bad thing first. The White Man has decided that he can no longer afford to keep us; from now on, we shall have nothing to eat but buffalo dung."

A doomed silence fell over the assembled tribe, until a brave rose in his place. "And what is the good news?" he asked.

"There's plenty of it," the chief replied.

This bitter little joke covers a great deal of the government's legislative programme as it has unrolled before the oppressed and underprivileged of Canada. The Indians, for a start, were told in a White Paper hastily advanced and reluctantly retracted that the federal government would just as soon be rid of them. The Indian Affairs branch was to be dismantled and their problems turned over to the provinces. Instead of legislation to meet the real and pressing needs of a people chronically under-fed, undereducated and underemployed, instead of the establishment of an Indian claims commission promised nearly a decade ago, instead of an attempt to meet the charges of broken treaties and shattered promises, the Indian was to be given a kiss good-bye. Buffalo dung: and plenty of it. I don't propose to re-examine here the plight of the Canadian Indian — the case is all too drearily documented elsewhere — but just to consider one tiny ripple in the sea of injustice that surrounds the indigenous people of this land. In 1950, the Ontario Hydro Commission put in a dam not far from Dryden that flooded the lands of the local Indians. A few years later, a large industrial company began to dump effluent into the waters of the nearby Wabegoon river.[7] The result of these two actions was to deprive the Indians in the area of their income from gathering wild rice, fishing and guiding tourists and hunters. The wild rice was flooded under, the fish were declared contaminated by government inspectors, and the tourists disappeared with the closing of the private fishing lodges. The Indians were destitute. In 1961 — five years after the dam went in — Hydro paid over to the federal Department of Indian Affairs a sum of slightly more than $20,000 to compensate the natives for rights of way for roads and hydro lines, and for the flooding; three years later, Hydro paid another $3,000 interest on the long-delayed first payment. The Indians calculated the loss of their rice crops at $500,000 annually; the Ontario government disagreed, and set the figure at $46,000 annually. So far, the Indians have received $23,000 over sixteen years. The loss of fishing, according to the Indians, cost them at least $380,000, and they put in a claim for that amount to the provincial government. When last I heard, it was still bouncing around the files of a body called the Federal-Provincial Loans Committee which, if it accepts the claim, may advance the Indians a loan — not a grant — of up to 70 per cent of the loss. The Indians did nothing to bring on their ruination, and the governments, federal and provincial, did nothing either to stop it or allay its brutal effects.

The response of the Trudeau government to this kind of situation has been simplicity itself — get rid of the Indian as a federal charge. There has been no legislation either to protect the native peoples or to give them the money, education and training to protect themselves.

The Trudeau government struck its stance on social issues early, with a 2 per cent "social development tax" embodied in Finance Minister Edgar Benson's first budget, in October 1968. The tax did two things at once: it made it clear that if Canadians insisted on having Medicare, as they mulishly did, they would see the cost of it written directly and separately into the budget; secondly, because it had a ceiling of $120, the tax ensured that the lower-income groups pay a much higher percentage of their incomes than the rich for the privilege.

Poverty has been a major social problem in Canada for some time; in 1968, the Economic Council of Canada described it as "a national disgrace", and commented, "We believe that serious poverty should be eliminated in Canada, and that this should be designated as a major national goal. We believe this for two reasons. The first is that one of the wealthiest societies in world history, if it also aspires to be a Just Society, cannot avoid setting itself such a goal. Secondly, poverty is costly (in terms of lost jobs, lost incomes, lost taxes)."[8]

The Council attempted to lay down a poverty definition which, while arbitrary and in some ways misleading (a man living on $1,500 a year as a fisherman in Prince Edward Island is clearly in a different position from the same man mired in a Toronto slum), is better than nothing. Later, the Senate Poverty Committee under Senator David Croll re-adjusted the ECC's figures to account for changes in the cost of living, and came up with a figure of $1,944 as the poverty line for a single person. For two people, poverty begins at $3,240; for three, at $3,888; for four, at $4,536; and the figure rises by $600 for each additional child. These figures defined nearly 20 per cent of all Canadians, and according to them nearly half of all Canadian farm families are poor. When the government unrolled a new Family Income Security Plan in late 1970, it set a series of maximum incomes for Canadians on assistance that were, in every case, well below the poverty line drawn by the Senate Poverty Committee.[9] A couple with four children, for instance, can receive a maximum $3,738 a year — $1,998 below the poverty line. A couple living on the old age pension will, if they qualify for assistance, receive a maximum of $3,060, still below the poverty line, and if the sly old rogues try to get past the line by earning extra money on the side they lose $1 out of every $2 earned. (The MPs who devised this scheme laid no such restrictions on their own generous pensions; an MP can fare forth at the age of forty as a $40,000-a-year ambassador and receive his full pension; he doesn't have to wait until age sixty-five to collect it, either.)

In short, the Trudeau government has not attempted to reduce poverty, but to do as little as possible consistent with the mounting demand — "to restrain, to deflate, to pacify and reconcile". Whether the poor will really be pacified with such half-measures only time will tell.

One of the areas open for action, had the Liberals truly set out to embrace the Just Society instead of merely its winsome daughters, was housing. It is not a problem that can be delineated with statistics, though the statistics are harrowing enough. (The Report of the Task Force on Housing and Urban Development, tabled in January 1969, noted, "There are about 5,500,000 housing units in Canada to serve a market of 5,700,000 family and non-family users" — a quaint way of saying that 200,000 families and individuals are just bung out of luck; they have, literally, no place to stay — ". . . At least 500,000 of those existing units are in substandard condition" — i.e., real or potential slums.) It is a problem, rather, of people, of mothers packed all day in tiny rooms with children from whom they can never escape, of whole families bedded down in armouries, gymnasiums, whatever shelter can be found in our crowded cities; it is a problem of families shuffling from overpriced home to overpriced home one step ahead of an angry landlord, of more honest families spending money that should be used for food, education, clothing, to pay exorbitant mortgages and high rents. It is a problem, the economists tell us, of supply and demand. Too many people want houses, and therefore demand for them is high, and therefore the price is high, and therefore people can't afford them. But to anyone who looks seriously at housing in Canada, it seems less a problem of supply and demand than of simple greed.

Take, for instance, Bramalea. Bramalea is a satellite city outside Metro Toronto; it is Canada's first satellite city, the answer to a nation's prayer; and, all in all, the homes in Bramalea are cheaper than comparable housing in the city itself. Bramalea is not really a housing development; it is a money-making machine for its owners, Bramalea Consolidated Developments Corporation.

The land for the satellite city was assembled in the mid 1950s, at prices of between $1,000 and $1,200 an acre. At the time of purchase, then, a fifty-foot lot suitable for the erection of a semi-detached house was worth $137.50. Services were required, of course — water, lights, roads, sewers — and these the developer installed at an average cost of $2,500 for a semi-detached lot, boosting the basic cost to $2,637.50. A few of the lots were sold, for $6,750 in cash, but most were leased, under the Ontario government's Home Ownership Made Easy plan, at a cost of $43.49 a month for each semi-detached lot. Over the period of a standard thirty-five-year mortgage, therefore, a couple will pay $18,265.80 for a lot that started at $137.50. But they still won't own it, of course, and the price of the house, of course, is extra. At these prices the Bramalea homeowner wins the right to live in a sprawling, overcrowded, under-planned city, where there are not enough schools, few stores, little parkland (and most of that along the banks of a stream where houses could not be squeezed) and almost no recreational or cultural amenities. (The only library is ensconced, suitably enough, in the basement of a bank building.) Bramalea, with a population of 25,000 and a projected population of 100,000, has fewer stores than Streetsville, a nearby town of 5,000.

The men behind Bramalea have built a fortune, rather than a community. Alan Taylor, President, and Arthur Armstrong, Executive Vice-President, of Bramalea Consolidated (neither of whom live in Bramalea) were given options to purchase company stock at cut-rate prices; by judiciously exercising those rights, Taylor cleared more than $600,000 and Armstrong more than $500,000 in the period between May 1967 and August 1969.

There is not much point in blaming Taylor and Armstrong;

they are not in the housing business, they are in the money business, and if they didn't sell Bramalea lots for a stiff profit, they would quickly be removed from their positions by the shareholders. What is needed is a radical new approach to housing in Canada, and it has already been made painfully clear that we are not going to get it, not in Trudeau's time. The government began bravely enough, with the appointment, on July 17, 1968, of a Task Force on Housing and Urban Development under Transport Minister Paul Hellyer. Hellyer's seven-man contingent criss-crossed the country and found, as expected, deplorable conditions in Canadian housing. The Task Force Report, tabled on January 29, 1969, set forth its goal in simple terms: "Every Canadian should be entitled to clean, warm shelter as a matter of basic human right." What is more, the report had a pretty good idea of how to bring that about: remove the 11 per cent sales tax on building materials used in residential construction, lend money to municipalities or regional governments to purchase blocks of land for future housing needs (a proposal that would have ended, at a stroke, much of the expensive land speculation behind sky-rocketting costs), establish a national department of housing and urban affairs, lower and eventually remove the down-payments on housing for lower and middle income groups, and raise the ceiling for loans under the National Housing Act.

The afternoon Hellyer tabled his report, Prime Minister Trudeau came to the Transport Minister's office for the celebration party. He accepted a drink, sat down and said, "I hope you won't be too unhappy if not much happens to this." In the stunned silence, he added, "What kind of priority do you people think this ought to get? Nineteenth?"

Three months later Hellyer resigned, because, as he told a news conference, "I have been unable to get approval for the submission I put forward . . . at the moment I have no indication when it would be approved. . . ." In private he indicated that he did, in fact, have some idea when the report might be acted on — approximately when Hell freezes over. In his letter of resignation, Hellyer noted, "I feel there is a lack of initiative in using federal powers to deal with issues such as housing, pollution, inflation and urban development, which are so vital to the needs of ordinary people in our modern, industrialized society."

The Prime Minister replied that the Hellyer proposals would

have interfered with provincial rights. For the federal government to intervene unilaterally every time it felt that a situation,
such as the housing situation, had reached crisis proportions
would be to betray the very foundations of federalism, he argued. (In that case, someone might have noted mildly, why in
tunket was the housing task force set up in the first place?) Hellyer had not, in fact, suggested that Ottawa take over housing;
he had suggested ways in which provincial governments could
be assisted, persuaded and pressured into action, and ways in
which the federal government might act alone. Just as, when
medical care became a crucial issue, the federal government
stepped in, Hellyer argued that it should step in again.
Trudeau, for whom housing has never been much of a problem,
turned him down cold.

Some of the report's recommendations did survive in piece-
meal form. Robert Andras was given a new Urban Affairs ministry (though precious little money), the ceiling on NHA loans
was raised, and more funds were pumped into public housing,
after an initial freeze brought on by the anti-inflation war. But
there has been no action on a scale sufficient to meet the problem. In fact, in 1970, housing starts were actually down over
1969, although they are expected to rise in 1971. People are still
living in shacks and slums, developers are still collecting enormous speculative profits, and the outlook is still grim. On
April 27, 1970, more than two years after the Hellyer resignation, and three years after Trudeau became prime minister, the
Canadian Welfare Council noted in a brief to the federal government that "Not since World War II have Canadians found it
so difficult to secure decent housing within their means". In
terms of rent levels, vacancy rates and mortgage interest charges, conditions had actually worsened over the crisis state of
1968, the Council said.

The government's housing record has been the rule of its
performance rather than the exception to it. The major problems of a modern state in peacetime are generally considered to
include housing, transportation, welfare, health, education,
employment and pollution. The serious student of the Trudeau
record will find some token gestures in all these areas em-
bedded in the legislative programme of the Prime Minister's
first Parliament, from upward tinkering with pensions to the
creation of a Ministry of the Environment, complete with its
own cabinet member, former Fisheries Minister Jack Davis

34 (who once argued seriously that Canada could solve its water pollution problems by zealous application of the Fisheries Act). But what no student of the regime will find is any coherent programme, or any thrust of action, to meet the commitment of the high-blown words that rumbled through the Throne Speech on that hopeful September day in 1968.

## Notes

1. Michael Oakeshott, "On Being Conservative", in *Rationalism in Politics* (London, 1962), p. 192.

2. See Newman, *The Distemper of Our Times*, pp. 523-8.

3. *Maclean's* Magazine, April 1970, p. 55.

4. The scheme is outlined in *Unemployment Insurance in the '70s*, a publication of the Queen's Printer. Free, too.

5. Takeovers are recorded by a single clerk in the Mergers Branch of the Department of Corporate and Consumer Affairs, who files clippings from daily newspapers and trade magazines. Honest. These become what is grandiloquently known as *The Merger Register*. It is only a partial record, since financial firms and service companies are excluded.

6. Eleanor Wright Pelrine, *Abortion in Canada* (Toronto: New Press, 1970).

7. The details are taken from a report of the Ontario Water Resources Commission on pollution in the Dryden area.

8. Economic Council of Canada, *Fifth Annual Review* (Ottawa, 1968).

9. Canada, Department of National Health and Welfare, *Income Security for Canadians* (Ottawa, 1970).

# 3

# Unity I:
# Go West, Young Man,
# But Go Armed

*We must remain whole and we must remain complete.
National unity is the framework to which everything
else is knit.*
Pierre Elliott Trudeau, April 2, 1968

Unity was certainly the theme Prime Minister Trudeau stressed
both in his search for office and after its attainment. The failure
to achieve anything like unity cannot be laid at his door alone,
but the fact is that we are now, if anything, more divided than
ever, with western separatism, Maritime discontent and Quebec unrest all on the rise. The causes are buried in our past;
they have as much to do with conniving in 1867 as intransigence in 1971, as much to do with the north-south flow of
trade and capital as with the oft-touted arrogance of central
Canada, as much to do with such fundamental changes in our
society as a revolution in education and the growth of the welfare state as with the failure of federalism. All that said, the
Trudeau government has not done much since 1968 to bring us
closer together and has done at least one thing, in the imposition of the War Measures Act on Quebec, which is almost certain, in the long run, to drive us apart.

Ottawa no longer has dealings with provinces — it deals
with power blocs, four of them: the Atlantic area, Quebec, Ontario and the west. (British Columbia looks on itself as a separate kingdom, and perhaps deserves the title, but it tends to get
lumped, in Ottawa thinking, with discontented farmers and

out-of-sorts Prairie premiers.) A useful way to measure the government's performance on the unity issue is to look at each of these areas in turn.

Of the four, the Atlantic area has probably received the most sympathetic treatment since Trudeau came to power. The eastern provinces were the first to receive grants under the Regional Development Incentives Act, and received the lion's share of them. (Of the twenty-two "special areas" designated for an extra $200 million in aid, twelve were in the Atlantic area.)[1] Provincial premiers from the east have not been involved in any head-on clashes with Ottawa and have been only too grateful, with some token grumbling, to accept whatever aid is proferred. (At the first federal-provincial conference I ever attended, I overheard a group of premiers discussing what they would ask for when the sessions opened officially a few minutes later. One of them turned to Premier Joseph Smallwood of Newfoundland and wondered "What will Newfoundland be after?" Smallwood growled, "Whatever's left when you bastards are through.")

What the Atlantic area wants, of course, is jobs, jobs the Maritimers argue they have been deprived of since Confederation, when central Canada began to set tariff policy. The eastern seaboard has been a captive market for the manufacturers of Ontario and Quebec since those tariffs went up, cutting off the natural flow of trade to and from the states to the south. With only a tiny local market available, the Maritimers were never able to compete effectively with central Canada, and the area's most valuable export for decades has been its people — especially the most talented, dynamic and restless of them. I remember talking to a Glace Bay coal miner whose five brothers and two sisters had all lit out for Ontario and whose two sons were just about to leave for the same destination. Why did he not go too? His answer was defensive: "No ambition, I guess. And no sense, neither." The pattern of flight, if anything, has been getting more pronounced. Between 1951 and 1956, an average of 7,400 people fled the Atlantic provinces every year; between 1956 and 1961, the figure reached 11,800, and in the next five years, it nearly doubled again. The exiles were those the area could least afford to lose: 81 per cent of those who left in the 1961-66 period were under twenty-nine; in those five years, 64,000 people between the ages of fifteen and twenty-nine grew up, looked around, said to hell with it, and moved out.[2] Who could blame them? Per capita income in the region has been the lowest in Canada for forty-four years, and unemployment the highest.[3]

Those who are left tend to blame central Canada for their plight, and central Canada tends to accept the blame for the very good reason that it appears to be based on fact. In New Brunswick, a successful sheep farmer (successful by Maritime standards: his gross income from a 350-acre farm was about $7,000 a year) put the point flatly: "Now if I try to ship my lambs into Ontario, why, a New Zealand or Australian farmer can land them on a Toronto dock a lot cheaper than I can, and you won't see the federal government doing a thing to protect me there. But if I want to buy a refrigerator or a freezer to keep my lamb carcasses in from just down the road apiece, in the United States [we were less than fifteen miles from the Maine border] well, no, Mr. Ottawa says I can't do that. It would be hurtful to some factory owner in Toronto, who can charge me twice as much and make me pay the freight charges to boot. That, my son, is what is known as co-operative federalism."

The Trudeau government, accepting the *mea culpas* of its predecessor, has fattened the grants to the Atlantic provinces, extended a hand to such ailing industries as the heavy-water plant at Glace Bay, and pushed, discreetly but persistently, for Maritime union (discreetly, because the one thing that could doom what seems the inevitable union of Nova Scotia, New Brunswick and Prince Edward Island would be proof that Ottawa favoured the union so that it could wash its hands of the region).

But Maritimers and Newfoundlanders are not satisfied that the federal government is doing its best for them. Many of the Ottawa programmes seem sops to the federal conscience rather than genuine attempts to help. I encountered a lobster fisherman on the south shore of PEI who was busily engaged in a Manpower retraining programme that would turn him out, eventually, as an accomplished plumber. Since he lived on a farm near the sea, and twenty miles from the nearest town of any size, I wondered where he would ply his new trade. "Oh, I don't intend to work," he said. "Gawd, there's no jobs for a plumber, not even in Charlottetown." Then why was he taking the course? "The sixty-five dollars," he said. "They pays me sixty-five dollars a week to take it. Gawd, that's more than I make at the lobsters."

If patch-work programmes are one source of discontent, the

---

-rib-
... he re-
... ational
... arguably
... e of star-

... have under-
... e accept that
... ur time and the
... will not practise
... God, let's starve
... e vanguard. After
... a foreign policy. In a

... any wheat farmers was
... 960 acres near the village
... e he would not participate
... meant a loss of money, be-
... ot to grow food in a starving
... my life studying how to grow
... growing."
... s in agriculture policy — the es-
... of federal marketing boards and a
... on Programme — incorporate the
... ss-like, no-nonsense nuttiness. Un-

... nt
the
made

federal government's preoccupation with the problems of French Canada is another. There is a strong feeling th[at] Quebec is the spoiled child of Confederation, that wha[t Q]uebec wants, Quebec gets, while the Atlantic area g[ets] [...] fact that this is simply not true has become [...] the average Maritimer feels it to be true, [...] Trudeau has done nothing to feed this [...] cited example is the federal contrib[ution] [...] Trudeau had nothing to do with tha[t] [...] assuage it, either. He seldom visit[s] [...] is usually for a one-day whirlwi[nd] [...] rounded only by the faith[ful] [...] phrases. The federal-prov[incial] [...] signed to provide each pr[ovince] [...] lar grievances, have be[en] [...] between Ottawa and [...] for believing that [...] There was a cer[tain] [...] Act was impo[sed] [...] child displa[yed] [...] bedroom [...] new un[...] board [...] can[...] is the[...]

I want to b[...] usual, a specia[l] vincial relations ha[...] 1968. Gone are the [...] Premier Mitch Hepburn [...] King pouted over the consti[...] burn refused even to acknowle[dge] mission on Dominion-Provincial [...] venge by calling, and winning, an e[lection] dared criticize his conduct of the war; neit[her] performance.) Gone, too, are the brusque ex[changes] Ontario Premier John Robarts and Prime Minist[er] son over such issues as the imposition — as Robarts [...] of Medicare on the province by the federal governm[ent] tario, the big brother of Confederation, has the most to [...]

---

on land left fallow for the year 1970, and delivery quotas to the Canadian Wheat Board for the next crop year were based on land used for forage or left fallow. Farmers who didn't take their wheat fields out of production couldn't sell the product anyway; they could accept $6 or nothing. If it seems insane that Canada should, in a starving world, take twenty-two million acres of wheat acreage out of production, it seems scarcely more rational to suppose that a programme of tight-fisted coercion would somehow soothe the savage western breast. I spent a considerable period of time poring over every scrap of evidence I could find — including the speeches of Otto Lang, the cabinet minister responsible for the operations of the Wheat Board — in search of a reasonable explanation of Operation LIFT. I finally found it in the writings of novelist Mordecai Richler, in the course of an article he wrote for *Maclean's Mag*azine:

We are to subvert hardworking, God-fearing farmers, [turn]ing them to become senior citizen hippies. Whatever th[eir] sponsibilities-of-office, the conundrums of inter[national] agreements, the mysteries of high finance, it is un[...] immoral not to grow wheat when 10,000 people d[...] vation every day.

And yet — and yet — it is just possible [...] estimated Ottawa's subtlety. If, for instance, [...] overpopulation is the surpassing problem of [...] ignorant peasants of the deprived countries [...] birth control no matter what, well then, b[...] the bastards. Canada, for once, in th[...] months of agonizing review, we do have [...] word, famine.

Not surprisingly, the reaction of m[...] sullen rage. Glen Willner, who farms [...] of Davidson, Saskatchewan, told m[...] in operation LIFT even though it [...] cause he thought it was immoral a[...] world and because "I've spent a[...] the stuff, not how to keep it fro[m] [...] Two other federal initiativ[es] [...] tablishment of a new system [...] Grains Income Stabilizat[ion] [...] same hard-headed, busin[ess]

der the Grains Income Stabilization Programme, grain farmers
pay about 2 per cent of the value of their sales into a fund,
which is matched by the federal government. Then, when sales
fall below their average for the past three years, farmers may
draw upon the fund. Rich farms, big farms, corporate farms
will benefit most; the farmers who are really in trouble will receive the smallest subsidies. This follows the American model,
where subsidies are based on farm sales, and the bulk of government aid goes to huge corporate farms.

The new marketing boards also are weighted against the
small producer. They will not be controlled by producers, but
heavily influenced by agri-business representatives, and they
are specifically enjoined not to discriminate against "efficient
regions" or "more efficient producers", which means there
should be no techniques used to discriminate against corporate
farms.

The new farm programmes are the result of the report of a
federal task force on agriculture, completed in late 1969. The
report was written by four university professors and an accountant — well, hell, you wouldn't expect an actual *farmer* in
on it, they have dirty hands — and is studded with phrases like
"Younger non-viable farmers should be moved off the farms."
It contemplates, with apparent equanimity, the decline of Canada's farm population from about 10 per cent of the total population to about 3 per cent, and suggests a cut-back in Prairie
wheat acreage of about 50 per cent in a period of four years. It
suggests that farmers who cannot meet international competition should get out of the business, a conclusion that prompted
Allen Blakeney, the new Premier of Saskatchewan, to comment
bitterly: "There is hardly one bloody industry in Canada that
could stand up to such a rule. If you were to apply that principle
to, say, the textile industry, the first thing you would do would
be to close every textile plant in the country."

Blakeney won the June 1971 Saskatchewan election largely
on the basis of rural rejection of the new farm policies. The late
Ross Thatcher, as a Liberal Premier, had attracted the wrath of
every farmer who saw, behind the gobbledygook of the task
force report, a direct threat to his way of life. If we are to have
fewer, bigger farms, run, in the report's unhappy phrase, "like
any other industry", inevitably many of today's farmers will
have to go off the land — and join the unemployment lines in
crowded, polluted cities. They do not look forward to the pros-

pect, and even staunch Liberals found themselves on the defensive during the June campaign. Ray Heinrich, Reeve of the rural township of Willner, in central Saskatchewan, and a long-time Liberal worker, told me: "There is a guarantee built into the new policies — they guarantee to keep us as poor as ever." Like most westerners, he sees no reason why he should be forced off the land to keep food cheap for easterners.

The assumptions that underlie federal policy are that Canada should cut back food production and get rid of farmers, and if that seems dim-witted in view of the world food situation, it is no dimmer than assuming that cash for wheat is the elixir that will set the dry prairies abloom for the Liberals. It simply isn't so. In three month-long swings across the west over the past two years, I expected to find the usual catalogue of historical western gripes — the tariff, wheat sales, oil exports and the iniquities of the wicked barons of Bay Street. I found all these, of course, but I found much more, a seething rage directed at eastern Canada and shared by an astonishing cross-section of the population.

I stood in a crowd of 6,000 farmers in Saskatoon and watched them shake their fists and boo at every mention of Ottawa or the federal government. I read the signs that said, "We Want Bread and Butter, Not Bullshit" and "We've Been Feeding the Wrong Hogs" and "Ottawa, Go To Hell" (which reminded me of those old placards that now sound so innocent, "Québec Oui, Ottawa Non"). I sat in a Regina pub, engaged in what I thought was the brisk give-and-take of debate on the subject of American investment in Canada, until a large, angry young man told me, "You'd better leave now, Easterner," and I left. I sat in farm kitchens and living rooms, in business offices and union halls, and in most of them I heard the same message that went winging with the ripe tomato somebody chucked at the Prime Minister during one of his fund-raising dinners in Calgary, a message of alienation, hurt outrage, and despair.

That message still hasn't seeped through to the Prime Minister, or if it has, he simply doesn't care. In Ottawa, he speaks of unity and the need to come together; in Winnipeg he tells the grain growers, "Why should I sell your wheat?" When he asked them to accept the Official Languages Act, he sent Secretary of State Gérard Pelletier out west to explain it, and Pelletier's brusque arrogance quickly convinced westerners that their fears were well founded — French *was* to be thrust down their throats.

It is, as always, by little things that westerners measure their treatment by Ottawa. Consider, for instance, the matter of Edmonton's educational television station, a miniscule matter, but one containing within it an important principle. Albertans lobbied for years for an educational television station and Edmonton seemed the logical site — far enough from the U.S. border to eliminate interference, close enough to a major concentration of population to justify its establishment. The lobbying succeeded, and permission for the station was granted. But, as in the wheat deal, Ottawa's largesse was conditional. Educational TV would be broadcast only part of the day; for the rest of the time, the outlet would become a French-language station. What's more, after three years, the French-language portion would be expanded and the educational television would have to move; it could either go onto ultra-high frequency — and few Edmontonians have UHF receivers — or disappear. Only about 4 per cent of the area residents speak French, while almost 8 per cent claim Ukrainian and another 8 per cent German as a first language; to Edmontonians, the decision seems not only wilfully stupid but malicious, and the station is nothing more than a daily reminder of how little their views count in Ottawa, a constant goad for western separatism.

Not that western separatism can fairly be compared — at least not yet — with the separatism of Quebec. For one thing, the thrust towards independence is not nearly so strong; for another, the ties that bind French Canada to Confederation are economic, while the forces that work against it are cultural; in the west, the reverse is true.

But discontent in both areas cuts across normal political lines; New Democrats, Conservatives, Liberals and Social Creditors in the west share a sense of outrage against the east; Saskatchewan farmers are mad at Ontario farmers; the Manitoba Federation of Labour is mad at the Quebec Federation of Labour; and British Columbia businessmen are sure that banks in Toronto and Montreal discriminate against them. When the federal government, in its zeal to smite the inflation bogey hip and thigh, placed tax strictures on new construction in fast-growth areas, it struck what seemed to westerners as a brutal and discriminatory blow against Vancouver, Calgary and Edmonton, which were to be penalized for doing well. That would have been hard to swallow in an atmosphere of enlightened camaraderie, but in the mood currently prevailing, it simply would not go down the gullet. "I think you people must have a certain attachment to us," a Vancouver businessman explained, "because you're always trying to screw us."

"You people" embraces all easterners, but especially Ontarians. In Edmonton, I attended a coffee-and-cakes party at which former Tory chieftain John Diefenbaker hurled his customary thunderbolts, and chatted afterwards with an elderly matron who revealed that except for "certain people", Diefenbaker would still be exercising his oratorical talents as prime minister. Which certain people? Not the dirty Grits, but Ontario Tories. "Those big power people . . . those people on Bay Street . . . all those Easterners," the lady said, and flounced away.

Western discontent did not begin with the Trudeau government; it is as old as blight and drought and mortgage foreclosures. It found expression in the Progressive Movement of the 1920s, in the CCF and Social Credit parties of the 1930s, and in the sentiment for annexation with the U.S. that blooms across the Prairies from time to time, then withers and dies in the same uncertain rhythm. None of this is new — and perhaps that is why the Prime Minister thinks it can be harrowed under with cliches about unity — what *is* new is that the malcontents are no longer weary-eyed farmers who have been pushed off their lands by drought or grasshoppers or bankers, they are the young, bright, trained technocrats, the movers and shakers. They are, by God, many of them members of the Establishment, and it won't do to call out the troops against them. A recently published collection of openly separatist essays, *The Unfinished Revolt,* was edited by John Barr, executive assistant to the Alberta Minister of Education, and Owen Anderson, executive assistant to Alberta Premier Harry Strom.

Eastern journalists who dismiss talk of western separatism as a banner-wave from the lunatic fringe haven't examined either its sources or its sponsors. It was no crack-pot, but Richard Baxter, an influential Winnipeg businessman and chairman of the Manitoba Export Corporation, who said, "I believe in the Canadian concept, but I believe it's being loused up. . . . Emotionally, I don't want to get out of Canada, but you have an infallible argument economically for getting out, and if some strong leader could be found to support the idea, it could be sold, because it is so right." It was no lunatic, but Dr. Hu Harries, former dean of commerce at the University of Alberta, and now Liberal MP for Edmonton-Strathcona, who said, "For years and years we'd cuss and swear at the east, but we had no place to go. Now we're a viable economic unit, and the rules have been changed. . . ." It was no political neophyte, but Art Coulter, executive secretary of the Manitoba Federation of Labour and a power in the NDP, who stabbed a square finger across the dining room of his suburban Winnipeg home and growled, "The more I look ahead, the less I can see that eastern Canada can do one damn thing for us."

Like the Maritimers, these men believe that whatever Quebec wants, Ottawa grants, while whatever the west wants is refused. The memory of Expo 67 and its Ottawa-financed deficit still burns brightly. Quebec wanted hundreds of millions, and got it, while a telescope for British Columbia was refused. When it made economic sense to transfer the Air Canada overhaul base from Winnipeg to Montreal, that was done, despite the loss of hundreds of jobs in Manitoba; when it made economic sense to extend the oil pipeline from southern Ontario to Montreal, opening the eastern market to western oil, that was not done, because, as westerners see it, it would bring a rise in prices at the pumphead in Quebec. ("They expect us to pay millions for their damn fair, but they won't pay an extra cent a gallon for our oil," complained an Edmonton oil executive.)

This western view of recent history seems simplistic and unfair, but to many westerners, the parallels I have just cited are the simple facts of life. There is no incident too large or small to be squeezed into this pattern of thought, from the Official Languages Act (one worrying aspect of that law, as the westerners speedily saw, is that almost all bilingual Canadians come from the east, from Ontario, Quebec and New Brunswick; jobs in the federal hierarchy will be even harder than ever for westerners to land) to the naming of a bishop to the Roman Catholic diocese of St. Paul, in northern Alberta. He was chosen from Quebec, overlooking all western candidates, a fact that caused great bitterness in the parish. The Reverend C. W. Poirier of Barrhead, in the centre of the diocese, commented, "We're at a pretty low ebb if we have to turn to Quebec for a bishop for Alberta."

Westerners feel that Quebec can not only get what it wants, it can block what they want. A leading member of the British Columbia bar said, "For twenty-five years meetings of the

Canadian Bar Association passed resolutions on constitutional reform, on divorces, on the Criminal Code, and for twenty-five years the Quebeckers blocked us. . . . There is not
one damn thing that Quebec opposed and we wanted that we
could get. Then, finally, when Quebec woke up, everything
became possible."

Dave Steuart, former Provincial Treasurer of Saskatchewan,
noted, "We're convinced that we've got a government at Ottawa that is totally preoccupied with Quebec and Ontario, and
if it has any time left over, it spends it on the Maritimes."

Increasingly, Steuart finds, a western politician can rouse a
crowd either by attacking Ottawa or Quebec. "I have to be
careful when I get talking about Quebec. Every time I get on to
anything that could be remotely construed as anti-French, you
can see the people come lifting out of their seats, shouting for
more. It's a terrible temptation to give it to them."

Trudeau simply shrugs away this bitterness. In 1969 he went
to Calgary to address a group of Liberals, most of them oilmen,
most of them seething because their wells were running at
about half-capacity and Ottawa had declined to push vigorously for markets either in the U.S. or eastern Canada. The oilmen expected some explanations from the Prime Minister.
They got, instead, a rambling and disjointed talk about NATO
and North American defence. When Trudeau was asked why
he had refused to discuss the one subject his audience was interested in, he replied, "I like to disappoint people sometimes."
No campaign by his political foes could convince Albertans of
Trudeau's indifference as effectively as that one flat statement.

A fundamental difficulty we face in trying to hold this nation
together is that our interests do differ sharply from region to region. To central Canadians, a tariff protecting our manufacturers from too-direct competition with American industries
makes sense, but a tariff against food imports does not; to westerners, this simply means that they pay more for almost everything they use to produce their crops, the price of which stands
naked to the blast of competition from all over the world.
Wheat prices were actually lower in 1970 than they had been in
1949, while the cost of producing the grain had risen sharply.
To many Canadians east of Thunder Bay, American capital
represents a threat, and U.S. exploration for oil in the Canadian
west and north makes our nationalists decidedly uneasy; to

many Canadians west of Thunder Bay this attitude is simply another plot to cut off money and jobs destined for the west. To those of us in Ontario and Quebec, the acceptance and accommodation of the French fact in Canada is a matter of urgent priority; to those in Manitoba, Alberta, Saskatchewan and British Columbia, it is simply another concession to Quebec, another slap in the face to the huge New-Canadian population of the west. There are few things so disheartening as to leave Alberta after several days of trying to explain the position of Quebec to hostile listeners who speak of "Frogs" and "whiners" and "quitters", and fly to Montreal for several days of trying to explain the position of the west to hostile listeners who speak of "Hunkies" and "squareheads" and "clod-hoppers". Bigotry flourishes in Canada everywhere, regardless of race, language, colour or creed.

These problems can be resolved; a balance between the needs of Canada as a whole and the needs of its parts can be met, but not by the Trudeau style of arrogance, ignorance and the well-lifted shoulder. Winnipeg businessman Richard Baxter worked out the cost of the tariff system as $687 for every Canadian family per annum — that is the price difference between a typical range of goods in the U.S. and Canada. He said, "That's the price of Confederation, and we've never minded paying it, but now we're beginning to wonder what we're getting for it. All we can see is the Official Languages Act."

There are more German Canadians than French Canadians in every western province, more Ukrainians than French in every Prairie province, more Chinese than French in British Columbia,[6] and the Languages Act might have been traded to the west for a little generosity, a little understanding, on other issues. If, for instance, the federal government had presented the western farmer with a two-price system for wheat instead of ramming the LIFT programme down his throat, that concession might have created an atmosphere of give-and-take. (If the government simply pays a subsidized price for wheat, the price must go up; since we sell most of our wheat on world markets, the effect would be to price ourselves out of business. One possible solution is a controlled higher price within Canada and a lower price for export, with the difference covered by federal funds. Then the farmer receives a fair return, yet remains competitive. Most of our international competitors have adopted some form of two-price system for wheat.) Instead, westerners draw a bitter parallel between the treatment accorded grain-growers, who get no direct subsidies and are located overwhelmingly in the west, and dairymen, who receive both price support and subsidies and are located overwhelmingly in Ontario and Quebec.

Ironically, both the west and Quebec are caught in the same trap, the trap of the simple majority. Out of 264 federal MPs, 162 come from Ontario and Quebec, and so on any issue that touches their common interest, even if it harms the west, Ontario and Quebec will have their way; there are 156 members in Ontario and the west, so on any issue that touches *their* common interest, even if it harms Quebec, Ontario and the west will have their way. Ontario is the key; her eighty-eight members can make, on any regional issue, an instant majority with any other power bloc. Sir John A. Macdonald used to say, "Myself and time against any two men"; Ontario can say, "Myself and anyone else against all comers."

Or, as a shrewd Vancouver politician once put it to me, "The reason you guys are regarded as the villains in the piece is that you goddamn well are the villains."

It is not just a question of tariffs or wheat subsidies, as far as western Canada is concerned. "The main question is psychological," said Senator John Nichol, a Vancouver businessman and former president of the National Liberal Federation; "The west has to be convinced that eastern Canada knows we're here, cares about us and is willing to do something for us."

There has been no sign so far that the Trudeau government even thinks of the west as a problem in Canadian unity, perhaps because it has been so busy trying to impose that unity at rifle-point in Quebec.


## Notes

1. See the 1969 *Annual Report* of the Department of Regional Economic Expansion.
2. Statistics prepared for the Maritime Union Study by the Atlantic Provinces Economic Council.
3. Per capita income figures are from successive issues of the *Atlantic Year Book* (Fredericton: Brunswick Press), unemployment figures from the *Canada Year Book* (Ottawa: Dominion Bureau of Statistics).

4. *Canadian Statistical Review*, February 1971 (Ottawa: Dominion Bureau of Statistics), p. 42.

5. See *The Unfinished Revolt*, edited by John Barr and Owen Anderson (Toronto: McClelland and Stewart, 1971) for an account of the strength of western separatism and the reasons behind it.

6. *Canada Year Book*, 1969.

# 4

## Unity II:
## Standing Together
## At Rifle-Point

*It is more important to maintain law and order than to worry about those whose knees tremble at the sight of the army.*
Prime Minister Trudeau, October 12, 1970

When Trudeau became Prime Minister, there was a general expectation that he would somehow sort out the problem of Quebec; English Canadians, counting on his sense of authority, expected him to put the French in their place; French Canadians, counting on the fact that he was one of them, expected a sympathetic hearing. He has given both sides enough, on the surface, to hold or perhaps even gain votes in the next election. On the one hand, he has imposed order vigorously in Quebec, on the other he has taken measures to give the French language a stronger position inside the federal bureaucracy. But as a nation we remain more divided than ever before, and Quebec separatism is more firmly entrenched than ever before, especially among the young intellectuals who will be the province's future leaders. Trudeau has failed in this crucial area because he has attempted to solve a delicate, complex question with what seems to be his only political weapon — the bludgeon. He began wielding that weapon against Quebec almost from the day he came to power.

The first incident that signalled a change from the soft, scrambling, fumbling approach of Lester Pearson was the Rossillon Affair.[1] In August 1968, Philippe Rossillon, secretary general to the French government's High Committee for the Defence of the French Language and a man who had, apparently, contacts with separatist groups in Quebec, turned up in Manitoba for a five-day visit to St. Pierre, thirty miles southwest of Winnipeg. The Prime Minister regarded this breach of propriety very seriously, as he told a news conference in Ottawa. A cultural accord exists between Ottawa and France, he said, which allows the French government to promote cultural activities among French Canadians after prior notification to Ottawa. Rossillon had given no such prior notification, and his sudden arrival in Manitoba's bosom made him nothing more or less than a spy: "I am afraid that a good many Canadians who are not French-speaking will be very much annoyed with this intervention, and I rather think that if French Canadians are going to plot with more or less secret agents of France in Canada, this can harm the French-Canadian interests in Canada. . . . I think that nothing could be more harmful to the acceptance of the bilingual character of Canada in the province where French-speaking Canadians are a minority than having free agents of a foreign state coming into the country and agitating, as it were, to get the citizens of that particular province to act in a given way."

Was Rossillon teaching Manitobans to build, as it were, bombs? Was he asking them to subvert the state, attack English schools? No. On the invitation of some members of the Manitoba French community, he was propagandizing them about the need to preserve their culture and language. But he had not gone through the right channels. He was inept, wildly misinformed about the spiritual state of French citizens in Manitoba — where apathy is next to godliness — and he was sneaky and rude. But to unveil him as a "more or less secret agent", and to call a full-blown press conference to excise him like a tick from the body politic, gave him an importance he did not deserve. The exercise was comforting to English Canadians, who could see that those Frenchies weren't going to be allowed to get away with anything, but it indicated that the election of a French-Canadian Prime Minister had done nothing to cool hostilities between the two main language groups.

Daniel Johnson was then Premier of Quebec and following a confusing "separatism if necessary but not necessarily separatism" line. After his sudden death in September 1968, he was succeeded by Jean-Jacques Bertrand. Bertrand was a convinced and dogged federalist, under attack from the nationalist wing of his Union Nationale party, and needed all the help he could get from Ottawa to maintain the federalist position. It was not to be; instead, we had more, and noisier, confrontation.

First there was the long, tedious battle over the Francophone Conference in Niamey, Nigeria. The governments of Ottawa and Quebec were summoned to the conference by separate invitation, although they had earlier agreed, after much bickering, that the Canadian delegation would be headed by a federal official assisted by provincial representatives. There seemed little doubt that, in accepting a separate invitation, Quebec was trying to establish an independent presence abroad which might later be parlayed into a lever for more independence at home. (Canadians have reason to be wary of this tactic; we used it as a nation ourselves; it was, as much as anything, our successful manoeuvering for separate representation at overseas conferences that cut the umbilical cord from Britain earlier in this century.) It was equally clear that Ottawa would not allow this to happen. Secretary of State Gérard Pelletier led the Canadian delegation and spoke for all of Canada. The conference itself was an anti-climax after the build-up; its highlight came when Quebec separatist and singer Pauline Julien shouted *"Vive le Québec libre"* during a Pelletier speech. It was, explained Marcel Masse, leader of the Quebec wing of the Canadian delegation, "an idea shared by part of our people". (Miss Julien had once publicly refused to sing God Save The Queen, and if you can not sing noisily, well, that's what she did.) But, for the time being at least, the point was made: Ottawa would not allow Canada to be represented abroad in fractions.

Firmness, in that instance, seemed appropriate; that was not the case in the next Quebec-Ottawa clash, over the placing of Quebec's new Montreal-area airport. The choice of the site was up to the federal Department of Transport, but Quebec, like any other province, expected to be consulted. Instead, when the Prime Minister had made his choice, he sent one of his aides down to Quebec City to inform Premier Bertrand that a location at Ste. Scholastique, twenty-six miles northwest of Montreal, had been chosen. Predictably, the Premier was unhappy. He said that the location would mean that Ontario would reap much of the benefit of the airport construction, since the site was so close to the provincial border. He preferred something in southern Quebec, where, as it happens, his own riding is situated. Whatever the merits of the dispute may have been, they were lost in the Prime Minister's off-the-cuff reply. Bertrand, he said, was "off his rocker".

The phrase was not merely mischievous, childish and inept; it was extremely damaging. Bertrand, who was having some difficulty convincing his own party that reasonable dialogue could be maintained with Ottawa, had been contemptuously dismissed. To his own great credit, he refused to reply in kind, but the lesson was there for anyone to see: to Trudeau, federal-provincial relations meant, We'll do it my way.

With the defeat of Bertrand's government and the election of Robert Bourassa's Liberals in April 1970, Canadians confidently expected, once more, a new era in Ottawa-Quebec relations. We got it, too, but not in the manner advertised. Bourassa seemed a man like Trudeau, shrewd, cool, pragmatic and, at heart, a federalist, though not as committed to the concept as Trudeau. However, the election that brought him to power contained some ominous portents, largely ignored by Ottawa. The separatist Parti Québecois, dismissed by Trudeau as *"une particule"*, rolled up an impressive 23 per cent of the vote. In fact, if you subtract the English and ethnic votes — which went overwhelmingly to the Liberals — the Parti Québecois gathered almost as much of the French-Canadian vote as the Liberals themselves. The fact that this achievement resulted in only seven seats in the national assembly — as Quebec's legislature was now called — seemed to indicate that the electoral system was disastrously out of line. (The new premier, Robert Bourassa, admitted as much, and promised to take early steps to rectify the situation; the province waits with eager anticipation for some action.) There had always been separatists who believed that the voting system would always be rigged against them, and the April results seemed to bear them out. The reply of some was to turn to violence.

Who knows when political disagreement becomes racism, when the voicing of dissent becomes sedition, when the imperative to maintain order becomes suppression? I remember the chill, disheartened feeling that came over me one night during the Quebec election campaign, when I was sitting in the auditorium of a school in Laurier riding, where Parti Québecois leader René Lévesque was seeking re-election. I saw Lévesque, a man I

had always admired and respected, disappear suddenly behind
a shrill mask. That day *The Montreal Star* had carried a dim-
witted editorial, in which it hinted that Lévesque was a latter-
day Kerensky, that however reasonable and fair-minded he
might be in dealings with English Canada, he was only preparing the way for a French-Canadian Lenin. Lévesque was tired,
emotionally drained, physically exhausted, and facing certain
defeat in his own riding. Instead of ignoring the editorial, he reacted with hysterical racism. His raspy voice squeaking with
rage, he lumped *The Montreal Star's* editorial writer with all
English Canadians; the English of Quebec, he said, spitting the
words across the auditorium, were White Rhodesians, vaunting
their alleged racial superiority on the French. "If it was colour,
you could feel it." But there was nothing to feel, there in that
innocent auditorium, nothing to feel but endless weariness and
despair. Lévesque's diatribe, naturally, brought a gutter response from the English electorate. (A Montreal cab driver told
me the next day he was oiling up his gun against the day he
now considered inevitable when "those French bastards come
to get me.") Suddenly we were in Alabama or Mississippi; suddenly Pierre Vallieres' graphic and wildly misleading phrase,
"the white niggers of America", would take on meaning because Lévesque, of all people, insisted on turning his political
aspirations into a racial slur. But who was to blame? Lévesque
for succumbing to weary bitterness, or the nameless editorialist
whose twisted view of history began the ugly confrontation?
(To their credit, an impressive number of the *Star's* reporting
staff wrote a letter to their own paper denouncing the editorial
and, on threat of resigning, saw it published.) There was no one
to blame, only a lesson to draw: the lesson that confrontation is
not the answer, that slugging it out, clearing the air, settling
this thing once and for all, will not work, any more than it has
down through Canada's troubled history. If confrontation
worked, Canada's French-English problems might have been
settled with Louis Riel, or the Boer War, or the Manitoba
School Question; if putting the French in their place was a solution, we'd have known it after the conscription crisis in
World War I, or that in World War II, or after the last Quebec
election, in the results of which the federalists claimed to find
the crushing defeat of separatism.

But Trudeau is, alas, no historian, but a lawyer (part-time)
and teacher (part-time) and dogmatist (always). When the
chance came for confrontation in Quebec, he seized it eagerly.

At 8:15 on the morning of Monday, October 5, 1970, two revolver-armed men gained access to the Westmount home of British Trade Commissioner James Cross on the pretext of delivering a birthday gift.[2] Cross was hand-cuffed and bundled into a taxi, which headed toward downtown Montreal. A witness on the street told police one of the abductors said "We're the FLQ." Not long after, the police received the first communique from the kidnappers. (The communiques issued throughout the crisis were normally left in telephone booths whose location would be indicated to one of the two Montreal radio stations the kidnappers regarded as trustworthy. On the communiques there was always a crude drawing of a musket-bearing *habitant*, copied from a famous painting of an *habitant* marching to battle during the 1837 rebellion in what was then Lower Canada.) The ransom note set forth seven demands that combined incredible naivete with ordinary greed. The kidnappers demanded: release of twenty-three "political prisoners", including seventeen convicted of terrorist acts and six others charged with terrorism and held without bail; payment of $500,000 in gold; broadcast and publication of an FLQ (Front de Libération du Québec) "political manifesto", which was thoughtfully provided; cessation of police manhunts for the kidnappers; publication of the name of an informer who had given police names of FLQ activists; provision of an aircraft to fly the prisoners, the abductors and their gold to Cuba or Algeria; and the re-hiring of postal truck drivers laid off in Montreal the previous April.

Clearly, no government could meet all those demands; the question was, would it meet enough of them to save the life of James Cross?

On Tuesday, October 6, Trudeau called a meeting of his inner cabinet, the Cabinet Committee on Priorities and Planning, of which he is chairman, to make what came to be the crucial decision. Canada would not follow the lead of the Latin American countries; we would not give in to the demands of the kidnappers. But the cabinet ministers, who were agreed on this tactic — and were supported by Quebec Premier Robert Bourassa, who was in constant touch by telephone — were also concerned to keep Cross alive while the frantic search for the kidnappers went on; they decided to pretend to negotiate.

A message went back to the Front de Libération du Québec asking for proof that Cross was still alive; in the meantime, negotiations were begun with Cuba to receive the kidnappers. In the House of Commons, External Affairs Minister Mitchell Sharp dismissed the FLQ demands as "wholly unreasonable", but said the government wanted to speak to the abductors. That evening, Montreal radio station CKAC reported receiving an FLQ note saying they would "do away with" Cross if the demands were not met by 8:30 a.m. the next day.

On Wednesday, pre-dawn raids by the police yielded thirty arrests, but no clues to the whereabouts of Cross and the kidnappers. The 8:30 deadline passed with no word from the FLQ. Then, in the early afternoon, the kidnappers extended the deadline and sent along a note in Cross' handwriting to prove he was still alive. In a late-night news conference, Sharp asked the kidnappers to name a mediator to treat with the federal authorities. That spokesman eventually became Robert Lemieux, a Montreal lawyer who had acted for FLQ members since 1968.

At 10:30 p.m. on Thursday, October 8, the CBC met one of the crucial demands; it broadcast the FLQ manifesto over French-language radio and television. It was also printed, in English and French, in the next day's newspapers. At this stage, the kidnappers had achieved an incredible propaganda coup; Trudeau, who had criticised the media bitterly for over-covering the kidnapping, which played, he said, right into FLQ hands, was now providing the terrorists with free air time. The federal government was visibly on the run; the police had turned up nothing, and the stern dismissal of the "wholly unreasonable" demands had been reversed. A number of prominent Quebeckers, including Claude Ryan, publisher of *Le Devoir*, and René Lévesque, began to suggest the release of "a certain number" of jailed terrorists to save Cross' life.

In Montreal, at that time, the mood on the street — as opposed to that in government offices — was far from outraged. Many French Canadians, while they sympathized with the captured Cross, were more than a little amused by the discomfiture being inflicted on official dignity.

The joke, if ever it was one, ended abruptly on Saturday, October 10, when Quebec Labour Minister Pierre Laporte was taken from outside his south-shore Montreal home at machine-gun point. The kidnapping came shortly after Quebec Justice Minister Jérôme Choquette had officially refused to release the prisoners demanded by the FLQ and offered instead safe-conduct to Cuba in return for the release of Cross. At the time, press reports linked the refusal and the second kidnapping di-

rectly; Laporte's abduction was "an instant response" to Choquette. It could not have been; the abductors were circling Laporte's home even while Choquette was speaking; this was the
work of a second FLQ cell that had decided the kidnapping of
Cross was a mistake and that what was needed was to take a
French Canadian. The accidental timing made the FLQ seem a
highly-organized, incredibly swift-moving organization.

That night, Premier Bourassa moved into a guarded suite on
the twentieth floor of the Queen Elizabeth Hotel in downtown
Montreal.

On Sunday, October 11, frantic meetings of government
officials in Ottawa and Quebec continued behind the scenes,
while police tried in vain to turn up some clue to the whereabouts of either kidnapped man. Robert Lemieux was charged
with obstructing justice and held in jail, while police seized his
files. (The charge was subsequently dropped.)

The next day, notes from the two FLQ cells were received
with contrary demands; the abductors holding James Cross
said they would release him in return for release of the twenty-
three "political prisoners" and safe conduct to Algeria or Cuba;
the second cell, which was holding Laporte, stuck to the original seven demands. A third note found late that afternoon said
that the satisfaction of the demands of the respective cells
would free the respective hostages. It was clear by now that the
FLQ was not monolithic or even well-organized. About the
time that third note was found, troops began moving out of
Camp Petawawa, 115 miles west of Ottawa, for the national
capital. While they rumbled towards the city, Robert Lemieux,
who now had been named negotiator by both FLQ cells, began
meeting with corporation lawyer Robert Demers, the Quebec
Liberal party treasurer, who had been appointed the government's representative in negotiations.

The next morning, Ottawa woke to the measured tread of
combat troops carrying FN automatic rifles or submachine
guns. I'll never forget the shock when I was out walking the
dogs that Tuesday morning and rounded the corner to see a clot
of soldiers swarming out of a truck outside Mitchell Sharp's
house. I had known they were there, from news broadcasts, but
I was somehow not prepared to see them in the flesh, embar-
rassed-looking men in battle fatigues with heavy weapons and
sullen faces. In our Ottawa neighbourhood, soldier-watching
became something of a sport, and the children of cabinet minis-

ters whose homes were being guarded basked in glory at school. When Defence Minister Donald Macdonald was asked why the troops were armed with automatic rifles, he replied that, well, Laporte's kidnappers had carried machine guns, and it was necessary to be armed with "equivalent equipment", as if what was at stake was a point of social etiquette. If someone turned out to be trying to kidnap a cabinet minister in Ottawa, apparently, the troops would let fly with their submachine guns, come what may: in the name of public safety, of course. In the end the only result of the soldiers' "equivalent equipment" was the tragic death of one of them, whose weapon discharged accidentally.

The Prime Minister's statement in the House that afternoon was, in the circumstances, astonishing. Among other things, he said, "I do wish that the media — radio, television and the press — would exercise a bit more restraint in talking about these problems. It is a mistake, I think, to give them publicity, which is the thing they hope for most." Outside the House, he began to hint, for the first time, what was on his mind. CBC reporter Tim Ralfe, visibly outraged by the presence of the troops, asked, "How far would you be willing to go in that direction?"

"Just watch me," Trudeau replied.

"To the point of using electronic listening devices and the suspension of certain liberties?"

"Yes, certainly. I think society must take means to prevent the emergence of a parallel power which defies the elected power of this country. I think that goes to any distance."

That same day, Lemieux was arraigned in court and released on his own bail so that he could meet with Demers to negotiate release of the prisoners and kidnap victims. Late that night, in a news conference at the Nelson Hotel in Montreal, where he lived, Lemieux announced that "in light of government refusal" to meet the FLQ demands, he could not go on. "My mandate is over."

Lemieux stuck to that position the next day, Wednesday, even though a note from the FLQ cells gave him carte blanche to negotiate new terms; he refused to go to Quebec City, where Premier Bourassa said he wanted him, because he said he had to remain in Montreal to stay in touch with the FLQ.

Clearly, the governments at Ottawa and Quebec were spinning out negotiations while planning something else. In the

House of Commons, Conservative Leader Robert Stanfield asked Trudeau if he was contemplating any kind of emergency measures. The Prime Minister replied, "Quite frankly, I do not think this type of suspension of civil liberties, if I understand the Leader of the Opposition, would be possible without some amendment to our statutes or some action by the government which would have to be brought before the House at some point."

The next day, October 15, Trudeau sounded a little closer to action: "I would not be truthful if I said that we had not considered such measures. However, the fact that we have not taken them indicates that we have not considered them in a way that would cause us to act on them, at least at this time."

The Prime Minister was not being very frank; that morning the cabinet had met to begin arrangements for imposing emergency measures on Canada. A second cabinet meeting at 2:30 p.m. authorized a security and intelligence committee — consisting of Trudeau, External Affairs Minister Sharp, Justice Minister John Turner, Solicitor-General George McIlraith, and two other ministers — to meet that night at 10:30 p.m. and impose the War Measures Act unless there had been some change in circumstances.

Premier Bourassa had set a deadline of 3 a.m. the next morning, October 16, for the kidnappers to respond to yet another offer of safe-conduct in return for release of the hostages. The deadline passed, the cabinet committee gave its go-ahead and, at 4 a.m., D. F. Hall, an assistant secretary to the federal cabinet, drove to Government House and asked that the Governor-General be awakened to sign an order imposing the War Measures Act and a series of supplementary regulations. Just before 5 a.m., all across Quebec, RCMP, provincial and municipal police pounced to arrest Quebeckers who were newly-made criminals under the provisions of the Act.

The new regulations permitted police to search without warrant, arrest without charge, and hold without bail persons they suspected of acting in contravention of the Act. It became a crime ever to have been a member of the FLQ — a retroactive law — and a crime to support the aims of the organization — a thought-control law. It was even a crime to make a statement "on behalf of" the FLQ, a provision that made the publicly owned Canadian Broadcasting Corporation, which had published the manifesto, open to such a charge.

Just as the crimes set out in the regulations were retroactive, so, apparently, was the gravity of the crisis. In the Throne Speech on October 8 — that is, three days after the kidnapping of Cross — Trudeau had practically purred about the state of Canada:

> An economy that is in need of adjustment; a society beset by a variety of tensions; an environment that has been abused and degraded; an international community that is under intense pressures — these are the problems that demand our immediate attention. But of those that are basically Canadian, none is insoluble. None takes the form of those dilemmas or irreconcilable issues which elsewhere fire the violence of despair. Notwithstanding its difficulties, Canada continues to enjoy social stability to an exceptional degree. This stability is not simply a matter of luck. Good fortune is a factor, but we should accept gracefully the fact that we are also more amenable to reason and, perhaps, more capable of wise decision than we are normally willing to admit.

Eight days later — that is, after the Laporte kidnapping — the Prime Minister was reading from a very different set of tea leaves:

> It is a matter of deep regret and grave concern to me, as I am sure it is to all honourable members, that the condition of our country makes necessary this proclamation. We in the House have all felt very strongly, I know, that democracy was nowhere in a healthier state than in Canada; that nowhere was there less need for frustrated men to turn to violence to attain their political ends. I still believe firmly that this is so. Yet in recent years we have been forced to acknowledge the existence within Canada of a new and terrifying person — one who in earlier times would have been described as an anarchist, but who is now known as a violent revolutionary. These persons allege that they are seeking social change through novel means. In fact, they are seeking the destruction of the social order through clandestine and violent means.
> Faced with such persons, and confronted with authoritative assessments of the seriousness of the risk to persons and property in the Montreal area, the government had no responsible choice but to act as it did last night.

What had happened to our social stability between October

8 and October 16? It was such a fragile thing that it blew away in two kidnappings, leaving us a residue of violent revolutionaries who had, it appears, been lurking there for years and had
somehow been overlooked.

In the subsequent debate, a number of opposition speakers,
led by John Diefenbaker for the Tories and David Lewis for the
NDP, suggested that no evidence had been produced of an
emergency that could not be met within the ordinary powers of
the law, and that if increased police powers were necessary,
they could be made through the Criminal Code. The government would have none of it. Justice Minister John Turner said,
"Why these powers? Because in the opinion of the attorney
general of the government of Quebec, an opinion which I share,
in the present situation . . . under the present law, the prosecution of this type of violent, criminal conspiracy is rendered
difficult, if not impossible, under the present provisions of the
Criminal Code."

This turned out to be balderdash. James Cross was found and
freed on December 3 as a result of normal police surveillance,
and his kidnappers were flown out to Cuba. Pierre Laporte
was found murdered on October 18, two days after the pro-
clamation of the War Measures Act, and his abductors were arrested December 28, again through the use of ordinary police
methods. As Tom Hazlitt, who covered the police operation
throughout for the *Toronto Daily Star*, noted, "The vast powers granted the police had no impact whatsoever on the all-im-
portant kidnapping investigations. . . . Pure police work, un-
related to any kind of extraordinary powers, led to the recovery
of British diplomat James Cross and the arrest of those believed
responsible for the murder of former labour minister Pierre
Laporte."

The War Measures Act was not used against the kidnappers; it was used against the more than 400 separatist sympathizers, musicians, writers, teachers and students, who were arrested, clapped in jail and, in most cases, released later without
any charge having been laid. The government made a number
of spirited defences of its action, none of which made much
sense.

Regional Affairs Minister Jean Marchand gave one explanation that bordered on hysteria. The FLQ, he said, were everywhere. "These people have infiltrated every strategic place
in the province of Quebec, every place where important decisions are taken. . . . There is an organization which has thou-

0d

sands of guns, rifles, machine-guns, bombs, and more than enough [dynamite] to blow up the core of downtown Montreal." However, the police raids failed to turn up the guns, rifles, machine-guns, bombs or dynamite, although they did sweep up Pauline Julien, whose misbehaviour at Niamey kept coming back like a song.

The Prime Minister advanced two principal explanations: the first was that there was a state of "apprehended insurrection" in the province of Quebec — although the term was never explained; the second was that Premier Bourassa and the Mayor of Montreal, Jean Drapeau, had asked for the emergency measures, and the federal government, after due consideration, had concurred.

The "apprehended insurrection" argument has never been clarified. Secretary of State Gérard Pelletier, who has devoted a whole book (*La Crise d'octobre*) to explaining the October crisis, placed the number of FLQ terrorists in the province at between forty and fifty, backed by 200 to 300 active sympathizers and between 2,000 and 3,000 passive sympathizers, who approve of the FLQ but will not belong to the organization. Neither Pelletier nor anyone else has ever explained how this handful was going to demolish civil order in the province. Justice Minister Turner hinted that, if only the government could tell all, we would understand its need to act quickly: "It is my hope that some day the full details of the intelligence upon which the government acted can be made public, because until that day comes the people of Canada will not be able fully to appraise the course of action which has been taken by the government." Turner was promptly contradicted by the Prime Minister, who told the Commons on October 23, "The facts that are known to the House are the facts on which we acted, and it is on that we stand." Trudeau was being more forthright than Turner: there were no secret documents presented to the cabinet to justify War Measures.

The argument that Ottawa was simply reacting to Bourassa's request also stands on shaky ground. The War Measures Act was subsequently replaced by a Public Order Act, whose provisions were somewhat less harsh, and which expired on April 30, 1971. Premier Bourassa wanted this Act extended indefinitely, and criticized the federal government bitterly for not complying with his wishes; but John Turner, who could see in the linking of his own name with the repressive

legislation (the Public Order Act was invariably referred to in
the French press as *la loi Turner*) the death of his own prime
ministerial ambitions, threatened to resign on the issue, and
the law died. Apparently the Bourassa voice that rolled like
thunder through Ottawa's council chambers in October had
been reduced, by April, to a squeak.

A theory widely held by those who admire Trudeau, but not
the way in which he abruptly suspended civil liberties in Canada, argues that the federal government simply panicked in
face of the October crisis; that the continuing reports of dissension and unrest in the Bourassa cabinet — which was badly
split in its reaction to the kidnappings — and the bom-
bardment of publicity that seemed to blow the FLQ into a major
political force, caused the Prime Minister to lose his perspective. In short, he blew his cool. This theory ignores everything we have learned about Trudeau. No one who watched
him under fire in the St. Jean Baptiste day parade in Montreal
during the 1968 federal election campaign, when he smiled and
waved under a shower of hurled pop bottles while other politi-
cos ran for cover, will believe that he is prone to panic.

In their study of the imposition of the War Measures Act,
*Rumours of War*, Toronto journalist Ron Haggart and lawyer
Aubrey Golden argue that the federal cabinet reacted to a ru-
mour that a provisional government was being plotted to take
over the province of Quebec. Haggart and Golden traced the
plot rumours down to a single meeting in the editorial offices of
*Le Devoir* in Montreal, at which Editor Claude Ryan suggested
that opening the Quebec cabinet to members of other parties —
including, if necessary, René Lévesque — might become necessary if government control of the situation broke down. Ryan
later discussed the possibility with Lucien Saulnier, chairman
of the city of Montreal's executive committee, who quickly dismissed it. "I don't think we will be driven to that extreme,"
Saulnier said. Ryan accepted that, and the idea died. But not
quite: word of it got back to Ottawa, where insiders were told,
"Ryan has been out to take over the government."

The story was obviously taken seriously, but my own cabinet
sources indicate that it was never advanced as *the* major reason
for imposing War Measures. After all, it is not illegal to propose considering a course of action, and while even discussion
of an all-party cabinet might indicate that Ryan thought there
was a good deal of unrest in the province, the most conservative

elements — and that certainly includes Saulnier — saw no basis for Ryan's concern.

There is only one explanation of the War Measures Act that makes sense: Trudeau saw in the October crisis a chance and a duty to meet what he considers to be the separatist menace head-on, and he took it. Consider the timing of events once more:

— On October 5, Cross was kidnapped.
— On October 8, the Throne Speech indicated an extraordinary degree of social stability, as the government saw it, in Canada.
— On October 10, Laporte was kidnapped.
— On October 12, troops moved into Ottawa.
— On October 16, War Measures were imposed and police rounded up hundreds of separatist — not necessarily FLQ — sympathizers.
— On October 18, Laporte's body was found.

Laporte's death has been used subsequently to explain the government's harsh measures, but in fact it had nothing to do with them. Nor was violence new to Quebec: there had been frequent bombings in the province since 1963, one of which had resulted in death. The conclusion is inescapable that the government action was not aimed at the FLQ at all, but at separatism; and certainly its first result was to bring a widespread revulsion against separatism both inside and outside the province. National polls taken immediately after the events showed that four out of five Canadians approved the Prime Minister's strong action, and a majority of Canadians were in favour, if necessary, of sending troops into Quebec to prevent that province from separating.

It is still too early to measure the long-term effect of the government's extreme reaction. At the time, a great deal of nonsense was written about it. Canada, we were told, had lost its innocence. What innocence? We have, in our short life-span, been through three wars, the Riel rebellions, a great many bloody riots, political suppression in Quebec's Padlock Law, economic suppression in the use of police to break strikes, and we have been busily engaged in recent years manufacturing armaments for the Americans to use against the Vietnamese, and chemical weapons for them to use against any and all comers. We have also been accused, with some justice, of con-

ducting a campaign of genocide against our own Indians and
Eskimos. But somehow, up until October 16, 1970, we were in-
nocents: it is an act as remarkable as the restoration of Doris
Day's virginity just before every movie.

The real effect of War Measures has nothing to do with innocence; it has to do with unity. The government must be
judged on the answers to two questions: was the action necessary? and will it, in the long run, aid or harm Canadian unity?
The answer to the first question, it seems to me, must be NO;
the government has never given an explanation satisfactory to
any but its most sycophantic supporters, and even they are beginning to waver. The answer to the second question cannot be
given yet, but the early signs are not hopeful. For every separatist the government arrested, it created a martyr and a hundred
sympathetic listeners; for every anti-separatist strengthened
in his views by what happened, a moderate was shifted towards separatism by the crisis. Claude Ryan, long a wavering
federalist, has indicated that, given a choice between Lévesque's separatism and Trudeau's anti-democratic tendencies,
he would choose Lévesque.[3] In the by-election to replace the
murdered Pierre Laporte, the Parti Québecois obtained 34 per
cent of the vote, slightly up from the provincial election of
April 1970. More significant was a survey conducted by political scientists Michel Bellavance and Marcel Gilbert of Laval
University, and reported in the May 29, 1971, editions of *Le
Devoir* and *La Presse*. The survey, taken between March 5 and
March 11, 1971, covered 1,194 people across the province, and
showed a decided shift in mood. Only 38.4 per cent of those
polled "approved entirely" the conduct of the Bourassa government during the crisis, although more than 70 per cent had approved the previous October. More Quebeckers worried that
they, or members of their family, would be taken by the police
or the army than by FLQ kidnappers, and an election call
would have seen only one party, the Parti Québecois, improve
its showing over the results of April 1970. (Fifteen per cent of
the respondents had voted PQ, and 17.5 per cent said they
would today; Liberals were down from 37.2 per cent to 28.6 per
cent and the Union Nationale from 8.3 per cent to 3.7 per cent.
The Ralliement Créditiste support remained constant at 5.5 per
cent.)

What's more, the PQ is moving to a more radical position.
On February 28, 1971, Pierre Bourgault, an extremist who had
been driven from office by the more moderate Lévesque, was

propelled back onto the party executive at the annual meeting, and at once began to mutter about the need for violence, in some circumstances, to work changes.

No one who travels in Quebec, no one who meets the young people in the colleges, the universities, or in the pubs of east-end Montreal, can believe that separatism died with Pierre Laporte or was even temporarily discredited by War Measures. Suppression, gun-point justice, arrest without charge and jail without bail have never stamped out the dissent they were aimed at in other nations; why should they work in Canada? If the Prime Minister's idea of unity is the brotherhood of the bull-pen, he may leave his nation even more divided than it was when he came onto the scene to save us from ourselves.

The October Crisis appeared to draw the governments of Ottawa and Quebec closer, but the phenomenon was temporary; by the time of the Constitutional Conference at Victoria, British Columbia, in June 1971, they were back in the familiar pose of antagonists. If the Victoria Conference was a failure — and at this writing it seems to have been that — much of the blame must be laid at the feet of an irresolute Premier Bourassa and an over-resolute Prime Minister Trudeau.

The conference was one in an endless, numbing series aimed at bringing Canada's constitution to Canada. After more than 100 years of Confederation, we are the only nation in the world without the power to amend the written part of our constitution. That part, the British North America Act, is a piece of legislation passed by the British Parliament, which alone has the power to vary its clauses (the rest of our constitution consists of unwritten traditions, such as the tradition of Cabinet government, and of the application of a number of key laws, such as the presumption of innocence, which have no place in the BNA Act). This situation is not only galling for the nation as a whole, it is particularly confining for the province of Quebec, which, rightly or wrongly, feels itself under siege, and wants greater control over its own destiny than the Fathers of Confederation ever envisaged when they drafted the BNA Act. For Quebec, constitutional reform has long been a matter of priority; for Trudeau, as he said in so many words, it is "a can of worms" he would just as soon not open. His attitude was not a helpful omen for the conference.

This was the seventh constitutional meeting since Lester

Pearson started the process in 1968. The way had been prepared not only by apparent agreement among the ten premiers and the Prime Minister that the constitution should be patriated, but by agreement on an amending formula to be applied after it was. (In brief, the formula gave a veto power to any of four groups: the federal government, any province with more than 25 per cent of the population — i.e. Ontario or Quebec — any two of the four Atlantic Provinces, and any two of the four western provinces, provided that they included half the region's population — i.e. either the three Prairie provinces in concert or British Columbia with any of the others.) Premier Bourassa had appeared to accept that formula in an earlier meeting in Ottawa in February 1971, but he quickly came under fire in his own province for his compliance. Quebeckers wanted more than an agreement to amend the constitution; they wanted a large measure of control over the crucial area of social security, and, just as important, over the money to pay for the new social programmes.

Since World War II, the federal government has moved more and more into areas of jurisdiction once thought to be within provincial control, because it alone had the money to finance the ambitious new schemes. Unemployment insurance and old-age pensions were given to the central government by constitutional amendment, as exceptions to the general rule that the provinces control social legislation (a rule set out in unequivocal terms in the BNA Act), and gradually, it came to be assumed that all the major planks of a modern welfare state should be laid down by Ottawa. Other provinces became restive under the new division of powers, which gave tremendous voting appeal, among other things, to the federal members, but Quebec's concern was always more vigorously expressed than that of any other government. Since the days of Jean Lesage, Quebec leaders have seen control over the vital areas of provincial development slipping into Ottawa hands; protests voiced by Quebec politicians of every political stripe have not reversed the process; at best, the province has earned the right to opt out of certain programmes, or, in the case of the Canada Pension Plan, to see its own, superior plan accepted by the rest of the nation. But we continue to become a more centralized nation, and when Bourassa appeared to be aiding the process, he faced repudiation by his own party. A meeting of the Liberal caucus, held before the Victoria Conference, denied the Premier the open mandate he wanted to take west with him; he was instructed to come back with control over social legislation, or to withhold Quebec's agreement. Faced with that political reality, and with the Prime Minister's blunt assertion that the conference would have to say Yes or No, at once and forever, to constitutional amendment, the Victoria meeting seemed doomed, despite some of the hopeful drum-beating that preceded it. (Among that hopeful drum-beating was an announcement by the Prime Minister that the federal government would, if all went well, agree to pay 50 per cent of the cost of a guaranteed income scheme for any province that wished it. The arrangement did not constitute federal support for guaranteed income; far from it, since the provinces most in need of such a scheme are precisely those least able to afford the other 50 per cent. The offer was never pursued in Victoria, and quietly disappeared.)

The three-day meeting in the British Columbia capital opened with the usual round of polite hokum and impolite denunciations. As part of the former, Premier W. A. C. Bennett arranged a 45-minute motorcade to get the visiting dignitaries from the Empress Hotel, where they were staying, to the legislature, a five-minute stroll away; as part of the latter, the same Premier Bennett attacked the federal equalization payments because they sent British Columbia money to Quebec, and suggested a crash programme to provide "a healthy moral environment in which our young people can grow to maturity". That out of the way, the leaders moved behind closed doors for the bargaining sessions. Since nothing really important was at stake, only the future of our nation, we were not allowed to see or hear anything that went on at these sessions. But from the coverage-by-rumour, which has become the traditional way of reporting such meetings, we didn't miss much. Premier Bourassa was indecisive and not particularly articulate in setting out Quebec's position, Trudeau was firm and articulate in rejecting it.

What emerged at the end of the conference was a document grandly billed as the "Victoria Charter", which was a mishmash of compromises. Characteristically, the Charter, although it contained sixty-one clauses, had no preamble, because none could be agreed upon by the assembled politicians. The main provisions of the charter can be simply stated:

— on language rights, the Charter recognized French and English as official languages and provided that either could be used in the seven provincial legislatures east of Saskatchewan. Citizens were assured of the right to communicate with their governments in either language, but only in five provinces — Ontario, Quebec, New Brunswick, Prince Edward Island and Newfoundland. There was no agreement on linguistic rights in the federal bilingual districts set up by the Official Languages Act, and no guarantee of bilingual instruction in the schools. (Here, Quebec was as much at fault as the other provinces, being as uncertain about enshrining the rights of its own English minority as the other provinces were about French.)

— on regional disparities, there was a clause committing Ottawa to attempt to eliminate them.

— on the amending formula, there was agreement to accept the provision already outlined above.

— on human rights, there was a vague clause entrenching such rights as freedom of opinion and thought, but careful avoidance of such legal rights as that to bail or *habeus corpus.*

— on the Supreme Court, a crucial issue for the provinces, which felt that legal interpretations could upset their rights and priorities, there was a complex system that gave the provinces, in effect, a veto over federal appointments.

— on social legislation, there was a hollow provision that gave the provinces paramountcy in such fields as family allowances, manpower training allowances and old-age pensions, but made no mention of reallocating the funds to support these programmes. Ottawa argued that it must have control to insure uniformity across the country, Quebec argued that it must have the control or lose the right to set its own priorities according to the needs of its own people. The resulting compromise gave Quebec titular control, but left the real power with Ottawa.

The Victoria Charter carried with it a Prime Ministerial ultimatum — the provinces were to accept it, as is, or reject it, within ten days, that is, by June 28, 1971. Although he sounded optimistic in Victoria — or perhaps not so much optimistic as befuddled — Bourassa could not accept the Charter, which was ringingly denounced from every corner of his home province. Claude Lemelin, chief editorial writer for Montreal's *Le Devoir*, asked the crucial question: "What other political leader in Canada, what other political leader in the world, would ever consider pushing through his legislature a law with which he was not altogether happy, given the facts that, in the process, he would have to accept the resignation of five key ministers, pit himself against organized labour, incur the wrath of the press, lose all sympathy from the academics on whom his government relies for expertise — and be faced with a mounting wave of protest and unrest that could easily boil over and then be put under control only by calling in the troops?"

Back in Quebec City, Bourassa announced rejection of the Charter on June 23 — five days before the deadline — and his province was promptly made the villain of the piece by the rest of Canada. Once more, French Canada was blocking progress. What those anxious to belabour Quebec missed was that the increasing incursion by Ottawa into fields of provincial jurisdiction is an issue that affects all provinces. Western Canadians who poured scorn on Bourassa are the first to complain about operation LIFT, but apparently they don't see the connection.

All too often, devotion to federalism in Canada means subservience to Ottawa, which is not the same thing at all. Federalism implies a division of powers, held in uneasy balance by continuing competition between provincial and federal governments; it does not mean a system in which Ottawa collects all the money and makes all the major decisions. A nation as large, sparsely populated and diverse as Canada is not suited to a unitary form of government, but we are drifting towards it. The failure at Victoria, which left the Prime Minister so unconcerned — he said his government would now be free to "get on with other business" — is just another disquieting landmark along that route.

## Notes

1. Source material for this incident, and for most of the events described in this chapter, is drawn from daily newspaper coverage. An excellent roundup of the Quebec–Ottawa clashes during 1969 is found in J. Saywell, ed. *Canadian Annual Review 1969* (Toronto: University of Toronto Press, 1970).

2. Again, source material on the Cross and Laporte kidnappings is from news accounts, although the shifting moods in the province are related from my own observations in Quebec during the crisis period.

3. "Claude Ryan's Answer", *Maclean's* Magazine, May 1971.

# 5

# Inflation:
# St. Pierre and the Dragon

*The objective of a just society must always include the
pursuit of a prosperous economy as well as the fair
distribution of its proceeds.*
Speech from the Throne, September 1968

*I go in and fill out an application if they'll give me one
but I don't really expect to get a job any more. . . . I
guess it shows. . . . I'm getting tired of walking and of
being told there's not a chance, nothing doing.*
Factory worker John Noseworthy, January 1971

When Trudeau came to power in 1968, the average rate of unemployment ran between 4 and 5 per cent. It had been as low as
3.6 per cent in 1965, as high as 4.7 per cent in 1964. For 1968,
the first year of his reign, it averaged 4.8 per cent. From that
time it marched steadily upward to a high of 8.1 per cent in February 1971.[1] At that time there were 675,000 Canadians out of
work, and another substantial number — about 100,000 — un-
dergoing Manpower retraining programmes; most of these individuals were also out of work. There were almost as many
jobless as there had been at the height of the Depression (although the percentage of unemployed was lower, and the support available for them was higher). The figures became a matter of heated controversy between the government and opposition parties. The opposition insisted on citing the unemployed
rate as the number of people without jobs compared to the total

labour force — the figure that produced an 8.1 per cent unemployment rate. The government insisted that only a seasonally adjusted rate could fairly be used. Seasonal adjustment recognizes that in a cold-weather country such as Canada, there will always be more people out of work in the winter than in the summer; therefore the rate of unemployment is jiggered to reflect, not the rate of jobless compared to the labour force, but compared to the number of jobless in previous years at the same season. A man out of work in June, by this standard, weighs more heavily statistically than he does in December. In December, apparently, you damn well expect to be in trouble. There was only cold comfort in this argument for those who were trudging the streets and pacing the parks, but for what it's worth, seasonally adjusted unemployment in February 1971 was 6.2 per cent. However measured, there were 675,000 Canadians who wanted to work and couldn't, and they found themselves in that predicament as a result of the brutal calculation, blind stubbornness and ordinary dim-wittedness of the Trudeau government.

For the first two years of its reign, the administration was obsessed with the dragon inflation, and its pursuit of the beast left in its wake broken lives, broken homes and broken hopes. The Prime Minister claimed that it was not he who had spooked the dragon; he had laid a clear choice before the people of Canada, and they'd chosen wrong. "It certainly wasn't the government's intention to create unemployment," he said, "on the contrary, we warned people what might come if we didn't get voluntary restraint. We didn't get it, and it came."

That is an interesting statement, well worth examining in the light of the economic policies pursued by the government.[2]

Inflation was already considered to be a nagging though not overwhelming problem during the Pearson years, and repeated attempts to bring it under some sort of control were unleashed from time to time. They had no perceptible effect. Then, in early 1969, the Trudeau regime declared all-out war on inflation. The first shot was fired by the Governor of the Bank of Canada, Louis Rasminsky, in a speech to the Overseas Bankers Club in London, England, on February 3, 1969:

> Expressions of concern about inflation sometimes draw the reply that we must choose between inflation and unacceptable rates of unemployment. . . . I think we are seeing more

and more evidence that this is an illusion. The idea that a certain rate of inflation must be accepted more or less
indefinitely as the price that has to be paid for keeping unemployment at some target level assumes that large numbers of people do not know what is happening to them when
prices rise persistently. But people are not so foolish. They
do observe what is happening and if it keeps on happening
they develop an expectation of continuing inflation and ad-
just their behaviour accordingly. . . . Tolerance of inflation,
by breeding the widespread expectation of continued
inflation, makes the job of demand management more
difficult and less reliable.

I'm not sure what all that means to an economist, but to me it
comes across loud and clear: if we insist on keeping people
working as a first priority— "keep unemployment at some target level" — instead of sticking to really important work, like
defending the dollar, then, by God, people will learn to tolerate
inflation, playing the veritable Hob with demand management.
Rasminsky talks about inflation as if it were a venereal disease.
Never mind why, the damn thing had to be scourged. Nor was
he reluctant about naming the folks whose illicit amours
brought on the pox; inflation came from high wages, high
prices and high government spending. Those were the sweets
that must be forsaken no matter how tempting their allure.
Think of the children; they could be born blind. The last pay-
raise Rasminsky got was $25,000 a year, to $75,000; a great
many Canadians were willing to join him on the battle-front
the moment they had reached that figure.

Rasminsky laid it on the line: "The most important immediate objective of economic policy in many countries from both
the domestic and external point of view is to break the
inflationary expectations that exist and to restore respect for
the value of money." A chap can hug a phrase like that to his
bosom from breadline to breadline; it will not keep him warm,
but it will keep him proud; it will not feed his wife and children,
the whining curs, but it will let him know that he is doing his
part, in his own small way, to protect the dollar.

Having prepared the foot-soldiers for what was to come,
Rasminsky laid down his next barrage in the Bank's annual report, released on March 20, 1969:

It is of crucial importance to all Canadians that the problem of inflation be dealt with successfully, that we bring to an end the excessive price and cost increases which are threatening to undermine our prospects for durable growth in the future. . . . We shall need a consistency of approach and a deep determination to persevere until we are certain that we have dealt effectively with the problem. The stakes are too great to warrant anything less.

Except for a certain gumminess in the phrasing, there is something in that that smacks of Montgomery at Alamein, or Henry V at Agincourt. And Rasminsky, needless to say, was first into the breach. Under prodding, the major chartered banks raised their prime lending rate to 7 per cent in mid-January 1969 and, a few weeks later, interest rates on savings deposits were raised. The interest rates on treasury bills also began their upward climb, from 6.38 per cent on three-month bills in January 1969 to 7.81 per cent by December of that year. Money began to dry up; for individual consumers the cost of borrowing became prohibitive, for small businessmen there were no loans available. (The big businessmen, of course, were not so hard hit; they don't have to borrow from the banks anyway, since the bulk of their spending is generated from internal funds.) Naturally, inevitably, the lay-offs began.

On April 11, Rasminsky gave the screw another twist with the announcement that, beginning in June, the chartered banks would be required to maintain a minimum secondary reserve— in addition to the current reserve set by law— of 8 per cent of the total Canadian dollar deposit liabilities rather than 7 per cent. The effect was to pull huge additional amounts of money out of circulation, and throw more people out of work.

That the federal government approved all this is a matter of proud record. In June, Finance Minister Edgar Benson lobbed his own hand-grenade into the inflation war with an anti-inflationary budget. It called for a budgetary surplus of $250 million — the first surplus since 1956-57— and unrolled a number of specific anti-inflation measures, which included a two-year deferment of depreciation allowances on commercial buildings in the cities of Ontario, Alberta and British Columbia, an extension of the 3 per cent special surtax on personal and corporate incomes levied by the Pearson government in January 1968, and immediate implementation of a series of tariff reductions which were to have taken place over a thirty-

month period. The surplus meant a severe slash in government
spending. (The turnaround was from a deficit of $575 million
in a single year, a change of $825 million.) The extension of the
surtax pulled yet more money out of consumers' and corporations' hands. The depreciation deferment was expected to
produce, and did produce, an immediate halt to construction in
the fast-growth areas of the nation; and the tariff reductions
were to bring in cheaper American goods and undermine Canadian prices. Uncle Edgar had a bullet for everyone.

Still, inflation refused to go away and, on August 13, 1969,
the Prime Minister rolled his own howitzer up to the front line
and fired off his expenditure guidelines at a special press conference. These guidelines froze the level of government spending, and cut the federal payroll by 25,000 jobs from the 1968
level (partly through attrition, by simply not hiring new people
for jobs that became vacant, and partly through firings). The
net effect was to end all hope of swift action in such priority
fields as housing and welfare, to put the federal civil service
into a well-justified state of panic, and to set a hard line which,
hopefully, the shock-troops of business and labour would follow. The Prime Minister justified his guidelines by that wonderful economist's stunt, the extrapolation. Since 1960, he said,
"Spending on general government services has more than
doubled. Spending on foreign affairs has doubled. Spending on
economic development has tripled. Spending on health and
welfare has almost doubled. The federal share of the cost of
post-secondary education has multiplied sixteen times since
1960."

The figures were a trick, of course. Spending on foreign affairs and economic development had shot up because we were
beginning to do some of the things we should have done years
earlier. Spending on health and welfare had doubled partly because we were providing a modicum of welfare services for the
first time, and partly because Medicare had been introduced.
Huge sums that had been spent in the private sector as individual doctor bills were now showing up in government spending;
it wasn't an increase, just a transfer. The federal share of post-
secondary education costs had skyrocketted mainly because
there were almost no such costs in 1960; again it was a change
in policy that had shifted some of the cost from the provincial
to the federal government. Trudeau skipped the central point of
whether these increases were a good or bad thing from the

viewpoint of ordinary Canadians, and went on to paint a scarifying picture of the future:

> We'd be on the road to financial disaster if nothing were done to bring spending under control. Spending on just the general government services that exist now would go up another 50 per cent by 1975. Spending on foreign affairs would double again in five years. Spending on economic development would more than double again. Spending on health and welfare would go from $2.4 billions to $4.3 billions. The federal share of post-secondary education costs would quadruple. Total spending by the federal government would go up to nearly $17.5 billions in 1974-75; but revenues would go up to about $15.75 billions — leaving a deficit that year of $1.75 billion or a cumulative deficit over the next five years of $7.5 billion.

"Clearly," he concluded, "something must be done, and done at once."

Land-a-mercy, what a disaster we all faced; except that the figures were phoney. Spending on foreign affairs will not double by 1975, according to the forward estimates of the External Affairs Department and the Canadian International Development Agency; nor was there any basis but financial spookery for any of the other figures given. The underlying argument was phoney, too. If expenditures on economic development "more than double again", they will result in more national income — that's what economic development is all about. And the deficit red-inked in by the Prime Minister could be covered as easily by tax changes in an expanding economy as by slashing away at spending in a collapsing one. But it was inflation the Prime Minister was after, and he meant to have its hide. Inflation hits hardest at those at the lowest end of the economic scale, he said, those on low and fixed incomes, and something must be done to protect them. What he proposed to do was to throw them out of work, for their own betterment, although it was never put that crudely.

In fact, the freeze did not hold government expenditures down; they rose by 9.5 per cent over the next year,[3] but the squeeze on money continued, stock markets remained depressed and the bond market became, in the jargon of the Street, "a stretcher case".

The rising interest rates meant, among other things, that the banks who were so vociferous in their support of the anti-inflation war were coining handsome returns. Some persons thrown into the street by tight money might have raised a quibble, had not Rasminsky stepped into the breach with more soothing words. Some people, he told the House of Commons Committee on Finance, Trade and Economic Affairs, felt that "high interest rates are themselves inflationary because they increase the costs of those who do succeed in borrowing money. While it is true that there is some effect in this direction, the much more important role of high interest rates is to provide an incentive for people not to spend and not to borrow."

Just as it is the duty of the poor to hurl themselves over the unemployment wall, it is the duty of the rich to coin profits on their misfortune. Mother Nature has a wonderful way of balancing things out for her children; for every bum thrown out onto Wellington Street in Ottawa, another mint julep for the chaps in the Rideau Club.

It was at this propitious stage that Dr. John Young and the Prices and Incomes Commission joined the Prime Minister, the Finance Minister and the Bank of Canada in the trenches. Dr. Young was appointed in May 1969 to head the Commission, which was to investigate the causes of continuing inflation and to recommend cures.[4] He was specifically enjoined not to single out villains, and promptly proceeded to so so. Labour, greedy labour, which would not hold its demands to the 6 per cent wage raise per year recommended by the Commission, became at once and forever the villain in Dr. Young's thesis.

There was a certain dim logic to this argument; wages were certainly moving up faster than profits, but this had nothing to do with the superior virtue and restraint of employers. Wage rates react more slowly to economic change than profits; a manufacturer can change the price on his goods overnight, whereas labour contracts run for from one to three years. The unions were still trying to catch up to the profits of the expansionary middle-1960s, while those profits were on the way down.[5]

Even so, Young's was a selective approach to villainy; it ignored the fact that only about one-third of the Canadian labour force is organized and is therefore able to keep up the clamour for higher wages; it ignored the thousands of Canadians in the professions, making huge incomes; it ignored the raises paid to company executives (one *Financial Post* survey indicated recent pay raises among executives averaged over 30 per cent per annum) and concentrated exclusively on two areas: wages and prices. If they could be held, all would hold. Profits were not part of it; thus if a company, through the increased productivity of its workers, was able to increase its profits, it could keep the increase, and as long as it did not raise its prices or share the wealth with its employees, it was doing its duty by the Commission and the government. Marvellous thing, economics.

The labour unions had made it clear long before the Prices and Incomes Commission was appointed that they would have no part of an anti-inflation war that did not contain profits and professional salaries, and that froze exploited and underpaid workers at the same level and on the same terms as the powerful and affluent. They would have no truck, in short, with the Commission's view that workers in Newfoundland, where the average wage during 1969 was $105.86 weekly, should hold the line with provincial doctors, who were making $49,000 a year on the average.[6] Business leaders, to whom the Commission's 6 per cent guidelines meant, as much as anything else, a powerful weapon with which to fend off their own workers (Gawd, I'd like to give you a big, fat raise, fellas, but you wouldn't want me to go against the *government*), proved more co-operative, and the Canadian Manufacturers Association accepted, at least in principle, the guidelines that the unions rejected. Thus labour became the implacable foe of the Commission, and the Commission's work was reduced to sporadic pious mumblings, because there could be no co-operation to hold the price line.

Those mumblings were just nicely under way when, in September 1969, the Economic Council of Canada came down with a disquieting report. Perhaps, the Council hinted, the anti-inflation forces were attacking on the wrong front at the wrong time. "With unemployment in the range of 4 to 5 per cent in 1968 and early 1969, it is difficult to argue that excessive general demand pressure has contributed to inflationary conditions. The general policy environment in Canada in 1968 has been restrictive."

The government's whole thesis had been that excessive demand in the economy was pushing prices upward, and the tight

money policies were designed to slacken that demand. The
ECC warned that much of the inflationary pressure was a slop-
over from the U.S., so that chucking Canadians out of their jobs
might have little effect on inflation while wreaking havoc in the
economy. The Council wrapped this up in difficult language
that is well worth wading into:

> In Canada it is difficult to maintain that current inflation is a
> reflection of excessive demand pressures, for the Canadian
> economy has been operating with at least a moderate overall
> margin of slack since 1968. On the other hand, in the United
> States the problem of price and cost inflation has been very
> much one of excessive demand, aggravated by the impact on
> the economy of the war in Vietnam. Until some easing of
> price and cost increases takes place in the United States, Ca-
> nadian policies to deal with domestic price and cost problems
> will be handicapped. Further fiscal and monetary restraint
> could conceivably result in higher rates of unemployment
> and economic slack with no more than marginal effects on
> current rates of increase in prices and costs. Moreover,
> tighter restraint in Canada this year is likely to have its main
> impact on the economy next year. And if excess demand
> pressures in the United States are brought under control by
> the latter part of 1969, the principal result of stringent de-
> mand policy restraints in Canada this year might well be ser-
> iously mistimed to push the economy into a poor economic
> performance.[7]

There, buried under all that economist's language, was a
warning that might have been put into five words: for Pete's
sake, watch out. If, as seemed likely, the U.S. economy went
into a nose-dive — and it did — Canada would be slowing
down precisely when we should be speeding up — and we
were. That warning came from the one independent economic
body appointed for the precise task of advising the government
on its fiscal and monetary performance. It was ignored. The
federal cabinet, apart from making denigrating side-references
to ECC Chairman Arthur Smith (who has since announced his
resignation), never once discussed the Council's report.

And it all came to pass just as the ECC said it would. In late
1969, unemployment began creeping upwards in response to
the government's tight-money campaign. On December 22,

when it hit 5 per cent, the Prime Minister called a press conference to unlimber a new salvo at inflation, which was, he said, our "worst enemy": "There are a lot of people in this country who are bargaining that, oh well, the government can't hang tough for too long because it will only get frightened when it sees unemployment go up to 6 per cent. But if people think we are going to lose our nerve now, they should think again. We're not."

At the same press conference, the Prime Minister said that a floating exchange rate for the Canadian dollar would result in devaluation and an exchange crisis. The German Deutschmark had just been revalued upwards, and other currencies seemed likely to follow; a number of economists (including, as we shall see later, a member of Trudeau's own cabinet, Eric Kierans) argued that removing the dollar from the limits imposed by the International Monetary Fund (for which read the United States) would act as a buffer between Canadian and American inflationary pressures. In order to hold the Canadian dollar at its pegged rate, we were buying U.S. funds, draining ever more money out of our own economy. That suited the Prime Minister right down to the ground.

Throughout 1970 the government hung tough, just as Trudeau had promised, provoking a long, bitter postal strike because it would not bend on the 6 per cent wage guidelines (in the end it had to give way; the strike did nothing but harass an increasingly plagued economy and underline the futility of the guidelines), holding fast to a tight monetary policy and ignoring the increasingly clear warnings of the economists that it was pursuing a wrong-headed and mistimed policy. Led by Finance Minister Benson who, from the sanctuary of a $65-a-day suite in Vancouver's Bayshore Inn, let the peasants know that it was perfectly possible for a Canadian family to get along on $30 a week, the government stuck to its guns. The U.S. did, in fact, go into a slump. In Canada unemployment lines grew longer, factories slowed, then stilled and, during the summer of 1970, hordes of young unemployed rolled across the land, a tide of discontent.

In May 1970, Canada went off the fixed exchange rate onto a floating rate. This came about because, while the government kept warning that increasing costs in Canada would hinder our goods on international markets, that was simply not the case.[8] Canadian prices were rising, but the prices of our international competitors were rising even faster; our goods were a very good buy on the export market. Our balance of trade was more than healthy; in 1968 we had a merchandise trade surplus of $1,375,000,000,[9] and in 1969 one of $860,000,000. There were more foreign dollars chasing Canadian goods than there were Canadian dollars chasing foreign goods. At the same time, our high interest rates were attracting foreign capital. The pegged Canadian dollar was thus worth more than the artificially low price tagged to it, and it was costing us more and more, in the purchase of U.S. currency, to cool off the demand for it. Finally the pressure threatened to become too great, and we went off the pegged dollar. The result was not, as the Prime Minister had predicted, devaluation and an exchange crisis. The dollar climbed rapidly to near-equity with the U.S. dollar; it became, in fact, too strong. This was because the government, in its obsession with inflation, insisted on keeping interest rates high, which drew ever more foreign dollars into Canada in search of profits. With a singular faculty for combining two wrong policies, the government had stumbled into a situation of a floating dollar and high interest rates. As Montreal economist Dian Cohen noted, inevitably, in such conditions, three things happen:

1. Because our dollar is more expensive, our international competitiveness is reduced, because exports cost more. Layoffs follow.

2. Investment at home is inhibited, because it costs so much to borrow. Layoffs follow.

3. Government revenues are reduced because incomes are lower. The government has to borrow or tax more, drawing on the already limited money supply. Layoffs follow.

None of these developments came as a surprise; all flowed from the government's obsession with inflation. The result was an unemployment crisis. Because the cutbacks fell unevenly, as always, some regions became disaster areas. In the Atlantic region the jobless rate hit 10.2 per cent;[10] in some towns almost the entire population was out of work.

Then, just before Christmas 1970, the Prime Minister made a startling discovery. He told the waiting world, "Inflation no longer exists in Canada." The new problem, he said, was unemployment.

In fact, inflation had not been licked, although Canada had done better, in terms of holding prices down, than other nations. (The Consumer Price Index rose from 122.6 in January

1969 to 130.3 in January 1971.) But goods were still costing more, and those on low and fixed incomes were still hurting. Soon the Prime Minister was out to the trenches again, for a dekko round. In March 1971 he discovered inflation once more, lurking out there in No Man's Land. He meant to have done with it, he said, either through voluntary price and wage restraints in the private sector of the economy or, by George, through a government-run system of price and wage controls. But by the time Finance Minister Benson put forth his new budget, on June 18, 1971 (of which more in the next chapter), all was serene again, at least in the government's view. Inflation was so well in hand that Benson felt safe in slashing taxes, withdrawing the 3 per cent surtax and raising personal exemptions. Since he had never admitted any connection between government policy and high unemployment, he was unable to say these moves were taken to stir the sluggish economy; instead, they were to "reinforce . . . expected growth" and reduce unemployment, which had crept mysteriously into the economy.

For the time being at least, the inflation war was over. As truce was declared, Canadians could count the cost in dollars and jobs, even if there would never be a reckoning of the smashed lives attributable to the inflation war. Unemployment, said Arthur Smith of the ECC, meant that "A significant portion of our national production resources are now running to waste — in total, perhaps at an annual rate of $4 billion. In other words, on the average, in each week in the latter part of 1970, perhaps about $70 million to $80 million of output is not being produced that could potentially be produced, and an equivalent amount of total income that could be generated is not being generated."

Another noted economist, Professor O.J. Firestone of the University of Ottawa, compared the Canadian performance to that of other nations in an article for the *Canadian Tax Journal*, and we did not come off well. Between mid-1969 and mid-1970, consumer prices rose by 3.3 per cent in Canada, compared with 5.8 per cent in the U. S. and an average of about 5 per cent for twenty-two industrialized countries surveyed by the Organization for Economic Co-operation and Development. The price we paid was fearful. We had the highest rate of unemployment of any of the nations surveyed, and our production fell further behind its potential than was the case in most

other countries. This meant, Dr. Firestone wrote, "That Canada could have produced an additional Gross National Product
of about $2 billion and provided new jobs for up to 200,000 Ca-
nadians had she pursued policies that would have made full and
effective use of men, capital equipment and natural resources
available."

It also meant, despite repeated government denials, that
Canada, unlike most countries, deliberately chose a course of
high unemployment and relative price stability. Firestone, a
former economic advisor to the federal government, produced a
reaction of sorts from the Prime Minister. In response to a
question in the House of Commons, Trudeau said that, had the
government known the Canadian performance in the international sphere was going to be so much better than that of the
U.S., it might not have pushed the anti-inflation fight quite so
hard (it should have known, of course, because the ECC had
told it so), a response that must have brought immense relief to
the breadlines of Toronto, Montreal, Halifax and Vancouver.

What was so irritating about the anti-inflation war was not
merely its inequity — there were no cabinet ministers on the
unemployment rolls, no bank presidents, no Chamber of
Commerce chieftains — but its wrong-headedness. The Prime
Minister and Finance Minister chose to ignore the ECC because
they had already firmly identified inflation as a monster, and
strapped on their armour to do battle. Once they had decided to
play St. George, it was no good pointing out that what looked
like a dragon was only a kitten, not when that handmaiden,
Commerce, was already on the scene, rolling her almond eyes
and heaving her handsome bosom in anticipation of the coming
slaughter. Consider for a moment the basic questions that faced
the government:[11]

What is inflation ?
What causes it?
Whom does it hurt?
How can it be dealt with?

The first question is easy. Inflation is a general and persistent
rise in prices. It is not inflation when you pay a dime more for a
steak, or a quarter more for a movie, but when you pay more for
steak, *and* movies, *and* cars, *and* most other goods and services:

that's inflation. When prices go up too much and too fast, the results on the economy may be disastrous. When, instead of taking a wallet-full of money to buy a wheelbarrow, it takes a wheelbarrow full of money to buy a wallet, life is bound to become unsettling for everybody (with the possible exception of wheelbarrow manufacturers). But because runaway inflation poses a serious threat, it does not follow that every upward price movement promises runaway inflation. Prices in Canada have been rising for the past few years; that's inflation, but it is not runaway inflation, and it does not help to react as if it were. The Prime Minister heard the baby crying and resolved to meet the emergency by garroting it.

What causes inflation?

When the demands of the economy approach the capacity of industry and the labour force to satisfy them, there is more money chasing goods than there are goods available, and prices rise. Inflation is the product of a full, or nearly full, economy. What's more, it is the inevitable product of such an economy. The choice, as Canada found to its sorrow, is between a growing economy and some degree of inflation or a slack economy and some degree of price stability. Professor Firestone put it this way: "Stable economic growth is proving to be an elusive target not likely to be reached in the foreseeable future either in Canada or in other Western industrialized countries."

Besides this demand-caused inflation, Canada faces the special problem of being next door to the U.S. and the victim of spill-over from the American economy. When demand in the U.S. is on the upswing, we are unable to insulate ourselves from its effects. Our exports to the U.S. increase, creating fatter prices. There is also a psychological reaction; our manufacturers look across the border, see higher prices coming and raise their own, and our unions respond to the gains of U.S. labour. This was the point underlined by the ECC, and it is worth bearing in mind when considering that panacea, wage and price controls. There are two problems with such controls: the first is the problem of administering such a complex system fairly; the second is the difficulty that controls tinker with the symptoms rather than the causes of inflation. Since these causes are mainly external, elaborate Canadian controls to ward off U.S.-induced inflation would be an exercise in futility.

Whom does inflation hurt?

The answer is not as simple as it first appears. Conventional wisdom, the wisdom that allows the Prime Minister to tell those he is throwing out of work that he has their own best interests at heart, argues that the real victims are those on low and fixed incomes. That's not necessarily so; a study prepared by Professor Rosalind Blauer of Brock University suggests that the distribution of income is not fundamentally altered by inflation or recession. Those who do badly in inflationary times also fare badly in depressions. In fact, they may do better when money is plentiful because then, and only then, is attention drawn to their condition. In times of rising prices, old-age pensioners are handicapped because they have to meet rising prices from fixed incomes. But when prices are stable, they are still at a disadvantage. Other groups in the economy are able to bargain for increases; the pensioners are not; their share of the national income continues to fall. Their best chance comes during inflation, when their plight is visible and money is available to meet it. It was in the boom year of 1957 that pensioners received a 30 per cent increase in government support; their share of the national income actually went up. In short, it is not the price squeeze that hurts our poor and elderly, but our miserly treatment of them in fair times and foul. They are certainly not helped by government austerity programmes that begin — as this one did — by freezing welfare.

At the other end of the scale, the wealthy do not, as advertised, clean up in times of inflation. People anticipate inflation today, and protect themselves by demanding higher wages and higher interest rates as a hedge against it. From a corporation's point of view, this means that costs of production rise. But depreciation allowances, which are fixed, do not. In effect, the companies pay taxes on a higher share of their profits; this cuts into after-tax profits and lowers the price of stocks — which is just what has been happening in Canada. Because only the wealthy own stocks in significant quantities, the net result of inflation is a tendency to distribute wealth more evenly.

Then why do governments turn so readily to unemployment to cure the ills of inflation? Because it is a sacrifice to be made by somebody else. Joblessness is not a threat to the fat cats who are its tireless advocates; it is a threat to the lumbermen of Newfoundland, the steelworkers of Quebec, the shop clerks of Vancouver. When the economy goes slack, the upper ranks bear the anguish of those below with that stoicism we reserve for the hurts of others.

The government's approach to inflation is entangled in a series of misconceptions. The first is the notion that everything should cost today what it cost yesterday. When incomes improve, prices advance — they always have, and they always will. What counts is our relative position in the wage-price tug of war, and inflation really has little bearing on that. The second misconception is the notion dear to the Prime Minister that government spending is somehow different from private spending in its effect on the economy. Welfare spending was up, he said, and that was inflationary, but the $175 million spent by Ford and Chrysler to produce new model cars in 1969 was somehow not. New industry wrings huzzahs from the government, but more money for education must not be tolerated. In fact, it doesn't matter who spends money or where; in terms of its inflationary effect, the only question is: how much? A third misconception, perhaps the governing one, holds that government spending is bad, and private spending good, because the former decreases our freedom of choice, while the latter enhances it. So, when inflation threatens, the first reaction is to carve up the civil service and cut government costs, even though those costs and those civil servants may be directed towards more useful ends than their opposite numbers in the private sector. Government spending need not limit choice; it may enhance it. Increased private spending may permit a choice between a new car and a TV set; increased government spending may allow us to choose between a new car factory and a new school, between financing another television station and improving the quality of Canadian cities.

When these misconceptions are linked, our response to inflation becomes very narrow indeed. Because we hanker, with Governor Rasminsky, after price stability, we miss the connection between rising prices and full employment, and resolve that Something Must Be Done. But what? We can tinker with monetary policy — and have done so — but because the major source of inflation is a spillover from the U.S., the main effect is merely to produce unemployment. We can tinker with fiscal policy — the raising and spending of public funds — but only within the bounds of a notion that demands we begin by cutting government expenditures and end by leaving the tax rate alone. In short, we are hindered from doing anything except to provoke a mild recession, with consequent unemployment to be borne by somebody else. And that is exactly what Prime Minister Trudeau did.

Instead of accepting a degree of inflation as inevitable, and providing for those on low and fixed incomes by tying them to a realistic cost-of-living bonus, he plunged through the thickets in search of a cure. What is depressing about the exercise is that neither the Prime Minister nor his principal advisors seemed to have learned anything from it. Inflation is still to be pursued, with different spears, perhaps, but no less diligently; and those who stand unarmoured, close enough to feel the dragon's breath, will be, next time as last, the poor.

## Notes

1. Dominion Bureau of Statistics, *The Labour Force*, bulletin of March 18, 1971.
2. The accounting of Trudeau's anti-inflation war is drawn mainly from newspapers and Hansard.
3. *Canadian Statistical Review*, February 1971, p. 42.
4. The Commission's mandate was "To inquire into and report upon the causes, processes and consequences of inflation", a mandate wide enough to drive a truck through. The government did insist, though, that there was to be no name-calling or finger-pointing.
5. Organization for Economic Co-operation and Development, *Economic Survey*, May 1970, p. 19.
6. Figure given by Newfoundland Health Minister Ed Roberts to a meeting of the Newfoundland Medical Association in March 1971.
7. Economic Council of Canada, *Sixth Annual Review*, p. 163.
8. I have adopted as my own the reasoning laid down by Montreal economist Dian Cohen in a series of articles that appeared in the *Toronto Daily Star* during the anti-inflation war.
9. *Canadian Statistical Review*, March 1971, p. 36.
10. *Canadian Statistical Review*, Weekly Supplement for February 22, 1971, p. 5.
11. Most of what follows is cribbed shamelessly from Professor Rosalind Blauer of Brock University, an acknowledged expert on inflation. I helped Mrs. Blauer prepare an article on the subject for *Maclean's* in April 1970, and have leaned heavily on that article. Errors of interpretation are, of course, my own.

# 6

## The New Politics:
## Participate Me In Violet Time

*Above all, it is our determined wish to make
government more accessible to people, to give our
citizens a sense of full participation in the affairs of
government, and full control over their
representatives.*
Prime Minister Trudeau
The Just Society election pamphlet, May 1968

Participatory democracy was the phrase that hovered like a
halo over Trudeau's head all during his leadership and election
campaigns. In a swing across Canada just before he became
Prime Minister, I talked to dozens of people who used phrases
like "He'll give politics back to the people," "He'll give *us* a
say," "He cares what *we* think." There were to be conferences
and resolutions and think-ins and meaningful exchanges and
dialogue and grass-roots participation and it was all going to be
glorious and grand. It hasn't been, of course; participatory
democracy has turned out to mean "I'll hold the microphone
and talk, and you listen." There has been a great deal of Input
— the obligatory word — from the grass-roots to the Liberal
party and the government itself, but it has all been a fog, a mist,
a haze at the Output end. Unlike many of the myths that have
sprung up around Trudeau (the myth that he was a radical, the
myth that he is a devil for work, the myth that he was the bone
and gristle of the anti-Duplessis movement in Quebec during
the 1950s), the myth of participatory democracy was actively
encouraged by the Prime Minister; because of that, it is fair to
call it not merely a misnomer, but a monstrous fraud.

Strong words. I call as my first witness the Liberal party itself and, in particular, that party's own booklet, *The Politics of
Participation — A Progress Report*, which is yours for the asking at Liberal party headquarters, 102 Bank Street, Ottawa. After seven pages of self-congratulatory prose peppered with
catchy phrases like "More Power To Everybody," the Progress
Report gets down to the heart of things with a sub-section
called — are you ready? — A Progress Report, which is here,
in the interests of fair play, the public interest and participatory
democracy, reproduced in full:


## II  A Progress Report
What have we done to meet this challenge? What has the
Party and the Government done in the past two years to
stimulate and ensure meaningful participation?

### THE PARTY
Since the election of 1968, we have talked of a mass party, of
the Party as society's radar or as a vehicle of participation,
verification and communication. These ideas gave rise to
considerable changes and innovations at various levels of
Party organization. Everyone is familiar with the traditional
structures for communication within the Party — constitu-
ency meetings, local, regional or national conventions, meetings with the local Member of Parliament.
What are the new tools that have been placed in the hands of
Party members?
— Circulation of the Canadian Liberal has been expanded,
and Party Members who read it will be more adequately informed — a prior condition for any real participation.
— There have been some changes in local structures. At the
regional level, there was established in Quebec, for instance,
Metropolitan Councils which concentrate on regional problems.
— At the provincial level, the Advisory Groups bring party
members, party heads, Members of Parliament and Cabinet
Ministers into regular contact with one another. Political
Cabinet plays a similar role at the national level. This innovation which few people are aware of, represents a direct
line of communication between party members and the Cabinet. Eventually, it will constitute a direct line of action.
— The best known and most important development is the

three-phase program which began at Harrison Hot Springs and which is being concluded at the Liberal Party Convention. [The pamphlet was prepared for the party's national policy convention in Ottawa, November 21, 22 and 23, 1970.] For a year, now, the Party has been involving more and more people in a discussion of vital Canadian issues instead of limiting participation in the debate to a few members of Parliament and Party leaders. This year's Policy Convention represents an attempt to recognize the increased significance and value of each individual member.

(Let me sum up so far for those who may have dozed off: as far as the party goes, more free copies of the free paper have been sent out, one province has established Metropolitan Councils, Advisory Groups have been formed "which few people are aware of" to allow the party brass to talk to each other, and there have been a series of policy conferences, of which more anon. That's the party end of it. But what about The Government?)

## THE GOVERNMENT

Political parties are only a part of the participatory process. The role of government in this process is vast and of critical importance.

Committed to the principle of participation, the Liberal Government has established a number of new channels for the citizens of Canada to influence the decisions that affect their every day lives.

— Hearings by Committees of the Senate and the House of Commons are held in all parts of Canada.

— Various task forces have conducted extensive enquiries amongst groups of interested citizens.

— The public has been encouraged to freely offer its opinions to the Government on many vital national issues.

— The White Paper technique or "White Paper democracy" has involved millions of Canadians in the creation of public policy.

— House Committees have been reorganized creating greater opportunities for the useful participation of Members of Parliament.

— Members of Parliament play an increasingly constructive

role in the participation of their constituents and the community at large in public affairs. Their appearances on hot lines, their use of questionnaires and write-ins, their involvement in public forums — represent a positive adaptation from traditional representative roles.

— All parties represented in Parliament have been provided with research funds which will help them present constructive suggestions to the Government on alternative courses of action.

— Information Canada has been created to assist Canadians in becoming more aware and better informed of Federal Government activity. This step is of vital importance as the cornerstone of participation is information.

— Regional Desks have been created in the Office of the Prime Minister to assist the participatory process. No one can deny that significant progress has been made in creating more effective participation in the Party and in Government. Nor can anyone claim, however, that the Party or the Government should be contented with these first few steps, which can hardly be called bold in the face of the challenge to be met.

To summarize once more: there have been committee meetings, task forces, white papers (all of which we had before), MPs talking on hot-line programmes and in public forums (we all know how shy they were about appearing in public in the old, non-participatory days), the MPs have more money to help them read press clippings, a government propaganda service has been created and the Prime Minister has set up regional desks to help him by-pass the MPs. Oh, I nearly forgot, "The public has been encouraged to freely offer its opinions. . . ." On some subjects, of course: for a while there if you were to freely offer the wrong opinion on the FLQ, your participatory government would slap you in a participatory dungeon and throw away the participatory key.

I have not left anything out, I have not made anything up. This is the progress of participatory democracy from the lips of the Liberal party itself. As a matter of fact, the party does itself an injustice; it has left out the $50-a-plate dinners where the elite meet to eat and where, if he has fifty bucks and sufficient push, a member of the public can get right up to the Prime Minister and shake his hand.

If you will study the Progress Report carefully, you will see
that nowhere is there any provision for members of the general
public to influence either the government or the party directly.
Policies are still firmly locked in the hands of the government,
the cabinet and the Prime Minister, in ascending order of importance. To drive the point home, let us consider those flowers
of the participatory garden, the Liberal party policy conferences — "the best known and most important" development
on the participatory front.

The first of these conferences was held at Harrison Hot
Springs, British Columbia, in November 1969. It was called the
"Canada 1970's" conference, and the Prime Minister attended
a number of sessions, flying out in his JetStar — at public expense — to rub a democratic elbow with the hoi polloi. A
number of interesting papers were presented at that conference
— sixty reports were received in all — and they touched on
such wide-ranging topics as urban blight and a guaranteed annual income plan. The Prime Minister spoke, with careful
woolliness, about the problems of rapidly increasing technology; he said that technology should not be seen as an ultimate
good in itself, but as a tool to improve society. There were no
nay-sayers. Some of the Liberals, however, grew a little restless
towards the end of the two-and-a-half-day conference, and indicated they had hoped to talk about real, honest-to-god problems like, say, urban blight, and to propose real, honest-to-god
solutions that might someday become policy. No matter, they
were assured, this conference was just a warm-up, the beginning of a long, exciting, participatory process that would wind
up with the policy conference in Ottawa a year later. No votes
were taken on any of the proposals put forward at the conference.

   It was just as well. Marc Lalonde, the Prime Minister's principal secretary, made it clear that resolutions percolating up
through the party structure receive short shrift at the top.
"People in riding associations don't have the sophisticated
knowledge required. They're uninformed. . . . Suppose that the
riding association in Burnaby had a meeting and somebody got
up and said, 'Wouldn't it be a great idea to stop all defence
spending?' Would you expect it to immediately become government policy. Of course not, it's silly."[1]
   But what if, someone said, what if 51 per cent of the Liberal

party voted for such a policy? Would it then be listened to? "No, not even if 75 per cent wanted it." If that happened, Lalonde said, it would indicate that the government had not done a good job of explaining its policies; the need was not to change them, but to improve communications.

That statement of how the government really viewed participatory democracy should have chilled the delegates at Harrison Hot Springs, but did not. The fog of self-satisfaction that rose from the meeting-ground might have been sighted in Winnipeg.

For the next year, warming up to the national policy conference in Ottawa, local Liberal associations, discussion groups, friends and hangers-on conducted an endless series of meetings, exchanged earnest position papers and voted on resolutions to be presented on the great gettin'-up morning in November 1970. Some of the resolutions passed were lulus. One youth group wanted to chuck out the Queen, another to chuck out the Americans. But, in general, there was serious discussion of serious proposals, and it seemed there might be something in participation after all.

The public began to get the notion something was amiss just before the Ottawa conference, when a ginger group from the University of Western Ontario, in London, released its first broadside (everybody hoped it was the first; anyway, it was headed Vol. 1, No. 1) about the convention and the Liberal record to date. The group, all Liberals, opened their remarks by pointing out that while representatives of the poor had been invited to participate in the goings-on, the financial assistance necessary to get poor delegates to Ottawa had unaccountably not been provided, so their voices would be missing from the policy discussions. The pamphlet went on to criticize the government's treatment of the poor. It said that in 1967, only 7.5 per cent of Canadian taxpayers earned more than $10,000 a year, that in 1965 "for each dollar of non-farm income, the bottom 20 per cent of families received less than seven cents, and the top 20 per cent more than thirty-eight cents" and that "This gap has not narrowed appreciably in the past twenty years."

There followed some blunt questions:

— Why was a London resolution calling for implementation of an income maintenance scheme eliminated from the convention ballot?

—— Why was the Willard Report on social development programmes not released? (I can answer that one; because it advocated an income maintenance scheme.)

—— Where were all the resolutions that had been submitted calling on the government to "stop sacrificing jobs to their obsessive fight against inflation"?

—— Why did the government not allow time for people to dissociate themselves from the FLQ before making membership in that organization illegal, the way Communists were allowed to purge themselves when that party was outlawed in the 1930s?

Oh, they were dandy questions, full of the spirit of participation. But they received no answers, not one.

When the convention opened, the key issue facing the Liberal party, and the country, was the government's recent imposition of the War Measures Act; but that subject was never given a full hearing at the conference, nor were the Liberals who opposed the action under any illusion that they would be invited to comment on it. A great many delegates, especially from the Toronto area, simply cancelled their plans to go to Ottawa; at one point, members of a Toronto riding association were asking strangers in a bar if they wanted to go to Ottawa, to replace dropped-out delegates. I asked a friend of mine, a long-time Liberal, a lawyer, and a strong opponent of the War Measures Act, why he hadn't gone —— he was an elected delegate —— to make his opposition known. "Because they just roll over you," he replied. "Because there is no way they are going to allow me or anybody else to say anything against War Measures."

He was too pessimistic; the policy convention delegates did, in fact, take a glancing swipe at the government's action in one of four resolutions —— out of 335 —— in which they stepped out on their own:[2]

—— They voted 595 to 250 in favour of a guaranteed annual income programme to be instituted by January 1, 1972.

—— They rejected the current legislation on abortion by an overwhelming vote, demanding the removal of abortion from the Criminal Code and insisting that "abortion should be permitted on the decision of the woman and her husband".

—— They asked the federal government to establish an independent review board to guard against abuses under the War Measures Act and its successor, the Public Order Act.

—— They supported a moratorium on prosecutions for possession of marijuana.

They were wasting their time. The evening the conference opened, Trudeau told the delegates Canada could not afford a guaranteed income plan. (He later modified that stance, as we have seen in Chapter 4.) He also made it clear that he would not be bound by anything the delegates said anyway. In the House of Commons, he noted, "We have already stated in the Speech from the Throne what we would do this session" about abortion. (And what the Throne Speech had said was that there would be a special debate — i.e., no legislation — on the subject.) He also told the House the government would not, repeat not, set up a review board on the War Measures Act arrests. Marijuana charges continued as before.

The ink was scarcely dry on newspaper accounts announcing the brush-off given to the resolutions when the Liberals were back in print announcing the first of a series of questionnaires to be sent out to the party faithful, to plumb their thoughts on matters of interest and excitement. The Liberal official who released the glad tidings informed reporters that the cabinet would be influenced "about as much" by the response to the questionnaires as it had been by the policy resolutions.

The 1970 policy conference was significant, but not in the way its sponsors intended; it showed clearly that the influence of party members had sharply declined during the Trudeau years. Remember the famous confrontation between Mitchell Sharp and Walter Gordon at an earlier Liberal policy conference — also in Ottawa — in October 1966? The issue then was economic nationalism and, on the resolutions put forward, Walter Gordon and the nationalist wing lost, and the continentalists won.[3] Subsequently, the Liberal government took a distinct step away from the nationalism that had been welling up through party ranks. The significance of the 1966 policy conference was that it had a direct effect on the party and the government; the significance of the 1970 conference was that it did not.

A month after the meeting, a delegate from Rexdale, Ontario, wrote the Prime Minister asking "to what extent will the government be influenced by" the resolutions passed there. Trudeau wrote back, "It may be that in respect of some, the government will not be able to proceed in accordance with the delegates' wishes; such cases will be rare I hope." It was a pious hope.

There are a number of reasons why it is difficult for a party in power to follow the wishes of delegates to a convention; but there is no reason, beyond self-serving cynicism, for a government to make a year-long show of plumbing the hearts and minds of party members and then to turn its back on anything they may say that disagrees with its own fixed intentions.

The process mires itself one step more in cynicism when the government asks for a reaction to a policy position, listens only to a tiny part of that reaction, and calls the result the triumph of participatory democracy. That is what happened in the case of the famous, now deceased, White Paper on Taxation. Indeed, the process by which tax reform was strangled is an object lesson in how government may, over a decade, receive, reject, revise and finally destroy an attempt to change the *status quo*.

The attempt began back in 1962, when Kenneth Carter, a sixty-year-old Toronto tax accountant, was named to head — this was back in the days before heading up — a royal commission on tax reform. The reason was obvious; everyone knew the Canadian tax system was a shambles, and an unfair shambles at that. The rich paid higher tax rates than the poor, but laid off so many of their gains in tax dodges that they paid on only a tiny share of their incomes, while salaried workers, with no expense accounts and no gimmicks, paid on almost everything. Economist Thomas A. Wilson, director of the University of Toronto's Institute for Policy Analysis, calculated last winter that, taking into account all taxes, direct and indirect, Canadian families earning less than $2,000 a year pay a tax rate of 60 per cent, families at the $10,000-a-year level pay 38 per cent, and the higher levels pay about the same, "due to the fact that so much income now escapes taxation".[4] Wilson, who had been research supervisor on the Carter Commission, said these figures "sound unbelievable, but they are true".

The Carter Commission held ninety-nine public hearings, received 346 briefs containing over 2,500,000 words and spent five years cogitating furiously. Then, on February 24, 1967, the Carter Report thudded onto the Clerk's desk in the House of Commons. It ran to six volumes, 842,000 words, and a 119-page index.

The Report set down its objective in simple terms: "To achieve greater equality of opportunity for all Canadians and make it possible for those with little economic power to attain a decent standard of living." It was a laudable objective then, and it still is.

The essential reform proposed by Carter also seemed to

make sense: "If a man obtains increased command over goods and services for his personal satisfaction we do not believe it matters, from the point of view of taxation, whether he earned it through working, gained it through operating a business, received it because he held property, made it by selling property or was given it by a relative." Or, in words that were to send a chill down the spine of every magnate, travelling salesman and head waiter in the nation, "A buck is a buck". Carter proposed a capital gains tax, but he proposed much more; he proposed that every scrap of income, from that gained through the advantageous sale of a house to that cozened out of an expense account, would become taxable. Carter was not a well-loved man in the expense-account set. A very good friend of mine, who happens to be the president of two companies, exploded, "Do you know what this means? Every goddamn good restaurant in the country will go out of business. You don't think we're going to lay out our own cash for business dinners, do you?" As it was, other taxpayers were picking up half of every one of his business tabs.

Because the tax base would be widened, the Carter proposals envisioned a decrease in taxation for everyone in the nation earning less than $20,000 a year. Carter warned that his proposals were all of a piece, and should be accepted or rejected *in toto*; to snatch away parts of them and leave the rest would be to defeat the purpose of the new tax system. Carter was a brilliant tax accountant, but he knew nothing about politics.

During the 1968 election campaign, Prime Minister Trudeau unburdened himself on the Carter proposals. He was not "emphatically opposed" to a capital gains tax, which is, after all, applied in virtually every modern Western nation, but he thought it could be worked into the tax structure without a total overhaul. He doubted if the government could swallow Carter whole and "that is why we are trying to bring in what we can of it".

The Carter proposals were ignored in Finance Minister Benson's first budget, in 1968 — indeed, it could be argued that there was not time to absorb them — but, in November 1969, Benson produced a bowdlerized version of them, in his now-famous White Paper on Taxation. The Carter premise — "A buck is a buck" — did not survive. Benson's White Paper embraced several kinds of bucks, including those earned by way of dividends, those earned by employers, and those earned by employees. Employers were entitled to charge any legitimate expense against their incomes, employees could charge only for such items as tools up to a maximum of $150 a year. Bucks earned in the form of unemployment insurance, health insurance premiums paid by a company, student grants and company-provided cars were bucks for tax purposes, too, but such fringe benefits as yacht club dues and free parking were exempted. Limits were put on expense-account living.

The White Paper did recommend a capital gains tax, at a flat 50 per cent rate (rather than integrating that income with other earnings, to be taxed at whatever rate applied, as Carter had recommended), and it proposed two measures that brought it instant odium with some of the nation's most powerful economic interests. The first was an end to the three-year tax-holiday for new mining projects; the second was a measure to tie the depletion allowances connected with oil exploration to spending on new exploration. (Oil depletion allowances are a curious phenomenon, much admired in the U.S. Because oil companies are taking precious resources out of the ground, resources that belong to the nation and can never be replaced, they are paid a tax kick-back by the government against the day when those resources are depleted. The notion appears to be that those who rape the country should be compensated for their ripped clothes; the hope is that they will use the money for more exploration. The White Paper asked the oil companies to undertake the new exploration as a condition of collecting the tax kick-backs to pay for it, and the oil companies screamed bloody murder. The mining tax-holidays are, if possible, even dumber. They encourage those with huge amounts of available capital — for which read Americans — into the rush development of new mining sites, whether those developments are in Canada's best interests or not. The crude ore is then bundled out of the country into the U.S. where it produces jobs and dollars throughout the manufacturing process, and re-enters Canada as finished goods, for which we pay handsomely.)

Benson's White Paper was a curious amalgam of Carter reforms, timid economic nationalism (there were special rates on income from dividends from Canadian-owned companies) and stolid conservatism. Personal tax exemptions were raised from $1,000 to $1,400 for individuals and from $2,000 to $2,800 for married couples. But the change was more apparent than real; the basic exemption had been set in 1949; just to keep pace with the cost of living, it would have had to go to $1,640 for individuals and $3,280 for families.[5] And the exemptions were more generous, of course, for richer people. A family with two children and a $100,000 a year income would pay $5,423 less under the tax rates proposed in the White Paper, while one with a $10,000 income would pay $17 more.[6]

Some of the proposals were palpably unfair. To close the tax loophole under which individuals turned themselves into corporations (in order to benefit from the low rate of tax on a corporation's first $35,000 of profit), Benson recommended simply wiping out that special bracket, imposing a new handicap on genuine small businesses. Having avoided the "buck is a buck" principle elsewhere, Benson suddenly applied it to such items as a man's home — a capital gains tax would be applied to its sale — and even to such items as personal keepsakes and works of art. Stocks, keepsakes and works of art were to be given a valuation, and a tax paid on the increase in their value with the passage of time. As critics were quick to point out, that would mean in many cases that owners would be forced to sell their personal property to pay the tax on it.

It was this White Paper, with all its flaws and pitfalls, and not the Carter tax reforms, that became the battle-ground. The result was predictable. One of the largest, bitterest and best-organized lobbies ever to descend on the nation's capital mounted a steady eroding fire on the White Paper proposals. The government invited criticism, in its participatory way, and got it. As usual it heard from, and listened to, the well-heeled. Advertisements financed by groups of "concerned Canadians" — led by an insurance executive, a public-relations director and a clothing-store owner — blossomed in the newspapers. They asked such pointed questions as "Will you be able to resist the attractive tax climate of the United States?" and "Are you trying to build your savings by investing in the stock market?" Clearly they were not aimed at those with no surplus income earmarked for investment (i.e., the majority of Canadians). There were also letter campaigns and telegram campaigns and petitions by the score. These were, again, the work of the well-to-do. In Ottawa, the president of the Maycourt Club, a charitably inclined ladies' group, gathered the girls at her place to fill out protests and address envelopes for the anti-White Paper lobby. There was a delicious irony in the performance. The girls were paid $1.35 an hour for this work, with the proceeds to go, naturally, to good works among the lower classes. They put in several industrious afternoons until the wives of some senior civil servants objected violently to working directly against their husbands, and got the project shelved.

Not all the petitions sent to Ottawa were genuine. In the middle of the campaign, an angry letter appeared in the Toronto *Globe and Mail*, which said:

> I strongly object to the use of fraud by the opponents of the Government's White Paper on Taxation. My name was forged on a newspaper clipping and sent to "Member of Parliament, P.O. Box 4430, Ottawa, Ontario." It was returned to me by postal authorities for lack of sufficient address. If it had not been returned to my address, I would not have known it was sent, because I have never expressed any opinion on the White Paper. If the opponents of the White Paper have to stoop to such childish dishonesty I question the value of their cause.
> Richard von Fuchs
> Durham, Ontario.

On a more serious level, there were books, pamphlets and letters by accountants, tax experts and other eminent personages. There were dark, rumbling speeches from the bowels of the Canadian Club, the Rotary Club, the Canadian Manufacturers Association, and other outports of enlightenment. There were long, blunt telephone calls to Ottawa from businessmen large and small, and Liberal MPs began to go atwitter every time a telegram arrived. The oil and mining companies, naturally, were in there pitching, with ominous bays and mournful cries.

There was no counter-lobby in favour of the White Paper. Because it had been so badly-drawn, because it was so clearly half-hearted, its natural defenders on the political left could think of nothing nicer to say of it than that it was better than nothing, and they were not willing to wake up their MPs in the middle of the night to bawl *that* into their ears. Finance Minister Benson walked away from his offspring with some of the fastest back-pedalling since the death of the sternwheeler. The White Paper did not represent the government's last word, he said; it was just an idea his boys were playing around with.

There was no serious attempt to solicit the views of ordinary people, as opposed to the bank presidents, insurance executives and other assorted moguls who so freely offered theirs. The November 1970 Liberal policy convention in Ottawa dealt with seventy-eight resolutions on economic issues, none of which included the White Paper. When the *Toronto Daily Star* held a public forum on the proposals in February 1970, the ground of argument shifted abruptly away from the essential question: Does Canada need or want tax reform? — to which the only possible answer was Yes — to: Does Canada need or want this half-formed series of measures? — to which the only possible answer was No. (I have heard it seriously argued, among Liberals, that the White Paper was deliberately botched in order to block any tax reform. I prefer to believe it was that typical product of the Liberal mind, a compromise so framed as to outrage every sector of the political spectrum.)

By March 1971, it was all over. In a speech to the Junior Chamber of Commerce in Kingston, Ontario, on March 10, Finance Minister Benson announced that the White Paper "will never be legislated". It had generated public debate, he said, as was intended. "The public's views have been aired. We know its wants, and, as a result of the White Paper criticism, we'll be able to legislate better taxation — a fairer system."

Benson's June budget was almost an anti-climax; it reduced the reform programme to a tinkering with tax rates and the imposition of a partial capital-gains tax. There was no fundamental reform, and a system that had always soaked the middle-class and poor continued to do so. The exemptions were raised to $1,500 for individuals and $2,850 for married persons, which brought them back near, but not to, the 1949 level in terms of real purchasing power. The rich were still given preferential treatment; under the new system, a family with two children and an income of $5,000 will pay $73 tax, a saving of $137; the same family with a $50,000 income will pay $20,675, a saving of $347. Half of capital gains are to be included in income, but there is to be no integration, as Carter proposed, of capital gains with all other earnings. The "buck is a buck" concept was not revived. The surtax of 3 per cent levied on personal and corporate incomes by the Pearson government was at last removed, and provision was at last made for exemptions for child-care expenses of up to $500 a year per child. The three-year tax holiday for mines is to be phased out gradually, but they receive instead earned depletion-allowances, which amount to the same thing. In effect, oil depletion-allowances continue for major companies until at least 1980. The White Paper proposal to end the low tax-rate on small-corporation income was varied; small businesses are to be taxed at 25 per cent on the first $50,000 of income. (It used to be 21 per cent on the first $35,000.)

Purrs of satisfaction strong enough to set the key block on the Peace Tower atremble were emitted from the business community following the Benson budget, which seemed to have something for everyone — higher exemptions for the poor and, for the rich, only a partial capital-gains tax, more than offset by the ending of federal succession duties. But what it did not have was any measure of tax reform. As the Toronto *Globe and Mail*, which heartily approved the new budget, noted editorially:

> Describing it as tax reform could be put down as verbal overkill. Real reform, the kind that significantly redistributes income, redirects the economy or substantially re-orients priorities — that kind of reform you will not find. Reform that would produce the kind of equity that Kenneth Carter sought with missionary zeal has not been proposed. Nor has the jungle been cleared away as Mr. Carter hoped it would be. The world this morning remains a safe and plush place for tax lawyers.

Why the *Globe* thought it was a good idea to walk away from equity and leave the tax system a jungle I do not know, but it did, along with most of the Canadian establishment.

Nine years after Kenneth Carter began studying a fair taxation system for Canada, we were back almost where we started. And the entire exercise, the government and Liberal party kept telling us, was a classic example of participatory democracy.

In a way, it was, because what the Prime Minister means by participatory democracy is not listening to people, but circulating among them. He moves out of Ottawa on long pereginations across the land, attending Liberal fund-raising dinners, pressing the flesh of the faithful and mixing it up with students, farmers and assorted radicals. He wins those debates, because he is very good in debating and because he holds onto the microphone. I watched him tangle with a group of young-sters outside the Lord Nelson Hotel in Halifax when the Biafran tragedy was still working to its bloody climax, and the city's radicals had come to vent their rage on Trudeau. Radio and television reporters kept thrusting microphones under the Prime Minister's nose, wrenching them away to one youngster, then another, then a third. Only the Prime Minister could fol-low a coherent train of thought, and only those opponents who shrieked — and they were not always the most intelligent members of the crowd — got anything said at all. It was not participation, it was entertainment, with no more genuine ex-change of views than you will see in a Saturday wrestling bout on TV.

Of all the actions of the Trudeau government to date, I can think of only one that seems to have come as the result of a gen-uine public outcry genuinely heard. That was the decision to press claims for Canadian sovereignty in the Arctic, of which more later. Other decisions, from the partial withdrawal from NATO to the continuing encouragement given to outside ex-ploitation of Canada's resources, have been taken in the teeth of opposition within Trudeau's own party. The Prime Minister does not believe in participatory democracy, but in leadership democracy, and among his confidants he makes no bones about it. In private conversation, from accounts his aides have given me, he says that the role of government is to govern, and the role of the public is to judge him on the quality of his perform-ance when he chooses to call an election. He contends, with Marc Lalonde, that the issues raised in a complex, industrial society are too subtle, too difficult for the general public to grasp. And if he does not believe that even Parliament should be allowed to swerve him from his purpose— as he does not— how much less should that amorphous mass beyond the gates on Wellington Street be permitted to interfere? Thus, when the Prime Minister goes over the heads of the MPs and into the liv-ing rooms of Canadians, as he does frequently, he is not in search of debate, but support; he is not seeking out dialogue, but understanding. That is a perfectly legitimate exercise, and well established in North American politics since the time of Franklin Delano Roosevelt's fireside chats. But to call it partici-patory democracy is misleading cant.

I have that on no less an authority than John Roberts, a

thoughtful Liberal MP for York Simcoe, who wrote, in the Toronto *Globe and Mail*:

> The attempt to establish improved direct relationships between the public and the Prime Minister, or his office, seems at first glance an effort toward direct democracy; it marks the use of communicational techniques of the global village to create the sense of participation found in the face-to-face democracies of, say, the New England town meeting.
>
> The problem with such techniques is that they give the image — the illusion — of participation, not its reality. They tend to ritual.

Incidentally, the Liberal policy convention strongly supported a resolution that "The Federal Government should examine ways of making the governmental process more open to groups in society that do not have access to money or the media for the purpose of promoting their cause."

I'm dying to see what marks the government gets on that one in the next issue of *The Politics of Participation — A Progress Report.*

## Notes

1. Quoted in Peter Reilly's article "When Trudeau's Out of the Country, Marc Lalonde Runs Things", *Saturday Night*, October 1970.
2. Summaries of the voting appeared in a special post-convention issue of *The Canadian Liberal*, from which these figures are taken.
3. An excellent account appears in Newman, *The Distemper of Our Times.*
4. Wilson's figures were presented to a *Toronto Daily Star* public forum on February 10, 1970. A full account appears in the *Star's* editions of February 11, on p. 9. The small jiggering involved in the June 1971 budget will not have changed this imbalance much.
5. The Consumer Price Index, at 100 in 1949, rose to 164 in April 1969, a rise of 64 per cent.
6. Canada, Department of Finance, *Proposals for Tax Reform* (The White Paper), 1970, pp. 24-35.

# 7

# External Affairs:
# Never Send to Know
# for Whom the Bell Tolls,
# You May Get Involved

*All of us need to ponder well what our national
capacity is——what our potential may be——for
participating effectively in international affairs. We
shall do more good by doing well what we know to be
within our resources to do, than to pretend either to
ourselves or to others that we can do things clearly
beyond our capacity.*
Prime Minister Trudeau, May 1968

No one could call that a clarion cry. There are no visions buried
in the assessment of "Canada and the World", which the Prime
Minister released as his policy statement on external affairs on
May 29, 1968. There is no idle talk of the next century belong-
ing to Canada, no reach that exceeds the grasp. Practicality,
that's the watchword. Pragmatism. Black South Africans are
suffocating? Will it do any good to cut off trade? Biafrans are
starving to death? God, it's a pity, but if you call the cops, there
are all those forms to fill out, all those questions. Canadian munitions are blowing little Asians to bits? Can anybody *prove*
they're our bombs? American fighter-bombers scream through
our skies, American nuclear bombs nestle atop our Bomarc
missiles, American anti-ballistic missiles are poised to explode
over our heads to defend U.S. cities? In the words of the statement, "Realism —— that should be the operative word in our

definition of international aims. Realism is how we read the world barometer. Realism is how we see ourselves thriving in the light of its forecasts." And realism tells us there isn't a damn thing we can do.

The new realism injected into Canada's foreign stance by Trudeau's 1968 policy paper displayed itself subsequently in a number of ways, some good, some bad.

On the positive side, Canada realistically pulled back on our military commitment to NATO, recognized Red China, and began to press for sovereignty in the Arctic. It was realistic, too, for the Prime Minister to visit Russia in May 1971, and sign a friendship protocol with that nation. The protocol didn't amount to much — we only agreed to talk to each other about mutual problems at regular intervals — but the move helped to shift us ever so slightly out from under the American umbrella.

On the negative side, it was realism that prompted us to stand discreetly aside throughout the bloody Biafran tragedy, realism that permits us to sell the U.S. hundreds of millions of dollars worth of equipment for Vietnam each year, realism that squeezes down our foreign-aid contributions and frames our timid approach to American economic intrusion.

In the short ten-page policy statement I have cited above, the Prime Minister used the words "realism" or "realistically" eleven times, and he meant it every time — as our foreign policy record attests. In general, that record is a mere continuation of the "quiet diplomacy" approach laid down in the days of Lester Pearson, an approach that is essentially conservative. Even our initiatives spring from conservative motives, a reluctance to tackle anything "clearly beyond our capacity", as Trudeau put it. If anything, Trudeau is *more* conservative in foreign affairs than Pearson was; Canada's role as a peacekeeper in the late 1950s and mid-1960s, however imperfectly realized, seemed to spring from a genuine desire to become involved in the world's problems and a genuine belief that we could make a contribution to their solution. Trudeau wants no part of that; we will not become involved in peacekeeping operations unless we can be sure they will succeed, and since that is never certain, our peacekeeping role is bound to wither. Government policy is clear on this: "There could be further international demands for Canadian participation in peacekeeping operations — especially in regional conflicts. The Government is determined that this special brand of Canadian expertise will not be dispersed or wasted on ill-conceived operations but employed judiciously where the peacekeeping operation and the Canadian contribution to it seem likely to improve the chances for lasting settlement."[1]

At least Pearson's quiet diplomacy stemmed from a desire to get things done from behind the scenes; Trudeau's appears to stem from having nothing to say.

Within the modest ambit laid down by the Trudeau approach, there have been two major developments in external affairs: the first has been to bring the bureaucrats who had been running this nation's foreign policy sharply to heel; the second has been to grope — always realistically, always pragmatically — with a whole new set of international problems.

Since the first development has had inevitable repercussions on the second, let us consider it first.

On January 1, 1969, in a television interview with Ronald Collister and Norman DePoe of the CBC, the Prime Minister lofted his first hand-grenade into the ranks of the External Affairs Department in one of those questions-that-are-not-questions from DePoe:

*DePoe:*
You just mentioned the external review. I am not trying to criticize the people concerned, what I'm at is the system, it seems to me that our representatives abroad spend most of their time on the air-conditioned cocktail circuit, they talk only to high officials and really they don't know enough about the countries they're stationed in because they're isolated from the real society of these countries. The people I met in Nigeria that knew most about the country were CUSO people and American Peace Corps people and our diplomats don't get down to that level. Surely we should be doing better than this?

*The Prime Minister:*
I agree with you to a fair degree, Mr. DePoe. But I don't think it's a criticism against our officials. I think that the whole concept of diplomacy today, the whole concept of my (*sic*) diplomacy as a career is a little bit outmoded. I believe much of it goes back to the early days of the telegraph when you needed a dispatch to know what was happening in country

A. Whereas now most of the time you can read it in a good newspaper. In that sense I believe there is a need for a basic re-examination of the function of the diplomat. I think that it should be much closer to the people in the way you suggest. I think it should be much more culture-oriented than pure news-oriented. We will still get down to a point, I think, where we will realize that we do need posts in many countries and we do need diplomats who can speak to the government officials in those countries because that's not often perhaps, only once or twice or three times a year we'll need somebody urgently to tell the President of Country A or the Prime Minister of Country B, this is a situation, we want to know your reaction and would (*sic*) be able to convey it to us. So every time we would have to send a crew of ministers down from Ottawa, or a diplomat from Ottawa, you know, we would probably spend more money, we would be less informed. But I accept your basic criticism.

The view represented in that confused exchange, studded with misconceptions about diplomacy in general and the Canadian Department of External Affairs in particular, is one held not only among the general public, but among the academics from whom the Prime Minister picked up most of his notions of diplomacy. Professor James Eayrs of the University of Toronto, one of our most respected commentators on the field, dismissed the whole Department with three sentences: "Most of its postings are expendable. Much of its work is redundant. Many of its officials are unnecessary."

Trudeau accepts that assessment; early in his reign, before Eayrs became a bitter critic of the administration, Trudeau aides quoted the Professor with relish. External, the glamour department of government since the end of World War II, has been in trouble ever since Trudeau came to power. Its staff has been frozen, some of its missions closed and the development of policy whisked out of its hands and deposited behind the green baize doors of the Prime Minister's office. I am not talking now about final policy decisions, which have always belonged in the realm of the politician, but of the preparation of policy positions, from which the final decisions are chosen. For the first two years of Trudeau's reign, the department's views and recommendations were virtually ignored; there has been some improvement since the appointment of Ed Ritchie as Undersecretary of State, but the friction between the civil-service officials and the Prime Minister's Office continues.

It is based, in part, on a misconception in the Prime Minister's mind about the role of the diplomat. As we have seen from his remarks to Norman DePoe, Trudeau regards the diplomat as a man in striped trousers we send abroad to lie for his country, and he believes the envoy spends most of his time filing redundant telegrams home to Ottawa. Well, Canadian diplomats *do* drink cocktails, occasionally wear striped trousers and send and receive an average of 10,000 telegrams per month, many of which merely repeat information already available elsewhere. (During a strike at the *New York Times*, there was a noticeable slackening in telegraph traffic to External.) The Prime Minister was right to attack the information-gathering capacities of our diplomats. But information-gathering is only a small part of their job. In Washington, where our most important embassy is located, between 5 and 10 per cent of staff time is devoted to this pursuit, the rest to the duller, traditional, and vital diplomatic chores — consular work, trade promotion, propaganda, negotiation and policy development.[2]

The Prime Minister's sneers would sit better if the Canadian consular corps had, in the past, done a bad job, but we have one of the most highly respected foreign services in the world — or we did have, before the Prime Minister's attacks decimated their ranks, destroyed their morale and drove off some of the most promising career officers. The sneers would sit better, too, if the result of the new thrust had been a clear, forward-looking, dynamic Canadian foreign policy but, with the exception of the moves to recognize China and pull back from NATO, the record is patchy at best. In the crucial area of Canada-U.S. relations, the hurt withdrawal of senior diplomats from policy discussion has not strengthened our flabby stance. In the past, it was the diplomats who pushed for a strong stand on such issues as Arctic sovereignty and the rejection of American nuclear weapons, and the politicians who overruled them. Well, that voice of dissent is stilled, and our record in foreign affairs has not, as a result, been a proud testament to the new politics. In fact, it has not been a testament to anything but pragmatism.

One of the early decisions faced by the government concerned the civil war in Nigeria. At first, the Prime Minister couldn't understand the fuss. When a TV newsman braced him on the steps of the East Block with a question about Biafra, he replied, "You fellows certainly ask some peculiar questions."

Later, when he had been briefed, he took the stand he clung to throughout the controversy: Nigeria was embroiled in a civil war, and for Canada to interfere would be improper. The Organization for African Unity had specifically enjoined outside countries not to interfere, and we would meet that wish. But for many Canadians the view that we could not help the starving Biafrans because to do so would amount to recognition of the breakaway regime smacked of legalism and inhumanity. Private funds poured forward to meet the emergency, and private organizations flew in supplies. Canairelief, sponsored by Oxfam and a number of church groups, dispatched a Super Constellation to Africa on January 11, 1969, and sponsored 1,200 flights into Biafra within the next five weeks. It asked for, but did not receive, government aid. There were a number of protests at this; they were led, inside Parliament, by Tory MP David MacDonald and NDP MP Andrew Brewin, and outside Parliament by a wide collection of people, from Edward Johnson, the Secretary for Overseas Missions of the Presbyterian Church, to unnamed student leaders who buttonholed External Affairs Minister Sharp and the Prime Minister on every possible public occasion. The Prime Minister told students they wanted to play the white hero to backward blacks; they called him a fascist. No points, either way. Behind the scenes, excited bulletins from Ottawa kept telling us, the government was working like the dickens to get permission for mercy flights. Prime Ministerial aide Ivan Head was dispatched to Lagos twice to try to melt Nigerian resistance to the flights. (The Nigerians argued that mercy flights might bring in arms, or provide cover for arms flights.) But nothing happened — except that Biafrans starved, pictures of their starvation flashed around the world, and Canada took the official stance that it was all very sad. Finally, on January 9, 1970, a year after the Canairelief flights began, the government reversed itself and found that it could, after all, contribute to Biafran relief. A sum of $2,250,000 was to be set aside, $1,000,000 of it for Canairelief. Four days later, Biafra surrendered. We managed to weather the war without spending any money.

Parsimony was certainly the keynote in our approach to Latin

America. There, the Trudeau regime began with a bright new look, sending a closetful of cabinet ministers on a junket in October and November 1968. (It cost $239,886.04, when all the bills were in.) The mission's report, tabled on January 24, 1969, was full of flatulent cliches: "In all countries visited the mission was offered a warm and most hospitable reception. . . ." "The atmosphere in the talks was at all times cordial, frank and, as a rule, quite informal. . . ." "There can be no doubt that Latin America is a very important part of the world. . . ." But of action, there was none, not even a firm position on the Organization of American States, which we have been poised to join, or not join, since its inception. We are still poised. The only perceptible policy shift in our dealings with Latin America since 1968 has been the closing of missions in Ecuador, the Dominican Republic and Uruguay.

The reason given for these closures was economy, and that, in a way, was the reason for *opening* a mission at the Vatican, announced in October 1969. The Vatican was a listening post for information not available elsewhere, according to the theory put forward at the time. The Prime Minister called it "the cheapest listening post in the world. I don't suppose there are as many cocktail parties there as elsewhere." Suspicious Protestant churchmen saw the move as merely an attempt to placate French Canada and dish the separatists. Reverend E. M. Howse, former moderator of the United Church, said, "For several years now progressive Catholics have been suggesting that the church divest itself of the trappings of empire. Now Trudeau allies himself with the reactionaries by hinting that Canada should officially recognize that 'empire'."

But the Prime Minister stuck to his explanation, even after he named the first Canadian ambassador to the Holy See — John Robbins, former president of Brandon University, and a lapsed Methodist. How Robbins, a man with no political experience more complex than that available on campus, could take advantage of the Vatican's keyholes has never been explained.

The reactionary label was also applied to the Prime Minister in his dealings with the Commonwealth, and perhaps in this case with more justice. His first Commonwealth Conference, in England during January 1969, was summed up in Conservative leader Robert Stanfield's snappish comment that "Never in the history of the Commonwealth had Canada made a contribution less important and less useful." David Lewis, for the NDP, was just as blunt: "It appears that Canada's participation . . . amounts to one big zero."

Those critical remarks seemed fair enough; at the conference, which struggled manfully to deal with such contentious issues as Biafra and Rhodesia, Trudeau seemed to have nothing to contribute but platitudes. His summation to Parliament was typical: "After looking at the [Rhodesian] problem in its exact dimensions, after closing in on its many difficulties, men holding opposite views admitted that the true nature of the difficulties was now understood better than before. . . . Of most importance, however, honourable men agreed honourably to disagree."

Outside the conference, he was more outspoken. This was the trip on which the Prime Minister, still a bachelor, chose to date Eva Tittinghausen, a blonde divorcee, who twittered to the ever-eager press that it had been "love at first sight" between her and Trudeau. When the papers played that story in headlines, and then hounded another Prime Ministerial date, actress Jennifer Hales, Trudeau read the reporters with him a little lecture. (It was wasted, really, because he attacked the Canadian reporters; the zealots on both stories had been the British.) "I thought some of you, the reporters, had some pretty crummy behaviour here in London," he said. "I do not think it is any of your damn business, frankly, what a particular person thinks of me and how we behave together." It was a silly outburst; the Prime Minister was able later to show, in his courtship of Margaret Sinclair, that it was perfectly possible for him to date, woo, even become engaged, with no one the wiser. The London dates, with the careful leak of details to the press, were a deliberate part of the dashing-playboy image Trudeau polished to a high gloss. When the reporters chased that image too assiduously, he turned on them, and came off looking no better than they.

Still, it was nice to hear him speak out forcefully; if only he had saved some of his tongue for either that conference or the next Commonwealth meeting he attended, at Singapore in January 1971. There, the crucial issue was the proposed sale of arms by the U.K. to South Africa. The African Commonwealth nations opposed the sale bitterly; while South Africa claimed it needed weapons to maintain security in the Indian and South Atlantic oceans, her black neighbours suspected they were really intended for internal use against restless blacks. Canada's official position was that we supported the African objection; but we did so from a flimsy moral stance. While we object to the sale of arms to the apartheid regime, Canadian trade with South Africa continues to increase, based on a preferential tariff system that should have been abolished when that nation was read out of the Commonwealth a decade ago. External Affairs Minister Sharp argued, rightly, that it would be pointless to cut off trade to South Africa — after all, we trade with China and Cuba, and no approval can be read into that — but he slid past the really relevant point that extending Commonwealth preferences to a non-Commonwealth member *does* look like a sign of approval, and we do it only for one reason — it pays.

The stink of hypocrisy was not dispersed by the Prime Minister's performance at the conference. He junketted around the Pacific, skin-diving, holidaying, cuddling up to an orangutan, but contributing almost nothing to the debate. Worried Canadian reporters on the scene wired back that he was holding his fire, and at any moment would step out of the wings and save the conference and the Commonwealth. He did too, the same reporters decided later, because it was a Canadian weasel-phrase that permitted the assembled leaders to sign the final communique. The key part of the declaration of principles agreed upon by the meeting read, "No country will afford to regimes which practise racial discrimination assistance which, *in its own judgment, directly* contributes to the consolidation of this evil policy." The five words "in its own judgment, directly" were Canada's contribution, and one that might have warmed the heart of Mackenzie King. With their insertion, any country could sell South Africa lashes, thumb-screws and Mace if in its own judgment, fortified always by the zealous quest for a trading buck, they were not going to contribute directly to putting down the blacks. (If they contributed indirectly, okay.) The conference ended without the Commonwealth breaking up, and the arms issue was shovelled off to a committee — headed by Canada — which was to consider the question of security in the Indian and South Atlantic oceans. The committee died aborning; it never met. Britain went ahead with the sale of helicopters to South Africa. The Prime Minister shrugged his way home. Pragmatism, that was the key.

Pragmatism was the key, too, to Canada's foreign-aid performance in Trudeau's first term. One of his first acts as Prime Minister was to turn his back on the modest goal we had agreed to in the Pearson years, of a foreign-aid contribution equal to 1 per cent of our Gross National Product annually. That wasn't practical, Trudeau said. Instead, we would make a contribution commensurate with our means, and hopefully it would go up. Admittedly there is something a little false about the statistical measurement that puts countries like France ahead of Canada in terms of foreign aid. The trick is that both corporate and government figures are included, so that even if France's cash gifts are negligible, the fact that she hustles for foreign-aid commercial contracts makes her look more generous than she really is. However measured, though, we do poorly. In terms of GNP our aid contributions come to just about one-half of 1 per cent; in per capita terms we donate about $15 a year for every Canadian, twelfth in a list of sixteen Development Assistance Committee nations.[3] The average per capita donation of those nations is over $20. Our foreign aid is expected to rise at a rate of about $40 million per year, from its present level of just over $400 million, but a substantial portion of that assistance is in the form of loans. Maurice Strong, just before he stepped down as president of the Canadian International Development Agency, pointed out that debt-repayments by underdeveloped nations threaten to cancel out the value of our foreign aid by the year 1975; already, he noted, more aid money goes to repaying loans than to building new projects. Again, the Prime Minister simply shrugged away the criticism: Canada's aid programme, he feels, is "realistic".

It was that cheese-paring realism that set the tone for the government's Foreign Affairs White Paper, tabled in mid-1970. That White Paper, much advertised in advance, turned out to be nothing more than a review of what everybody already knew about Canada's foreign policies, spun out into five neat little volumes. No, that's not quite fair: most Canadians knew more than the White Paper, because they knew about two major issues that received scant notice in the five volumes — the United States and Vietnam.

I've never been able to understand the reluctance of our government to acknowledge our role in Vietnam. I mean, the Americans acknowledge it; Henry Kuss, Undersecretary of Defence in Washington, once told me feelingly, "We really appreciate the contribution you people are making." I tell you, it brought a lump to my throat. I've always felt that way about Vietnam.

When I read about an American soldier firing a clip of tracer bullets into a group of women and children in some Mekong hamlet, I feel a quiet thrill of pride. The vivid description of a fighter-bomber snarling across the hills near Khe Sanh, spraying napalm, sends a surge of patriotism coursing through my veins. An eyewitness account of bombs wrenching at rice paddies along the Ho Chi Minh Trail stirs me like a cry of bugles. After all, it's our war, too. The bullets for that soldier's weapon may have ridden in a De Havilland Caribou built at Malton, Ontario; that napalm-spraying fighter-bomber was almost certainly equipped with a Canadian-made Marconi Doppler Navigation System; those bombs along the Ho Chi Minh Trail may have been made from dynamite shipped out of Valleyfield, Quebec, and disgorged by a bombing computer fashioned in Rexdale, Ontario.

Why should the Americans have all the glory? We do our part, too. Oh, I know we don't send troops in. After all, we are members of the International Control Commission and, as then-External Affairs Minister Paul Martin once told the House of Commons, "Our membership in the Commission makes Canada an independent witness, and this role we must continue to exercise objectively and impartially." We do this by selling the Americans some of the weapons they need to kill Gooks, Dinks and Slope-Heads. I like to think of this as "creative impartiality", or maybe even "profit-oriented objectivity".

We furnish arms under the Canada-U.S. Defence-Production Sharing Agreement, which allows us to bid for military contracts across the border, just as if we were Americans, and at war with Vietnam. Under that agreement, we have sold more than $3 billion worth of war materials since 1959,[1] from fill for land mines to jackets for bullets, from complex electronic gear to the Green Berets worn so proudly through many a smashed hamlet. (They're sewn together in a Toronto loft.) We even put out an annual catalogue, "Canadian Defence Commodities," a sort of warmonger's shopping guide, with illustrations of the goodies we have to offer, and we send troops of salesmen around the U.S. to drum up business. I remember reading an account in the *New York Times* about a U.S. soldier throwing an elderly peasant into a well and dropping a hand-grenade in after him; I couldn't help wondering if it was one of Ours.

While we don't go around big-mouthing our role the way some nations do, we are appreciated in the U.S. A senior officer in the Pentagon's Procurement Branch told me that in some fields our expertise is unmatched; nobody turns out better bombing systems than we do, and our navigation systems are installed in nearly all U.S. military aircraft.

Some lily-livered ninny-hammers think we should scrap the Defence-Production Sharing deal; Trudeau put them in their place. If they were serious about harming the U.S. war effort, he said, why not cut off steel shipments to the U.S.? Not that he was going to do it; he wanted *them* to. For himself, he wasn't doing anything.

At one time, I thought it wasn't such a good idea to sell arms to the Americans. Article Seventeen of the Geneva Convention of 1954 specifically prohibits importing arms into Vietnam and, as members of the ICC, we are pledged to enforce that convention. Somehow it didn't seem quite right that we should be in the business of breaking it. Paul Martin used to say that, well, we didn't know for sure that our arms were going to Vietnam, but then one time I traced a shipment of dynamite from the Canadian Industries Limited plant at Valleyfield, Quebec, to a munitions plant at Crane, Indiana, where it was loaded into bombs which were stacked on trucks for transport to Vietnam. "When your bombs go out of here," the deputy director of ordnance told me, "they're still warm."

That gave me a kind of queasy feeling, so I raised the issue with the ranking military attache for Canada in Washington. He set me straight. He said just about what Trudeau says, that the Defence-Production Sharing deal began before the Vietnam war, that to abrogate it would not end the war, but would affect 100,000 Canadian jobs, and that it would make the Americans very, very cross. (Should a country already facing unemployment problems create more? Well, yes, if the alternative is to continue as munitions-makers for Vietnam, but there are other solutions to unemployment than cashing in on wars.) It's as if we ran a large department store, and our best customer bought, among other things, a lot of guns. Then it turned out that he used our guns to rob banks. Should we stop selling him guns just because of that? After all, he was a customer before he was a bank-robber. What if he stopped buying from us altogether?

The attache told me, "The question is not our view of the ICC, but our view of the piece of real estate we call North America, which we share with the U.S. We may not agree with what they're doing in Vietnam, but you don't forsake your friends just because they do something you don't like."

"It's as if," he went on, drawing a brilliant parallel, "you had a neighbour whose dog was destroying your bushes. Now you might not like it, but you would learn to accept it." Especially, to continue the parallel, when any attempt to trifle with the dog might result in having your throat torn out. If we broke the Defence-Production Sharing Agreement, our friends and neighbours would be, as Henry Kuss told me, "pretty goddamn upset", and we might expect economic reprisals.

Well, we are an accommodating people, especially where the Americans are concerned. When India and Pakistan went to war, we suspended arms shipments to both at once; when the Arabs and Israelis squared off, we did the same; but not in Vietnam. We don't even take it amiss that, although we can send arms over there, we can't send over medical supplies to the victims of those arms, because most of our big drug firms are U.S.-owned and barred from shipping anything to North Vietnam by the U.S. Trading With the Enemy Act. However, we *can* help the Americans with chemical warfare experiments at Suffield, Alberta. There, our scientists study gas weapons and run tactical exercises so we'll know what to do if ever the bad guys try them on us. This research is turned over to our allies, and what they do with it is none of our business. If we can swallow that, we can swallow our role as butcher's helper in Southeast Asia without even blinking.

The same "realism" that sends our arms to Vietnam lurks behind much of our acceptance of American leadership, not only in the world, but in our own backyard — not only across the blood-stained fields of Vietnam, but over the wheat-strewn fields of Saskatchewan, where U.S. fighter-bombers on NORAD exercises writhe across our skies in the name of common defence. It is not common defence, it is American defence, just as the establishment of U.S. anti-ballistic missiles is for American, not Canadian, benefit. Trudeau was no more successful in blocking those missiles than he was in trying to end Canada's nuclear role. (It was acceptance of that role that set off his famous tirade against the Pearson Liberals, already quoted, in 1963. The warheads went into place in 1964, and are still in place. *Sic transit*.) It was because of his outspoken opposition to nuclear weapons that many Canadians expected Trudeau to attack, and perhaps influence, the American decision to install an anti-ballistic missile system.

That system, now abuilding, consists of two parts, both manned by a different type of missile. The Spartan is to provide the outer defence, and explode incoming ICBMs 400 miles from the ABM site by means of a two-megaton warhead. Those that get through will be taken care of by the short-range, faster-moving Sprint, a comparative light-weight, with only a ten-kiloton nuclear capacity. President Nixon, over stiff opposition in his own country, approved the system in March 1968, with a beginning price tag of $8 billion. The first two sites are under construction in North Dakota and Montana, not far from the Canadian border.

Canada objects to the system, not so much because the bombs will explode over our territory (as External Affairs Minister Mitchell Sharp has pointed out, if a major nuclear exchange begins, territorial boundaries won't mean much in the ashes), but because it is bound to lead, indeed has already led, to another round of arms escalation. Trudeau promised to take the issue up with the President on his first call at the White House soon after Nixon gave the ABM go-ahead. He told the House of Commons that Canada had been "consulted" about the decision, but, pressed by the then-leader of the NDP, Tommy Douglas, he admitted "There was no consultation in the sense that we might have been in a position to change the decision."

Trudeau made it clear that he was not happy about the ABM system and the Americans made it clear they didn't much care. When Defence Secretary Melvin Laird told the Senate Foreign Relations Committee that he could not say whether the Nixon administration would drop the system if Canada objected, Senator William Fulbright replied, "But you have already answered . . . if they don't like it, they can lump it."

We lumped it. Trudeau went to Washington on March 25, 1969, and won a strange accolade from U. S. journalists, who found him attractive, but "shy". Nixon might have felt the same way. As Anthony Westell noted in the *Toronto Daily*

*Star*, "One common impression . . . was that Trudeau appeared altogether too much like the nervous junior visiting a superior. He even wore in his lapel the red button with the gold stripe and number that was the White House security pass for the day. . . . 'Can you imagine de Gaulle doing that?' one newsman asked."

The President and Prime Minister got along famously, and parted with a one-paragraph reference to the subject of ABMs in their joint communique: "Over the years the United States has regularly informed Canada of plans and developments in the ABM field; it has been agreed that this practice will continue."

On May 23, Trudeau told Parliament: "If the Canadian government had power to make decisions in this area I think we would suggest the ABM should not be proceeded with."

But we don't have that power, apparently; our role as defence partner with the U.S. is to keep our head down and our eyes shut. The ABM disagreement could have been taken to the Permanent Joint Board on Defence, which exists for just such purposes, but both Canadian and U.S. members of the PJBD took the view that it was strictly an American matter. In short, none of our business.

We proved a little harder for the Americans to control in our relations with Russia, where the Prime Minister paid a state visit in May 1971. U.S. reaction to the initiative was generally cool. They needn't have worried, however; the trip appeared to be as much for the folks back home as for the Russians. During the twelve-day visit, which encompassed calls to Moscow, Tashkent, Samarkand and even Norilsk, in the Soviet Arctic, Trudeau confined himself to banalities, at least in public, and to clowning for the television cameras. His new bride, Margaret, was along on the trip, an attraction that drew a forty-member press contingent that had little to report beyond hand-holding, warm glances and a little playful pushing and shoving between the newlyweds on the gangplank of the nuclear ice-breaker *Lenin*.

If Trudeau's private talks with Kosygin produced anything substantial, it has not yet come to light; the official communiques spoke only of the new protocol signed in Moscow, which enjoins Canada and Russia to meet regularly to discuss issues and exchange information on Arctic development. On the plane trip home, Trudeau told reporters he wasn't sure himself of the significance of his visit or, really, why he had been invited. He rejected the notion that Canada was playing its old role of "honest broker" between the superpowers of East and West; he had not been given any messages to bear from Moscow to Washington, he said, and if any had been proferred, he would have "told the Russians to peddle their own papers". He was subjected to the criticism that the trip was a waste of time and money, that there was no need for a state visit to sign one meaningless protocol or sanctify information exchanges that had already begun.

For once, I think Trudeau was too modest. This was, after all, the first visit of a Western prime minister to Russia; the choice of Trudeau and the warmth of his reception made it clear that the Russians are willing to regard Canada as more than a supine satellite of the U.S. Whatever game the Soviets were playing — and clearly they were, as usual, up to something devious — it was to Canada's advantage to accept the invitation and the compliment implied. To have refused, or to have played down the stay, would have been impolitic as well as impolite. It is not so much a question of Canada becoming pro-Soviet as becoming a little less slavishly pro-American. The Prime Minister made it clear during his press conferences in Russia that we continue to regard the U.S. as our closest ally, but there was still a certain amount of anxious hovering on the part of American diplomats until he got home. The way in which U.S. officials descended on our officials after the return to Ottawa was reminiscent of an anxious Momma pouncing on her daughter after her return from the prom. (Did he try anything fresh? Who else was there? You didn't go for a drive after, did you?)

Trudeau managed to wipe away some of the advantage of the trip by his dumb account of it afterwards. On CBC Radio's *Sunday Magazine* programme, he was asked why he hadn't asked the Russian leaders about the jailing of Ukrainian nationalists, a subject on which many Ukrainian-Canadians were exercised; he replied by comparing the Ukrainian nationalists with the FLQ. "My position in the Soviet Union or in Canada is that anyone who breaks the law to assert his nationalism does not get too much sympathy from me.

"I didn't particularly feel like bringing up any cases which would have caused [Communist Party Leader Leonid] Brezhnev or [Prime Minister Alexei] Kosygin to say 'Well you know, why did you put in jail certain FLQ leaders? After all they think they are only fighting for the independence of Quebec. . . . Why should you put your revolutionaries in jail and we shouldn't put ours?' "

The inept comparison between the systematic murder of Ukrainian nationalists by the Soviet state and the terrorism of the FLQ brought immediate protests from every sector of Canada; Trudeau withdrew into an explanation that he had been "misinterpreted". He had not; he came through loud and clear saying, as he always says, that nationalism is an evil and he has no sympathy for its adherents, no matter who, no matter where.

It is this attitude that explains our weakness in dealing with the Americans. Trudeau did make one stab at pushing off the U.S., when his government laid claim to sovereignty over Arctic waters. I mean to come back to that decision in Chapter 9, but for the moment it is enough to note that our claim was made, characteristically, by indirection; we said that we were out to control pollution in the north. The claim has not been seriously challenged by the U.S.; what will happen when it is challenged remains to be seen, but if past practice is any guide, "realism" will dictate that we speak softly and carry no stick at all.

It is this failure to deal with the U.S. on anything like equal — or even adult — terms that has left the Trudeau government with its blackest mark: its incapacity to meet the problem of American domination of the Canadian economy.

## Notes

1. Canada, Department of External Affairs, *Foreign Policy for Canadians* (The External Affairs White Paper), 1970, p. 23.
2. Internal study conducted at the embassy by Ed Ritchie and supplied to the author.
3. See Clyde Sanger's superb, and disturbing, book, *Half a Loaf* (Toronto: Ryerson, 1969), a study of Canadian aid programmes, from which these figures are drawn.
4. The exact amount used to be shown in the annual report of the Department of Defence Production, now part of the Department of Supply, but after what a public-relations man called "misuse by the media" — i.e., newspapers kept publishing the guilty total — the

figures were dropped. I asked an official in the Department of Industry, Trade and Commerce to verify this figure, and he did. A Pentagon official told me it erred on the conservative side.

# 8

## The Independence Question:
## What Am I Bid for Canada?

*There is some hope that in advanced societies, the glue of nationalism will become as obsolete as the divine right of kings.*
Pierre Elliott Trudeau, June 1964

Trudeau's anti-nationalist philosophy was born, as we have already seen, in Duplessis' Quebec, where nationalism was the rallying-cry used by the province's Establishment to consolidate its grip on power; it was reinforced by his world ramblings, during which he witnessed violence brought on by excessive nationalism in half a dozen nations. So it is not surprising that the Prime Minister remains suspicious of nationalism, and it is commendable that he believes — or appears to believe, although his government's record does not provide much evidence — in internationalism. However, Canadian nationalism, as presently practised, has nothing to do with cutting throats or burning buses or waging war to annex our neighbours' territory; it is not aggressive but defensive, and aimed at preventing the absorption of this nation into the United States. (In this context, the discredited term "nationalism" is clearly a misnomer — perhaps what we need is an equivalent of the French-Canadian term *indépendantisme*.) Furthermore, the alternative to nationalism in Canada is not internationalism, but continentalism; if we throw off our national ties we will acquire, not those of the U.N., but of the U.S. By his insistence on applying the lessons learned in the 1940s to the Canada of the 1970s, Trudeau does himself, and his nation, an injustice. Worse, he threatens to sell us out to the U.S. not because that nation wants Canada — she has troubles enough of her own — but because the increasing American encroachment on our economy must lead one day to the point where the border between our two nations makes no more sense.

Quite early in his reign, the Prime Minister appeared before a student audience for the television show *Under Attack*, and his response to questions put by moderator Fred Davis was revealing.

*Davis:*
Many Canadians regret the extent to which we have come under American domination economically. What do you think the chances are for Canada becoming master of her own house, or indeed should we try?

*The Prime Minister:*
Well, you're using "master of your own house" — if you're using it in psychological terms, you can be the master of your own house. If you're using it in economic terms, or in technological terms . . .

*Davis:*
That's what I meant, sir.

*The Prime Minister:*
. . . the question is much more complicated. . . . It's easy to say: we own it all; we won't let foreign capital in, or we will let it under very strict conditions. The next thing is to be able to do it and why do you do it? Do you do it just to satisfy a nationalistic feeling, a feeling that this is mine and I feel great, or do you do it in order to ensure the greatest progress for the people that live in the country?

*Audience:*
Survival.

*The Prime Minister:*
National survival, sure. If you want to do it in order to ensure that there will be continued progress in economic and technological and sociological terms, then you don't do it the same way as if you're mainly obsessed with national survival and think that you are going to get rid of all foreign ownership. You know, I've said this before. It's easy to get rid of foreign ownership — Cuba did it in about fifteen days. You just kick a few companies out, expropriate them without compensation and foreign capital leaves. It's no trick to do that . . . I won't do it. I certainly wouldn't do it because I

don't think Castro has the right solution for the Canadian people. I don't think, for one, that the people in this room would consent to descend to the standard of living which came in Cuba as a result of this getting rid of foreign capital. . . . There is another way of getting rid of foreign capital; that is replacing one foreigner with another, which the Cubans also did. You know, get rid of the Americans and bring in the Russians or the Chinese which is fine, too. I don't suppose we would have gone great lengths towards the pursuit of national survival if we replaced the Americans by the Chinese. I don't think they have as much to teach us in terms of technology and in terms of the production of real wealth and in the production also of the kind of society, of political institutions, social institutions, to which we are accustomed. I don't see any reason for replacing one type of foreign domination by another. I think we should try and get the kind of policy which makes sure that we have the least possible foreign domination in those areas which are most important for the preservation of the kind of ideas and values which we believe are right for this society.

I have quoted this extensively from the Prime Minister because his answers illuminate two important things about the man. The first is his argumentative technique, which is at once skilful and outrageous. He takes whatever the other side is saying — in this case a suggestion that perhaps we should be doing something about the domination of our economy by the U.S. — attaches implications to it that are a monstrous distortion, and attacks the implications. Do we want to become masters in our own house? Very well, there are only two ways to do it. One is to seize foreign assets, as Castro did. The other is to call in the Chinese. In one case, we reap poverty, in the other, a new domination. No sensible person wants either of these; ergo, we can't do anything about American domination except to "try and get the kind of policy which makes sure that we have the least possible foreign domination in those areas which are most important".

The second thing apparent from this exchange is that the Prime Minister does not intend to do anything about American control. He sincerely believes that nationalism is "an obsession" that makes people want to squat on a piece of land, steadfastly refusing either to develop their own resources or to let others do so. In the past several years nationalist sentiment has been growing in Canada, partly as a rejection of some of the worst, and most visible, outcroppings of the American Dream, partly because U.S. economic control is measurably growing. The nationalists have not suddenly discovered an ancient phenomenon, they are alarmed by the quickening of continentalism that has been taking place over the past two decades, and the consequences it holds for our political independence. In 1948, 42 per cent of all Canadian manufacturing was owned by non-residents,[1] and by 1968 the figure had risen to 58.1 per cent.[2] More than three-quarters of the foreign control is held in the United States, and that proportion is increasing every year.[3] Our resource industries are also overwhelmingly owned by outsiders; 99.7 per cent of petroleum and coal products are in foreign hands (76.4 per cent U.S.), 82.3 per cent of mineral fuels (67.1 per cent U.S.), and 62.8 per cent of mining (50.9 per cent U.S.).[4]

Foreign investment is concentrated, naturally enough, where the profits are highest. According to returns filed under the Corporations and Labour Returns Act, our furniture industry made a meager $4.6 million profit in 1968, and is 18.8 per cent foreign-owned; profits in the petroleum and coal industry were $375.4 million, and it is 99.7 per cent foreign-owned. Our knitting mills cleared $5.1 million and are 78.1 per cent ours; chemicals made $203.6 million and are 81.3 per cent theirs. We have a firm grip on sliding industries, Americans have a stranglehold on expanding ones. As our resources develop and markets expand, others will be there to reap the profits; Canadians will be left in command of farming, fishing and wood-chopping.

When he was asked on a television programme whether Canadians suffer because of the domination of our economy by Americans, Prime Minister Trudeau replied, "They don't, I think, suffer in an economic sense, or even for that matter in a technological sense. It is because of American capital investment, and the technology that came with it, that we enjoy one of the highest standards of living in the world."

In short, without massive injections of U.S. capital, we would be poor; to interfere with that capital is to endanger our well-being. This has been a chronic assumption on the part of successive Liberal governments, but it is now being attacked with increasing vigour by Canadian economists, led by Professor Kari Levitt of McGill University. In her study, *Silent Surrender*, Professor Levitt pointed out that "The acquisition of control by U.S. companies over the commodity-producing sectors of the Canadian economy has largely been financed from corporate savings derived from the sale of Canadian resources, extracted and processed by Canadian labour, or from the sale [of products] of branch-plant manufacturing businesses to Canadian consumers at tariff-protected prices." Those aren't American dollars expanding our economy; they are Canadian dollars manipulated by Americans. In the period from 1957 to 1964, U.S. direct investment in mining, manufacturing and petroleum was derived mainly from Canadian sources — 73 per cent from retained earnings and reserves, 12 per cent from Canadian financial sources, and only 15 per cent from new U.S. funds.[5] The trend is ominous; in 1968, of $2.61 billion new American investment, only $127 million, or 4.9 per cent, came in the form of U.S. funds.[6] We pay through the nose for that tiny injection of capital; in the period 1960-67, U.S. subsidiaries in Canada sent home $1.8 billion *more* in profits ($5.9 billion) than they received in new capital inflow ($4.1 billion).[7]

Americans aren't financing our takeover — we are.

According to the Liberal, continentalist view — a view held by Trudeau, Finance Minister Benson and External Affairs Minister Mitchell Sharp — it doesn't really matter who owns Canadian companies as long as they behave as "good corporate citizens". But we cannot make foreign corporations follow Canadian policy when so many of them are owned and controlled from outside, and respond to a trumpet played in Washington. Already we have lost the right, in many cases, to legislate for our own industry.

American laws, such as the Trading With the Enemy Act, determine with whom our corporations may trade. No U.S. subsidiary has been allowed to deal with North Korea, North Vietnam, China or Cuba except by special dispensation from the U.S. State Department. (In the spring of 1971, the ban was lifted as it applied to China.) We have lost orders ranging from baby-food and flour for Cuba to trucks for China. More important, there has been no attempt to develop trade with those countries by our most vigorous and well-placed firms; the advantage we might have had in dealing with the one-quarter of the world represented by China was denied us by American fiat, and now that it is open territory once more, the Americans are in a position to plunge in with, or even ahead of, us.

American anti-trust legislation not only determines how U.S. subsidiaries in Canada may act (the 1970 report of the External Affairs Committee on Canada-U.S. relations [the Wahn Report] noted "legal action has been taken by the United States authorities under their anti-trust laws in approximately twenty important cases which directly or indirectly affected or might affect the operations of Canadian industries"), it also affects the prices Canadian consumers pay for a wide range of goods. The Canadian refrigerator market of 400,000 units per year could be efficiently served by two factories. In fact, there are nine, seven of them American branch-plants. If they were to combine, they would (a) bring down the price of refrigerators in Canada, (b) compete more effectively in world markets and (c) face prosecution under American anti-trust legislation.[8]

If U.S. law determines how individual firms may operate in Canada, U.S. policy determines their collective behaviour in the crucial matter of capital flows. Three times — in 1963, 1965 and 1968 — American presidents have asked or demanded that U.S. companies abroad bring home more capital. In each case a hapless Canada, faced with a massive haemorrhage of funds, has begged for an exemption; in each case, we have been granted it only for a price — the handing of an increasing control over our monetary policy to the U.S.[9] As Earle McLaughlin, President of the Royal Bank of Canada, told his bank's shareholders: "Under the new arrangements, our own monetary authorities appear to be attached to a string . . . the business end of which is held in Washington." We agreed not only to hold a fixed reserve in U.S. dollars, which ties up billions of Canadian dollars and restricts our freedom of action, we even undertook to police the behaviour of American subsidiaries here, to see that they followed the U.S. guidelines.

. American subsidiaries buy components largely from their parents and compete only timidly for export sales, which means that more than half our manufacturing industry has opted out of competition for the export markets by which we live. A 1967 study by the Department of Industry, Trade and Commerce revealed that 82 per cent of the output of foreign-controlled companies was sold within Canada. The study showed that 50 per cent of the export sales of the subsidiaries was to their parents, and 70 per cent of their imports came from that same source. The president of a large U.S. branch-plant in Peterborough, Ontario, told me bitterly how his firm tried to open a market in the West Indies, only to be shut out by its parent. The Canadian company had opened negotiations for a contract in Barbados that had to be approved by the international office. That office added book-keeping costs to the Canadian bid that made it non-competitive, then submitted a lower bid on behalf of the American parent, which got the contract.

We pay for American ownership also because the decisions to expand or retract, to open new plants or close old ones, to conduct research here or buy it elsewhere, are made in the U.S., subject to American political pressures, guided by reasons that make perfect sense across the border, but make no sense to us at all. When economic retraction begins, foreign companies start their lay-offs in Canada — as in the case of the foreign-owned Dunlop Tire company outside Toronto in early 1970 — which is perfectly proper conduct from their point of view, but leaves more than half our manufacturing firms naked to the wind. Sometimes we even subsidize the process. When, in December 1968, the Ontario Development Corporation approved a $77,067 subsidy to help the U.S.-owned Selkirk-Metalbestos Company to expand its factory in Brockville, Ontario, it thought it was helping create jobs for Canadians. Instead, the American parent company bought another Canadian firm in Hamilton, closed the Hamilton plant and moved its operations to the expanded Brockville factory. In Hamilton, fifty workers lost their jobs; in Brockville, ten new positions were created, at lower wages than those paid in Hamilton.[10] The operation made perfect sense to the American owners, but for Canada it was just another illustration of the price we pay for dependence.

In face of the challenge of U.S. domination, the Trudeau government has had four opportunities to act, and has dodged every one of them. They were:

1. The government review of foreign policy in mid-1970.
2. The report of the External Affairs Committee on Canada-U.S. relations, tabled on August 17, 1970 (the Wahn Report).
3. The establishment of the long-promised Canada Development Corporation, through legislation introduced on January 25, 1971.

4. The government's own Task Force on Foreign Ownership, chaired by Revenue Minister Herb Gray, whose report was completed early in 1971.

The government review of foreign policy, tabled on June 25, 1970, and already discussed in Chapter 7, is an astonishing document. In five volumes, it manages to avoid the central issue of Canadian foreign policy — our relations with the U.S. — except for glancing references, and then comes down with two paragraphs reflecting perfectly the Prime Minister's view. They are worth reproducing in full:

> On the assumption that reasonable civil order is preserved in the United States and that such international involvements as the Vietnam war are scaled down and avoided in future, the economic and technological ascendancy of the United States will undoubtedly continue during the next decade, although it will be tempered by the economic integration of Europe and the industrial growth of Japan. This ascendancy will continue to have heavy impact on Canada, with political, economic and social implications. The dependence of Canadian private industry and some government programmes on United States techniques and equipment (not to mention capital) will continue to be a fact of life. United States markets for Canadian energy resources and more advanced manufacturing goods will be of growing significance to the Canadian economy. Increasingly, the Canada-United States economic relationship will be affected by agreements between governments and arrangements by multinational corporations and trade unions.

> While such developments should be beneficial for Canada's economic growth, the constant danger that sovereignty, independence and cultural identity may be impaired will require a conscious effort on Canada's part to keep the whole situation under control. Active pursuit of trade diversification and technological co-operation with European and other developed countries will be needed to provide countervailing factors. Improvements in United States relations with the Soviet Union and China — which would seem quite possible within the decade — would enhance Canada's peace and security but would also reduce trading advantages which Canada now enjoys with Eastern Europe and China. In general, United States developments and policies are

bound to have profound effects on Canada's position during the seventies, even though there is no reason to believe that the United States Government would consider intervening directly in Canadian affairs.

In short, Canada stands on guard, ever ready, ever alert, ever deeper in debt, and we have no intention of changing our policies in the future.

The External Affairs Committee, under the chairmanship of Liberal MP Ian Wahn, took a far tougher line. Reviewing the degree of U.S. penetration and the price we pay for it (one tidbit the Wahn Report dug out is that a huge proportion of Canadian government grants go to U.S. firms; in the 1967-68 fiscal year, 95 per cent of grants given to defence production industries went to non-Canadian firms), the Committee suggested stern measures: a provision that firms operating in Canada should eventually have 51 per cent of their shares owned by Canadians; establishment at once of a Canada Development Corporation; and installation of a Canadian Ownership and Control Bureau, with the power to approve or disapprove the takeover of Canadian companies, the power to disallow establishment of foreign firms and the power to ensure that subsidiaries did not turn down export orders.

The Wahn Report had barely hit a House of Commons desk before it was flatly disavowed by the Prime Minister and Finance Minister Benson. There would be no action on the recommendations, they indicated; Canada still welcomed, nay begged, foreign investment.

The Canada Development Corporation as finally established by the government bore little resemblance to the original model designed by Walter Gordon when he was Finance Minister in 1963. Under the legislation, the CDC is designed to "Help develop and maintain strong Canadian-controlled and Canadian-managed corporations in the private sector, and to provide greater opportunities for Canadians to invest and participate in the economic development of Canada."

A worthy goal. It is to be attained through a corporation that will eventually have $2 billion in capitalization, beginning with an infusion of $250 million in government funds. At first the government will own all the shares, but they will be made available to the public for purchase, probably at $5 a share. The CDC will funnel investment funds into private companies, but "Will not seek to exercise direct operating control of the corporations in which it invests." The government will always be the single largest shareholder; it will probably hold at least 10 per cent of CDC shares, while no other individual or company will be allowed to own more than 3 per cent.

All of this, unless you are a committed socialist, makes perfect sense. "As outlined by Mr. Benson," said the then NDP leader, Tommy Douglas, when the bill landed, "it sounds like a complete sellout to private enterprise." But the purpose of the CDC is not to settle political arguments, it is to safeguard the Canadian economy. That purpose is betrayed, not by its share ownership or control arrangements, but by the role given to it by the Trudeau government. The CDC's first task, said Benson, "is to make a profit". It will not interfere in the takeover of Canadian companies unless the company about to disappear is a profitable one. If a Canadian firm in a crucial but unprofitable area is to be gobbled up — a book or magazine publisher, say — the CDC will keep its hands to itself; a nice, fat hotel chain, now, that's something else again.

The logic involved boggles alike the thoughtful capitalist and normal socialist mind. It makes no sense to the capitalist for the state to interfere brutally in the marketplace of private enterprise just to turn a buck. Profit-making is the preserve of private entrepreneurs, and the CDC smacks of socialism run amuck. But to the socialist, the arrangement makes even less sense. The socialist argues that the role of government-owned enterprises is to express national priorities and advance national goals; profit-making has nothing to do with it. The CDC manages to outrage and offend at one and the same time both British Columbia Premier W. A. C. Bennett of the Social Credit party and radical socialist Mel Watkins — no mean feat. No one but a Liberal could love it, for it manages to wring the worst out of two possible alternatives.

The CDC as presently constituted will not halt the takeover of Canadian firms, now proceeding at a pace of about 170 companies per year.[11] It will only interfere spasmodically and quixotically with *some* takeovers. But will it provide venture capital for new Canadian enterprises? Perhaps, and if so it will be better than nothing — a phrase that may well encapsule its chief virtue.

The fourth chance the Trudeau administration has had to exert some influence on foreign ownership was through the Task

Force headed by Herb Gray. The appointment of a Windsor-area MP to the job should have been the tip-off — Gray's riding is, in the main, merely an across-the-border suburb of Detroit — but continual rumblings in the press about the hard look the Task Force was taking and the firm steps it was going to recommend, kept hopes high through most of late 1970. They were vain hopes. The Gray Report was ready in mid-February 1971, but by July had still not been tabled. It was not tabled because Gray was not to be given the final word; his report was sent to the Privy Council Office and the Prime Minister's Office for re-writing; there, it was decided that no report should be issued for the present, and the public may never know exactly what the Task Force had in mind. The material, said the Prime Minister, was to be for government guidance only, and the *official* position would emerge in the form of legislation at some future date.

I don't know what was in the Gray Report; I do know, from a source close to the Task Force, that it did recommend action to repatriate the Canadian economy; I assume, by the fact of its strangulation, that it was not well received by the Prime Minister, and that nothing is going to be done while he is in office effectively to halt the absorption of our economy into the American one.

I do not contend that there is a U.S. plot — an imperialist plot — to take us over; the astonishing thing about our absorption is its accidental quality, and the way in which we ourselves work to bring it about. Consider two typical cases, one from Newfoundland, the other from northern Saskatchewan, that show how the process works.

Come By Chance is a small town about eighty miles northwest of St. John's, Newfoundland. It was here, last fall, that bulldozers began to carve out a dream held dear by Premier Joseph R. Smallwood and his friend, the New York financier, John Shaheen. Shaheen, a slim, wiry, aggressive man, is a capitalist in the classic American mould. A mid-westerner of Lebanese descent, he served in the U.S. Navy during World War II, first in intelligence, later as an officer in charge of oil shipments. It was in this second capacity that he conceived the idea of a series of oil refineries strategically located around North America, to feed the endless maw of the U.S. market. ("Submarines might blockade one oil supply in a future war," he said, "they could never blockade four.") He went broke trying to build one refinery complex in Puerto Rico — "I dropped a quarter of a million dollars. I was too green." Then he came to Newfoundland, drawn by the generous terms Premier Smallwood offers almost anyone who promises jobs and industry for his province, and established a small refinery at Holyrood. In time, Shaheen built a financial empire under the corporate umbrella of Shaheen Natural Resources, Inc., and won rich and influential friends, including Richard Nixon, lawyer, and Joseph Smallwood, politician. With the Holyrood refinery an obvious success, Premier Smallwood approached Shaheen with a new scheme — to build a huge refinery and later a petrochemical complex at Come By Chance. The agreement subsequently entered into between the province of Newfoundland and the financier was remarkable for its generosity to Shaheen — so remarkable, in fact, that two of Smallwood's cabinet ministers cited it as a reason for marching out of the Liberal cabinet and setting up in dutiful but futile opposition to the Premier.

The refinery will cost at least $155 million to build, and the money is provided in two blocks — $30 million that the province of Newfoundland has borrowed to lend to Shaheen (originally, Shaheen's companies were to have raised this money with provincial guarantees, but, because of restrictions imposed by the province, Shaheen says, his fund-raising activities went for naught, so Newfoundland put up the sum) — and $125 million provided by a group of British banks and secured by a first mortgage on the property. For his part, Shaheen has put up $10 million and has spent, he says, about $3 million in development costs. The federal government will provide a wharf, at a minimum $16 million, to be paid for out of usage fees.

So, of all the partners in the operation, Shaheen has put up the least cash, and the province of Newfoundland, a province already much burdened with debt, has put up more than twice as much. But the refinery will not be owned by Newfoundland. No, indeed. It will be built, managed and owned by a series of crown corporations, which are run in turn by Newfoundland Refining Co., a wholly-owned subsidiary of Shaheen Natural Resources. The company that operates the complex will receive a sales commission of 5.1 per cent of gross sales (estimated at about $100 million per year) and 27.8 per cent of the net profits. The province will get 5 per cent of the gross profits, but not until after the first eight years of operation. After fifteen years, when the refinery has discharged its debt and mortgage, Shaheen Natural Resources has the option to purchase the crown corporation that owns it for a mere $1800. Then it must pay the province 5 per cent of the net profits until $10 million has been paid, after which the refinery will belong to the New York company.

If the project fails, Shaheen will simply not exercise his option to purchase; if it succeeds, he will own, for an outlay of $13 million, a complex worth $155 million, paid for out of its own operating profits and made possible by the aid of the federal and provincial governments. The federal government has also allowed the company to write off 100 per cent of the refinery costs as depreciation any time during the first eight years — in effect, a five- or six-year tax holiday.

Not only has Shaheen been given, with the aid of the Canadian taxpayer, an extraordinary opportunity to make huge amounts of money; he has also been given a virtual monopoly on any similar scheme in Newfoundland for the next quarter-century; one provision of the agreement gives the Shaheen interests first refusal for that time. There is no danger that any Canadian entrepreneur will be in a position to challenge Shaheen's supremacy in Newfoundland for some time to come.

Note that it is not American capital that makes the scheme work, and not the American entrepreneur who takes the major risk — all he takes is the major profit.

Almost as generous in its treatment of foreign investors was the arrangement provided by the province of Saskatchewan to Parsons and Whittemore, Inc. of New York — an arrangement that hopefully will be renegotiated as a result of the change in government in Saskatchewan, but the details of which are worth noting as an object lesson. On February 18, 1971, the late Premier Ross Thatcher called a press conference to announce "the single largest economic development ever to establish in Saskatchewan", which turned out to be a $177 million pulp mill at Dore Lake, in the northern part of the province. The mill was to be built, and mostly owned, by Parsons and Whittemore, although the timber was to be Canadian timber, the labour Canadian labour, and most of the risks were to be taken by Canadians.

Premier Thatcher anticipated what was bound to be the crucial question, and answered it. He said, "There will be some who will say that we should have signed an agreement with a Canadian company. We invited numerous major Canadian pulp and paper companies to build and operate a pulp mill in this area. They were not interested."

At the Premier's side was Karl F. Landegger, president of the U.S. firm, which also owns another pulp mill at Prince Albert, eighty miles south of Dore Lake. Landegger added, "Each of these deals was rejected by at least ten other Canadian and American companies. We were the only ones who had the courage to do it."

The words, the setting, the philosophy, all had a familiar ring. As usual, only Americans were willing to gamble on Canada's future. The funny thing is that I could find no trace of the approaches made to "numerous major Canadian pulp and paper companies". I wrote to the seventeen largest pulp companies in Canada, all of those that, in the opinion of an expert in the industry, would be large enough to take on such a project. Of the seventeen, nine are Canadian-owned, two British, five American and one Finnish. Of the seventeen, fifteen replied that they had never been approached in connection with Dore Lake; two — MacMillan-Bloedel of British Columbia and the Price Company of Quebec— said they had been invited to look at the feasibility of a sawmill, not a pulp mill, but since the only market would be the pulp mill already owned by Parsons and Whittemore at Prince Albert, there was, as Price President T. R. Moore wrote, "no assurance of a satisfactory return".

Most of the other pulp companies were bitterly critical of the new venture. Juan de Valle, president of the Ontario-Minnesota Paper company, put it this way: "The pulp and paper industry in Canada is in poor health because of increasing costs and the unpegging of the Canadian dollar, coupled with a serious overcapacity situation. . . . It seems to me very strange that we are expected to support additional capacity through our tax dollar when this is given in only certain circumstances."

Another pulp company president, who chooses to remain unidentified, was much blunter: "Another pulp mill is bound to have a disrupting effect on the market. They're dumping pulp all over the place at any price because they have to get rid of it. . . . The whole approach is goddamn stupid. . . . You're forcing the issue with these goddamn government-assisted things."

The assistance involved was certainly enough to force the issue at Dore Lake.[12] In fact, of $177 million involved, $141.7 million was to come from, or be guaranteed by, the Canadian public: $107 million as a provincially guaranteed loan, $12 million as a federal grant, $7.2 million as equity investment by Saskatchewan, $19.1 million more from the province to cover a road grant, half a contingency fund, an equipment loan and a line of credit for roads and a rail line. That makes $145.3 million, but the province would get back $3.6 million as a guarantee fee.

Parsons and Whittemore was to put $16.8 million into equity investment and $3 million as its half of the contingency loan fund. An equipment-financing loan of $12 million would be guaranteed by the U.S. Export-Import Bank or the Export Guarantee Credits Department of Britain, depending on which country supplied the material.

The U.S. firm was to get a lot for its $19.8 million. Ownership of the mill would be held in the ratio of share equity, that is, 70 per cent by Parsons and Whittemore for its $16.8 million, 30 per cent by Saskatchewan for its $7.2 million. By putting in about 10 per cent of the cost, the U.S. firm would get 70 per cent of the profit. It would also receive about $12 million in contract fees for building the mill (if all went well; if the cost escalated beyond a certain point, this figure would decline), profit on sales of machinery from one of its wholly-owned subsidiaries to the mill, and a commission of about $2 million annually on sales. If the project went according to plan, the American company would cover its investment with its services; the real capital outlay would all come from others.

In addition, the Americans would acquire exclusive timber rights on 23,000 square miles of Saskatchewan, an area about twice the size of Belgium, and an effective monopoly on pulp mills in the province — there wouldn't be enough timber left for anyone else. What's more, the province, not the company, was to be responsible for replacing slashed timber; the company would pay a flat rate of twenty-five cents per cord for re-seeding.

The mill would consume about fifty-six million gallons of water per day from the Dore and Beaver rivers, and the company undertook to minimize pollution of the outgoing water. Hopefully, it would do better than at its Prince Albert mill, where bacteria counts of 85.8 million per millilitre of water were measured by a biologist at the mill outlet. ("Fairly clean" water has a count of 5,000 bacteria per millilitre.) A Dore Lake housewife wrote, "Four years ago my family and I spent happy hours angling in the North Saskatchewan river for Winnipeg Goldeye. . . . That was before the Prince Albert pulp mill went into operation. The following year we fished again. The Goldeye were inedible. They tasted like skunk. Now, the North Saskatchewan north of the pulp mill is closed for sport fishing, but the American owners assure us that the water they are dumping back into the river is purer than that which they take out."[13]

All of this, from the giveaway of provincial resources to the spoliation of provincial rivers, was urged in the name of jobs. Premier Thatcher reported that the mill would employ 1,200 people during construction and 1,600 during operation. Joseph Condon, vice-president of Parsons and Whittemore, told me there would be an average of 450 jobs in the mill and between 700 and 800 in the woods. About 10 per cent of the top positions would go to experts brought in by the U.S. company. So, if the project provided 1,125 new Canadian jobs for a $177 million investment, the ratio of jobs to dollars would be one to 157,333. That's a bad deal for Canada, even if it did not involve giving away the pulpwood resources of a province and control over "the single largest economic development ever to establish in Saskatchewan". The deal was attacked by Saskatchewan NDP leader Allan Blakeny, who became Premier on June 23, 1971. He has promised to renegotiate the deal or kill it, but at this writing it is not certain which course he will follow. The deal was not a major election issue; it was largely by fluke that we avoided it.

I am not suggesting that either John Shaheen or Karl Landegger is at fault for taking advantage of Canada's extraordinary generosity; I am suggesting that we cannot afford any more bargains like these. But we are going to have them; we are going to have them, particularly, in relation to the development of Canadian resources. Outwardly, Canada has rejected the concept of continental resource development; behind the scenes, it has already been accepted. Three examples from my own observation should make this clear.

1. During a visit to Washington in mid-1970, I asked an attache in the Canadian embassy to explain our attitude on continental resources. He replied, "Which would you like, our

official policy — which is to say we don't know what the hell you're talking about — or the one we're working on with the Americans?"

2. Last winter, while federal cabinet ministers were still saying that we would make up our own minds in our own time about whether to permit a pipeline to be built down the Mackenzie River Valley, a cabinet minute proposed the hiring of 200 botanists and zoologists to study the ecological effects of such a line. They were to be hired because, with the normal staff available, such a study would take nine years, and the Americans weren't willing to wait that long. It was not to be a line for the transfer of Canadian oil and gas — oil and gas have not yet been discovered in exploitable quantities in the Canadian Arctic — but for the transfer of American oil and gas from Alaska to the U.S., and the decision to do the hurry-up study was based on American needs. The cabinet ministers who signed that minute were Northern Affairs Minister Jean Chrétien, Energy Minister Joe Greene and Fisheries Minister Jack Davis.

3. On the question of our water resources, Canada has been working on the presumption of a continental policy for years. Our official position, once more, is an enigma: on the same day in February 1970, that alternating-current nationalist, Joe Greene, was telling a dubious House of Commons that Canada was not contemplating any sale of water to the U.S., while the Prime Minister told a university audience "I don't want to be a dog in the manger about this. But if people are not going to use it, can't we sell it for good, hard cash?"

The answer to that question is No: not and retain our nationhood too. The water-sale question, an ancient one now in Canadian political annals, bears closer examination; it may be the most crucial one Trudeau has ever shrugged away.

It was on September 2, 1964, that Arthur Laing, then Northern Affairs Minister, described water export as "probably the greatest issue that will confront Canadians during the next several decades". At that time, Canada was examining a $100 billion plan to tap northern Canadian and Alaskan rivers for use in the parched southwestern U.S. The plan was called the North American Water and Power Alliance — NAWAPA — and it is still alive and well. Publicly Laing took the stance that "We deny categorically that there is anything like a continental resource in respect of water," but he told me privately, in an unguarded moment at the end of an interview, "Something like

NAWAPA is not merely feasible, it's inevitable." When I asked why, then, he was saying the opposite in public, he replied, "We are establishing a bargaining position, and the best bargaining position is to say NO."

We are still establishing a bargaining position. Our politicians may say no, no, but there's yes, yes, in our deals. A vast array of plans, projects, schemes, concepts and proposals has blossomed in both Canada and the U.S. aimed at moving our water south. None has received approval in either Washington or Ottawa, but one of them, the Central North American Water Project, was outlined by a gifted engineer, E. Roy Tinney of the University of Washington, not long before Tinney was made Acting Director of the Policy and Planning Branch of the Canadian Department of Energy, Mines and Resources.

Water importation has been taken under study by two key U.S. groups, the National Water Commission in Washington, and the Western States Water Council in Salt Lake City, Utah. While there have been no government-to-government exchanges on the subject at the official level, exchanges at the unofficial level are alarmingly frequent. For instance, Lewis G. Smith, a Denver engineer with an imaginative concept for a scheme much less expensive than NAWAPA, flew to the Yukon at the request of Commissioner James Smith to lay his plan before the Territorial Council, and Jay Bingham, Director of the Western States Water Council, has been to Ottawa a number of times.

Just as American entrepreneurs can hardly be blamed for our gullibility in financing their takeover of our industry, American engineers can hardly be blamed for trying to control large quantities of our water. The western and southwestern U.S. faces a critical water shortage. A generally dry climate and a rate of population growth far greater than the U.S. national average are pressing on the available reserves. Already, Arizona uses 3,000,000 acre-feet (an acre-foot is 326,000 U.S. gallons) more per year than it receives in rain, snow, and river flow. The deficiency is met by mining underground supplies from a water table that is sinking at the rate of twenty feet per year. In Utah, the lack of water is hampering industrial development — to build a steel mill at Provo, the state took 1,500 acres of irrigated farmland out of production. The Colorado River, which is the chief supplier of water to the southwestern U.S., is so heavily used that virtually none of it ever reaches the Gulf of California, and lawsuits over use of the precious fluid break out among the river-side states like prairie flowers at every available opportunity.[14]

If the situation is bad today, it will soon be worse. The Western Water Development subcommittee of the U.S. Senate reported in 1964 that "This water crisis is a problem of serious and far-reaching implications. It will grow steadily worse until it reaches alarming proportions in the years 1980 and 2000." The subcommittee's solution? Import Canadian water.

There are a number of ways in which the Americans could solve their own problem. Current supplies could be cleaned up and re-used; the Columbia River could be diverted on the American side of the border and run south; desalination of sea water could be perfected. But all of these solutions present difficulties, chief of them the fact that the states involved cannot agree on what should be done. How much simpler, how much more natural, to look north, where the water abounds, north where the stuff flows by the trillions of gallons, untasted and untouched, to the sea. North to Canada.

We have more water per capita than any other nation in the world, and much of it spills off our north and northwest coasts into the ocean. Why not turn this flow south and put it to work for the Americans, thus earning their undying gratitude, to say nothing of a fast buck?

Many schemes have been propounded to this end since NAWAPA unrolled to a deafening beat of public-relations drums in 1964. NAWAPA is a proposal to block off parts of north-flowing Canadian and Alaskan rivers and to pump the water 1,000 feet up through huge pipelines into the Rocky Mountain Trench, a 500-mile-long natural gorge in the Rockies. From there, the water would spill eastward across the Canadian prairies to the Great Lakes, and southward across the American drylands to Mexico. Hydro-electric power generated along the way would provide the push to lift the water where it was needed, and a handsome surplus to sell at a profit.

NAWAPA had the blessing of the U.S. Senate's Western Water Development subcommittee, but its huge cost, complexity and the hard sell that surrounded its launching caused Canadian politicians to shy away. The principal fact about NAWAPA — as about every other water export scheme — is that it would turn our water into an American resource, to be used as they want it, where they want it and when they want it, no matter what we subsequently say or do.

Any water scheme with the U.S. will bring benefits to Canada, including huge amounts of money, both during construction and in payment for water and power. Also, undoubtedly, any such scheme will open new areas to development, mainly in the U.S. but also in this nation. Against these undoubted advantages, however, must be measured the fatal flaw — that any such scheme will link our resources irrevocably to U.S. needs. Export is a tap that, once turned on, could never be shut off. We have already seen, in the long-term sales of Canadian oil and gas, that our energy resources are regarded by Americans as a natural part of their heritage. (For example, on July 20, 1970, the American Federal Power Commission approved construction of a $37.2 million gas pipeline from Michigan and Wisconsin to Canada before the Canadian National Energy Board had even approved export of the gas.[15] They knew we would not disappoint them, and we did not.) The Americans now believe, with some reason, that our water will be equally available. Prime Minister Trudeau encouraged them in such a belief by one of his key appointments, that of Jack Austin as Deputy Minister of Energy, Mines and Resources. Austin is a convinced continentalist, who hopes, as he said in a speech to the Canadian Bar Association in the year before his appointment, "that the practice of resource sharing as explained in the Columbia River Treaty is an indication of the tendency of the same parties to deal with other resource problems in the same way". The 1964 Columbia River Treaty began as a scheme to control flooding on Canadian rivers that cross the U.S. border; it ended by turning those rivers into rich resources for American use. The U.S. pays Canada for only a part of the electrical energy generated and for flood control, and nothing for consumptive use of the water in industry or home.[16] The Columbia River Treaty was a water export scheme; it should be the last such arrangement.

This is not a question, as the Prime Minister would have it, of being "dog in the manger". If the Americans were dying of thirst, we would have no choice. But our water will not slake American throats, it will drive American factories — factories that are our major competitors in world trade. What is at stake is not American lives, but the speed and direction of U.S. development, and to put that ahead of our own development is not righteous, but stupid. What we sell when we sell water is not American survival but American convenience; it is cheaper to import Canadian water than to desalinate sea-water, re-route

the Columbia or straighten out the squabbling states along the
Colorado. The crisis is a crisis of cash; the only survival at stake
is our own.

If, after a diversion scheme sent Canadian water across the
southwest, we discovered that we needed and wanted it back, is
there any chance the Americans would say, "Well, it's your water . . .?" Not bloody likely. Once a large area of the U.S. became dependent on our supplies, it would be immoral, illegal
and politically impossible to change our minds. More than
that, the temptation to interfere in Canadian politics to
safeguard that precious supply would be overwhelming, and
the American track record on intervention, from Santo Do-
mingo to Saigon, and including Ottawa, has not been reas-
suring.

Former Prime Minister John Diefenbaker has stated that it
was, in part, direct American intervention in Canadian politics
that cost him power in 1963; the Americans were anxious for
Canada to accept nuclear weapons, and a statement critical of
the Canadian attitude by the American NATO chief, Gen.
Lauris Norstad, was certainly a major factor in that election.
Direct American intervention also took place, according to
Walter Gordon, when the Canadian government threatened to
apply a tax on advertising in U.S. periodicals published in Canada. Gordon contended, and the Davey Commission on the
Media confirmed, that Canada granted exemptions to *Time* and
*Reader's Digest* — the two magazines at which the law was
chiefly aimed — because of pressure from the U.S. State Department. If we can be interfered with on such issues, we need
have no doubt that the U.S. would act in any way it saw fit to
protect the continuous flow of water across the border once export began.

The Prime Minister's failure to grasp the realities of Canada's precarious position on this continent can be attributed to
two factors. One is his abiding distrust, already mentioned, of
anything that smacks of nationalism. The other is his isolation
in power, his failure to grasp — or even to heed — the very
clear messages that are coming to him from that ultimate barometer of Canadian moods and needs, the House of Commons.

1. DBS figure quoted in W. H. Pope's *The Elephant and the Mouse* (Toronto: McClelland and Stewart, 1970), p. 28.

2. Latest figure available from the 1968 *Annual Report of the Minister of Industry, Trade and Commerce under the Corporations and Labour Returns Act (CALURA) Part I, Corporations*, p. 76.

3. A detailed table appears in the *Report of the External Affairs and Defence Committee on Canada–U.S. Relations* (The Wahn Report), p: 33:40.

4. CALURA report for 1968, p. 176.

5. Kari Levitt, *Silent Surrender* (Toronto: Macmillan, 1970), p. 64.

6. U.S. Department of Commerce, *Survey of Current Business*, November 1970, p. 16.

7. Levitt, *op. cit.*, p. 94.

8. *Ibid.*, p. 136.

9. The Wahn Report, pp. 33:26–33:32.

10. Details given in the Ontario legislature, during debates on the Ontario Development Corporation in February 1971, and reported in *The Globe and Mail*.

11. *Merger Register*, annual issues 1966-70.

12. Details are from the agreement between the company and the province tabled in the Saskatchewan legislature.

13. Letter to the author.

14. *Water for the West*, pamphlet of the Los Angeles section, The American Society of Civil Engineers.

15. James Laxer, *The Energy Poker Game* (Toronto: New Press, 1970).

16. A full account appears in Donald Waterfield's *Continental Waterboy* (Toronto: Clarke, Irwin, 1969).

# 9

# Parliament:
# Ain't Gonna Need
# This House No Longer

*If I were to summarize my feelings on my first year in
office, I would say it has been a year in which I have
had the satisfaction of seeing the Government
gradually take control of the mechanism of politics.
We have instituted reforms in Parliament, making it
more efficient under the new rules. . . . Beyond that,
we have reorganized the machinery of government in
general.*
Prime Minister Trudeau, May 1969

The place is a den, a cockpit, a cave; it is the most exciting place
in Canada; it is a fusty old chamber where nothing happens,
and happens, and happens. It is the glory and heart of Canadian democracy; it is the frustrator of government, the bane of
order, the barbed wire that blocks the path of progress. The
House of Commons, in short, is what you make of it, and what
Prime Minister Trudeau has made of it is a shambles. He has
pushed through a great many reforms of the *system* of Parliament — most of them changes already under way in the Pearson years — but he has moved most of the effective *power* of
Parliament out of that maddening green chamber, where you
can never be sure what is going to happen, never know when
some whippersnapper from Newfoundland, for God's sake, or
Portage La Prairie, is going to bring the whole business of the
nation to a halt by asking questions of those who sit in the seats

of the mighty; he has moved power from there into the cooler, calmer atmosphere of the East Block, where *he* is the chairman, where there are no votes, and where the only questions asked are among friends, colleagues and non-equals. The Prime Minister is not, in John Diefenbaker's oft-repeated phrase, a House of Commons man, and his inability to grasp the role of that institution threatens to destroy it.

First, the setting. The House of Commons is a huge chamber — ninety-two feet long, seventy-two feet wide and fifty feet high. Above is the elaborate painted ceiling, of Irish linen, framed by an ornate golden cornice; below, Tyndall limestone and Canadian oak frame yellow curtains, brown desks and the ubiquitous green carpet. At the north end is the Speaker's chair — occupied during Trudeau's reign, fortunately, by one of the most effective Speakers we have ever had, Lucien Lamoureux. His chair is superbly carved, and raised on a dais. Below him is the long desk occupied by the Parliamentary clerks and, beyond, the Hansard desks spaced along the Parliamentary centre aisle — which is, as tradition demands, just over two swordlengths across, to keep hot-tempered Members from having it out. To the Speaker's right are the government benches, fronted by the cabinet, with the Prime Minister about one-third of the way down; to his left are ranged the opposition parties, with the Progressive Conservatives, the official opposition, closest to the Speaker, then the New Democrats and finally the Ralliement Créditiste. Above the Members, all around the chamber, are a series of galleries. Just over the Speaker's head is the Press Gallery, from which a disrespectful babble rises most of the time; along the walls are the Senate and diplomatic galleries, and those set aside for guests of the MPs. At either end are the public galleries.

It is an impressive chamber, made more so by the rituals practised there. At first those rituals — sombre-suited page-boys dashing to and fro, the Sergeant at Arms stalking solemnly forward to place the Mace in its accustomed resting spot on the Clerk's desk, the daily parade into and out of the chamber, the formality that requires an MP entering or leaving to bow to the Speaker — all that strikes an observer as nonsense. You want the MPs to quit playing games and get on with the job. But none of the ritual is empty; every tradition is a reminder of a liberty bitterly fought for and dearly won. When the Governor-General comes to Parliament for the Throne Speech, he may not enter the House of Commons, but goes to the Sen-

ate — a place of much ritual and no power — and summons the
Commoners there. A foolish point? Perhaps, since no modern
monarch, or his representative, is likely to storm the Commons
as in the days of Charles I, but it serves to keep the record
straight. It would not matter, really, if the page-boys neglected
to bob to their feet whenever the Speaker rose, or if the Mace
was not removed from the Clerk's table to its cradle below
when the House went into committee, or if the Gentleman
Usher of the Black Rod — the Senate's Sergeant at Arms —
forgot to knock three times before begging admission — but all
of these rituals are reminders of the independence of Parliament, of its special place in the governing of this nation.

Polite myths surround much of what goes on: the myth that
MPs never lie, and therefore no member can be directly accused
of falsehood; the myth that the Queen has something to do
with legislation; the myth that the Speaker is the strongest
power in the House, and deserves the deference of the Prime
Minister, who must, if called to heel in mid-speech, take his
place like a chastened schoolboy. Myths are the grease that
makes the machine work, for if the MPs are allowed to call each
other cheats and liars, Parliament will break down; if there is
no chairman who can rule impartially over the savage debates
that shake the chamber, democratic government, with its open,
sometimes brutal questioning of the ruling powers, will become
impossible. During the infamous Pipeline Debate of 1956,
when Speaker René Beaudoin acted like a government enforcer
instead of an impartial umpire, that mild-mannered man, M. J.
Coldwell, then leader of the CCF, came storming out of his
place, shaking his fist; Parliament ceased to function. Parliamentary traditions are not the by-laws of the YMCA, to be
changed at will; the rules must evolve, not disintegrate.

Our history was hammered out in the Commons, much of it
in this same chamber. It was here that Laurier tossed his silver
mane and wriggled for power, here that Meighen stabbed and
Mackenzie King, dodging and feinting, turned his blade; here
R. B. Bennett blustered and harummphed, and Louis St. Laurent, that cool and gracious gentleman, dispensed power and
favour. Here Lester Pearson and John Diefenbaker locked
horns like ancient moose, and stirred the mud with frantic
stampings. Here Pierre Trudeau shrugs and smiles and, only
mouthing, mind, tells Honourable Members opposite to fuck
off.

No harm was done, of course, that afternoon in February

1971 when the Prime Minister, goaded by continual and un-answerable questions on the high level of unemployment, mouthed the obscenity across the chamber at the Tories. Nor did his repetition of the phrase to Lincoln Alexander, when the Hamilton MP rose to protest, do any permanent damage. It seemed a little foolish, a little cowardly, for Trudeau to declare, "Mr. Speaker, I challenge any member opposite to say that they heard me utter a single sound," and to insist, later, that the phrase he mouthed was "fuddle duddle". But no matter. The importance of the incident was not its strain on the Tories' feelings or the threat to public morality, but in the careless contempt shown by the Prime Minister for the institution of Parliament, its traditions and rules. Under pressure, the worldly Prime Minister reverted to being the Montreal snob and demonstrated not merely that he doesn't care for the Commons, with all its tedious questions, but that he doesn't understand what parliamentary democracy is all about.

Trudeau conceives of the Commons as a place where, on occasion, the government may be required to explain its actions to the people, but mainly as a place where the nation can keep score until the next election. If the government does something you don't like, Trudeau argues, the place to take that up is at the polls. Opposition MPs may criticize the government — and he has given them research grants to help them do so more effectively — but they may not block it or deflect it from its purpose, and the role of government MPs, besides keeping the cabinet informed of swings in opinion back home, is to hustle out the necessary votes on division. This is how he put it to a group of questioning university students:

> I think that if you want to govern, if you want to govern effectively, it's very useful for the executive to have the support of the legislative arm. We don't always have it because we've got backbenchers who don't always agree with the government — that's fine. But as a general rule this is the way it works, and it's certainly the system I prefer.

Compare that notion of the supporting legislative arm with the classic view of Parliament laid down by the late R. MacGregor Dawson, still our most respected authority on the subject:

> The House of Commons is the great democratic agency in the

government of Canada; the "grand inquest of the nation"; the organized medium through which the public will finds expression and exercises its ultimate political power. It forms the indispensable part of the legislature, and it is the body to which at all times the executive must turn for justification and approval. . . . It presents in condensed form the different interests, races, religions, classes and occupations, whose ideas and wishes it embodies with approximate exactness. It serves as the people's forum and the highest political tribunal; it is, to use Mill's phrase, "the nation's committee of grievances and its congress of opinions". . . . No Cabinet which keeps in constant touch with this body can be very far removed from fluctuations in public opinion, for the House is always acting as an interpreter and forcing this opinion on the attention of its leaders.[1]

Trudeau rejects this definition out of hand. He believes he has been elected to rule as best he can for a period of five years, or until he calls an election. At the end of that time, the people may judge him at the polls according to his performance, but in the meantime he must be allowed to get on with the job. What that implies is not parliamentary democracy, but an elected dictatorship of limited duration. As Ivan Head, Trudeau's legislative assistant and a man who reflects the Prime Minister's thinking accurately, put it to me, "The opposition may criticize us all they like, but we must be allowed to get our legislation through."

No matter what the legislation is? Yes, clearly, in Trudeau's mind, for the legislature is merely the government's supporting legislative arm. The opposition parties do not agree, of course. Gerald Baldwin, the Conservative House Leader, has his own definition of the Commons as the "place where you can say to a Diefenbaker or a Trudeau, 'All right, you so-and-so, you've gone far enough. Now back up.' "

Since he came to power Trudeau has made it clear that it is Parliament, and not he, that must do the backing up.

He began his campaign "to take control of the mechanism of politics" with a series of wide-ranging rule changes that came into effect on January 14, 1969. Many of the changes had the approval of the opposition parties; there had been, for years, a clamour to speed up and streamline the functions of Parliament, and an all-party committee had worked out some ground rules during the Pearson era. These included the establishment of a regular yearly session of Parliament divided into three semesters, lengthening of the hours of the House, strengthening of the committee system, and the downgrading of the process of second reading of government bills. (In the past, second reading carried approval in principle; under the new system, most bills are given automatic second reading and shuffled off for detailed study by a committee; the crucial vote comes on third reading; in effect, a whole stage is by-passed and Parliament's work speeded up.) The Committee of Ways and Means, a clumsy committee of the whole House which used to debate each budget resolution, was abolished, and replaced by a six-day debate on the budget and fixed-length debates on tax bills. The work of another committee of the whole House, the Committee of Supply, was given to the standing committees, a change that moved the nit-picking over expenditures out of the Commons and into the hands of committee experts, where it belongs. Non-confidence votes were limited to six a session — they had been a traditional time-wasting gimmick — and the opposition was given twenty-five days a session for debates on subjects of its own choosing.

These proposals met approval on all sides of the House and were passed without a quibble. Some proposed changes, however, were bitterly, if futilely, opposed. One set up a rotation system for cabinet ministers in the Question Period. For decades, Question Period has been a time of salutary terror for governments, even those with huge majorities. For the cabinet minister who has run roughshod over some individual or some law, there always comes that dreadful moment of reckoning, when an opposition MP rises to ask the unanswerable in the full glare of the Commons while fellow front-benchers crane to watch their pinioned colleague and, overhead, the pens of the Press Gallery are poised to record his discomfiture. The Question Period is the single clearest advantage the Canadian parliamentary system has over the American; the presidential press conference, its nearest American equivalent, is not a clash between equals, but the feeding of carefully selected tid-bits of information to the American people.

Trudeau has largely defused the Question Period, in part by his steadfast refusal to answer questions, and in part by the rotation system. Under its rules, cabinet ministers are no longer required to attend the House every day; some attend three days a week, some less, some more; only the Prime Minister is scheduled to attend daily. If a vital issue arises overnight and the relevant cabinet minister is not in the House the next day, the question is simply taken as notice, and he has twenty-four hours in which to think up a noncommital reply, or some reason why no reply would be in the public interest. The rotation system would undermine Parliament even if the cabinet ministers stuck to it, but they do not; normally there are fewer than a dozen of the thirty ministers in the House, and the major activity of Question Period has become the taking of notice for queries that will never be answered adequately.

Another controversial rule change was the one that set a final date for the passage of all supply motions. Supply is the parliamentary permission for the government to spend money, and in the past, a favourite opposition tactic was to mount a filibuster during a supply debate; as money threatened to run out, even the most overbearing government had been known to compromise to get the debate over and a vote taken. Under the new rules, however, the supply motion comes to a vote automatically on a fixed date around the end of May. The change makes sense in many ways, but it robs the opposition parties of their most formidable weapon.

The third, and bitterest, clash came over a rule change that was aborted by the government's own dim-wittedness, although it thought it was being remarkably clever at the time. All parties were agreed on the need to establish some sort of timetable for dealing with legislation. The Great Flag Debate, in 1964, was a classic example of wrangling that dragged on and on, long after every conceivable debating point had been made and every shred of public opinion had been brought to bear. But the government proposal to solve this time-honoured problem was not acceptable to the opposition. That was Rule 16, which would have allowed a committee of House Leaders to establish a timetable for Commons business but, where agreement could not be reached on any item, would have allowed the government House Leader to set the schedule. Conservative leader Robert Stanfield called the proposal "wholesale closure", and so it was; every piece of controversial legislation would have been settled, in the end, on the government's timetable. The clash over this rule became so bitter that the opposition parties gave way on the other points, and agreed to accept all the new rules, provided that 16 was held over for further study. Trudeau was jubilant. He told a press conference on December 23, 1968, that Rule 16 had been made objectionable on purpose, as a bargaining ploy for the other rules. "We pulled the ground out from under them, and Parliament has a completely new set of rules . . . done by unanimous agreement."

Rule 16 went back to the all-party committee set up to study procedures, and re-emerged, in the summer of 1969, as another government proposal, Rule 75. This was really just a more sophisticated version of Rule 16; the amount of time to be spent on each piece of legislation was to be allocated by a majority of the House Leaders from each party, but where there was no majority agreement, a sub-clause, Rule 75C, would allow the government House Leader to impose a time limit which could be as short as ten days, and could allow as few as four days' debating time. The opposition wanted no part of 75C; four days might be far too short a time to debate a major issue, ten days too short a time to mobilize opinion across the land. They wanted a minimum time limit of thirty days, and, to meet the objection that this would prevent swift action in times of national emergency, they agreed to work out a formula that would allow the Speaker, on his own or under direction from the Prime Minister, to set aside the thirty-day limit. That proposal seemed fair; it would give the government the efficiency it needed (the occasions on which the House Leaders cannot form a majority to set a timetable are bound to be rare), while safeguarding the ancient right of Parliament to sit as "the grand inquest of the nation".

All the opposition, and a good many Liberals, were prepared to accept the compromise when the Prime Minister, through House Leader Donald Macdonald, stepped in. Parliament was going to have Rule 75, including 75C, and that was that. The opposition, naturally, set up a howl, and tried to block the change. The government applied closure to force the rule through by brute force. In the bitter debate before the closure time-limit ran out, Trudeau unleashed a sneering attack on the critics who dared to oppose the government's will. "I think we should encourage members of the opposition to leave," he said, "every time they do, the I.Q. of this House rises considerably. . . . When they get home, when they get out of Parliament, when they are fifty yards from Parliament Hill, they are no longer Honourable Members. They are just nobodies."

Rule 75C was rammed through — and proved unworkable.

It contemplated a situation where one opposition party refused to go along with an arrangement agreed to by other House Leaders; then the government could invoke the rule and set a ten-day time limit. But what if all the opposition parties agree, and the government is odd man out? Then there is no lack of a majority, and 75C cannot be applied. It has not been, not once; the net effect of the entire exercise was merely to underline the administration's intransigence, and convince the opposition parties that there was no dealing with such a government.

A much more useful exercise was the change that gave increased stature and heavier work loads to the parliamentary committees. There are two major kinds of committees— standing committees, which are permanent fixtures on the parliamentary landscape (External Affairs and National Defence, Agriculture, Finance, Trade and Economic Affairs, etc.) and special committees, set up to consider a single subject, such as drug prices. Both kinds were given more scope, more time, and even a dribble of funds with which to carry out their tasks. It is now the committees that consider bills, including spending estimates, in detail and bring them back to the House in almost finished form. The changes have resulted in a measurable improvement in Parliament's performance. During the 1967-68 session — the last before the new rules came into effect — House committees met 254 times and sub-committees fifty-four times; in the 1969-70 session, there were 797 committee meetings and 180 sub-committee meetings; they put in 530 hours of work— virtually a whole additional session of Parliament, and the results showed in legislation passed. During the 155-day session of 1967-68, thirty-nine government bills were passed; in the first 152 days of the next session, fifty-five bills went through.

But Trudeau gave the committees work, not power. That he kept for himself. In late 1969, the House Committee on Indian Affairs and Northern Development, a committee with a Liberal majority, concluded after much study that the time had come for Canada to assert sovereignty in the Arctic, where American oil exploration seemed to indicate we might lose our hold by default. Trudeau saw the move as simply another ugly rash of nationalism, and, through House Leader Donald Macdonald, asked that the committee report be withheld from Parliament.

The committee's Conservative vice-chairman (the chairman was Liberal Ian Watson) waited for a month, then rose in the Commons to ask that the report be concurred in. Macdonald tried to block the move on the technical point that only a committee chairman could bring such a motion, but he was overruled by the Speaker. The ruling put the Liberals on the spot; should they vote for acceptance of the report, and court the wrath of the Prime Minister? Or should they vote against the report, and repudiate the unanimous finding of a committee dominated by their own members? (And repudiate it, incidentally, in the teeth of a good deal of propaganda about the new power of committees.) In the end, they did neither; when the motion for concurrence came up, Liberal MPs talked it out; the time-limit was passed without a vote ever being taken. The Prime Minister went on to set his own Arctic policy. Eventually he did make a declaration of sovereignty over shipping and pollution in the Arctic, but it had nothing to do with the committee findings; it was a result of the voyages of the U.S. supertanker *Manhattan*, and the consequent public outcry over American intrusion in what Canadians considered to be *our* Arctic.

The powerlessness of the committees became clear again when Ian Wahn's strongly worded report on foreign ownership passed the External Affairs Committee. As related in Chapter 8, it was at once repudiated by the government and is still, like the Northern Affairs Committee report on the Arctic, tacking around in a parliamentary limbo, a legislative Flying Dutchman searching for a port.

I am not arguing that committees should be given the right to lay down government policy — that right belongs properly to the ruling party and to cabinet — I am simply pointing out that it is not true, as the Prime Minister has alleged on a number of occasions, that he has given the committees more power, made them into what he calls a "countervailing force" in government. The committees were not reformed to wield power, but to crack out more work, and with no sass either.

The Prime Minister does not like sass from Parliament or any of its officials, and one of the most serious mistakes he has made was his attempt to de-fang that sassy watchdog of Parliament, the Auditor-General. Once a year, a slim, grey volume lands on the desk of every MP — and all hell breaks loose. That volume is the annual report of Maxwell Henderson, a slim, grey-haired, pleasant-looking man whose normally mild voice rises to a shrill "Stop, Thief!" whenever he detects bungling, bumph or burglary in the government's accounts. Henderson is always snooping around, uncovering overpayments on the HMCS *Bonaventure* refit here, criticizing government accounting procedures there; he is a damn nuisance. That is what he is paid for, of course: to be a nuisance and to save public money. He does his job embarrassingly well.

On November 16, 1970, the Trudeau government introduced a bill to put him in his place. Henderson and his pack of bloodhounds operate under a double legislative fiat; they are enjoined to report any "fraud, default or mistake" in the government accounts, but they are also empowered by a catch-all phrase to point to "any other case" they think merits disclosure. Henderson could drive a whole government department through such a clause, and frequently does. (For one thing, he objects bitterly, every year, to the government practice of paying huge amounts of its spending by Governor-General's warrant instead of bringing it before Parliament.)

The new legislation proposed to eliminate the catch-all phrase. It also required the Auditor-General to submit his report privately to the government three months before it was to be tabled in the House, presumably so that censorship could be exercised or alibies concocted. When the legislation was introduced, it produced not only howls of outrage from the opposition, which was to be expected, but cries of alarm from virtually every editorialist in the land. (They were not only safeguarding the right of inquiry but protecting a good source; Henderson's report supplies an annual injection of scandal; it is must reading in every newsroom in the land.) Even the tame Liberal MPs began to whinny uneasily at their government's latest caper. Unable to think of any reason for the legislation — beyond the real, but unmentionable one, that Henderson's sleuths were too active for comfort — the government let the legislation drop, and had to content itself with continuance of its old habit of hampering Henderson by refusing him the money he needs for adequate staff.

The attempt to curb the Auditor-General was not quixotic, but part of a pattern we have already seen, an attempt to streamline — for which read emasculate — Parliament. The pattern continued throughout Trudeau's first term. There was, for instance, the attempt in early 1971 to slip through $2 million in funds without the approval or even the knowledge of Parliament, for the purpose of hiring 250 French-speaking civil servants from Quebec. (The goal, to increase the number of French Canadians in the federal service, is no doubt laudable; but the technique, making language the basis of civil service appointments, was questionable, and attempting to hide the transaction from Parliament was even worse.) Henderson's sleuths sniffed that one out, and the scheme was abandoned. Within weeks there was another attempt to by-pass Parliament, when the government used $1 estimates to make major changes in legislation. Opposition MPs caught the move, and Speaker Lamoureux supported them and disallowed the estimates in two cases; in two others, he said, the government was entitled to the benefit of the doubt, and the changes stood.

But there is no example of the government's habit of working by indirection to gather power unto itself so apparent as Bill C-207, "An Act respecting the organization of the Government of Canada and matters related or incidental thereto", which was given first reading on December 9, 1970 and passed in the early summer of 1971.

The bill had four major goals:

1. To reorganize the cabinet and the system of parliamentary secretaries;

2. To establish a new Department of the Environment, with a minister responsible for pollution control, and to dismantle the old Fisheries Department;

3. To provide improved early superannuation benefits for civil servants;

4. To move the Post Office, which had disappeared into the bowels of a new Communications Department, back out into the sun again, as an independent department with its own minister.

The thing was a dog's breakfast. How could any MP vote for or against it? An eastern MP might be very much in favour of a Department of the Environment, but object to the dismantling of the one department — Fisheries — that seems oriented to Maritime interests. An Ontarian might not care about that, but object to the new cabinet system; yet if he voted against it, he was knocking the federal civil service, and that is no smart thing to do. A westerner might regard all that as fair enough, but believe that the Post Office belonged in Communications where, only a few short months ago, the government was telling us it belonged.

No matter; the MPs were not to quibble with the thing, or try to take it apart, they were damn well to vote for or against all of it, and stand by the consequences. For Liberal MPs, those consequences were very sweet indeed. The cabinet reorganization section of the bill created a whole new phalanx of cabinet ministers, some with enchanting names. There are to be up to five new Ministers of State for Specific Purposes, another clutch — no set number — of Other Ministers of State, and up to nine new parliamentary secretaries. All of these, along with the kudos, get more money — $15,000 on top of their salaries for the ministers, $4,000 extra for the secretaries. The changes give the Prime Minister the right to hand out goodies and titles to a huge proportion of his following — thirty-five cabinet ministers, twenty-five parliamentary secretaries, twenty-four committee chairmen, a caucus chairman, a whip, a deputy whip and a Deputy Speaker. (The Speaker is an Independent, although he entered politics as a Liberal.) That makes eighty-eight Liberals, out of 154 presently in the House, who would hold a direct gift from the Prime Minister, and for the remainder there is always the inevitable day when all the parliamentary secretaries are changed. If that doesn't bring the backbenchers to heel, nothing will.

When members of the opposition began to question the wisdom of swallowing Bill C-207 at a single gulp, the Prime Minister rounded on them. Criticism of the bill had passed the point of debate, he said; it amounted to "obstructionism". His charge was levelled in one of those corridor conferences for which he is justly famous, on February 26, 1971, while he was talking to a group of visiting French-Canadian students. He said the opposition parties "try to stop the government programmes by following the clock. They say Parliament is rotten because they sit for weeks and don't pass any bills, preventing the government from passing all the laws and measures that are important, gabbing for two weeks on government reorganization. They are blocking other things. The tactic of the opposition is to stop the government from doing anything." The solution was obvious — it always is, to the man with the stick — closure. "Reform the parliamentary system and introduce the guillotine — closure — and then we take a vote."

At the time of that petulant outburst, the opposition was not, in fact, blockading the bill, although it was asking for more time to consider it. Less than four hours were taken to give the measure second reading, twenty hours were spent on the wide-ranging environmental aspect of the legislation, less than six hours on the question of the Ministers of State, one hour dealt with a change in the Department of Energy, Mines and Resources, and one hour had been spent on the change in the Post Office. Tory House Leader Gerald Baldwin commented, "If the Prime Minister spent more time here he would realize that when legislation which is introduced which in part or in whole is obnoxious and repugnant to the opposition parties, those parties would be derelict in their duty if they did not oppose that legislation vigorously, actively and, if necessary, to the point of arousing public opinion."

MP Stanley Knowles, the NDP member for Winnipeg North Centre, used the incident as the occasion to make an eloquent, moving and, in the end, pointless plea to the Prime Minister: "I do not rise in anger, or with any thought of trying to return blow for blow or to castigate the other side, but to make an earnest plea. I make this plea on behalf of Parliament. I believe that this is a tremendous institution and that it can continue to do a job for the people of Canada. My plea is that it be permitted to do so without remarks of contempt and derision that destroy the goodwill necessary for the work of this House of Commons. As I have already said, and I shall endeavour to stick to my statement, I do not wish to return blow for blow or to castigate the Prime Minister, but I do make a plea to him to make a real effort to understand this place and to give it an opportunity to function as I believe it can."

Trudeau rejected the plea and the criticism, and accused the opposition of "wasting the time of the House" by bringing it up. In the end, two tiny concessions were made: the Ministers of State, it was agreed, would be appointed only after consultation with the House, and not simply on government whim, and a fisheries branch, though not a department, would be maintained. Essentially, however, Trudeau got his way, and the re-organization bill gave even more power to a government that already has too much.

The essential problem remains the fact that, for the Prime Minister, the proper way to run the House is clear: the government introduces legislation, the opposition attacks it for a civilized and tightly controlled period of time, and then the government uses its majority to ram the legislation through. That's all; the legislature is the supporting arm of government, and for that arm to turn around and attempt to seize the government by the throat is damned impertinence.

It is impertinence, especially, for MPs on the Liberal side to step out of line. Phil Givens, former mayor of Toronto and later a government backbencher (he has since retired to provincial politics), did so when he attacked the government on its treatment of urban issues. As a result, Givens was by-passed, despite his considerable municipal experience, and left to languish on the backbenches. He continued to set off firecrackers, but not where they could do much harm. "The average MP," he says, "is as useless as tits on a bull."

Justice was also swift for David Anderson, a British Columbia Liberal MP, whose sin was to make a direct attack, without government sanction, on American plans to ship oil down Canada's west coast by tanker. He was promptly removed from membership on a U.S.–Canadian parliamentary committee, and blocked from taking the Commons Special Committee on Environmental Pollution — of which he was made chairman before his intransigence became a matter of record — to the west coast to investigate the danger of the American proposal. "All they want around here," said Anderson, "is people who stay in line, lick boots and keep their noses clean."

What is distressing in all the changes that have been made in Parliament during Trudeau's reign is that, instead of streamlining and strengthening the institution, they have curbed and weakened it; to knock some of the chrome off our Cadillac, the Prime Minister has run it into a wall.

Responsible government, in its usual meaning, has disappeared, for what it means is that the party in power is responsible to the House of Commons, which in turn is responsible to the electorate. In theory, if enough MPs decide that a government's course of action is objectionable, they can band together and throw the rascals out. In fact, of course, nothing of the sort happens. Parliament is run by parties, and the parties by leaders; decisions are made on the basis of party loyalty, reinforced by the promise of elevation and more cash and by the threat of ostracism and the withdrawal of party support in the next election.

But the ultimate threat remains — or did until recently — that a government could still be toppled by the attacks of its foes and the indifference of its supporters. Parliament was still the master. Trudeau has changed all that. His supporters have become hangers-on and his opponents have been de-fanged by the rules changes. The Commons is no longer "the nation's congress of opinions", but an echo chamber where it is not only permissible, but even clever, to mouth obscenities at the enemy across the way.

The substance of power is gone from Parliament and cabinet, vanished to the inner sanctum of the Prime Minister's Office; it was the realization of this fact, more than anything else, that led to the resignation of Communications Minister Eric Kierans.

## Note

1. R. MacGregor Dawson, *The Government of Canada* (Toronto: University of Toronto Press, 1948), p. 158.

# 10

## The Vanishing Cabinet: Why Kierans Quit

*The political philosophy of the Liberal party is simplicity itself. Say anything, think anything you like. But put us in power because we are best fitted to govern. . . . What idiots they all are. . . . I have not yet agreed to tramp on democracy. It is for this reason that on April 8 it is my intention to vote for the NDP. It is for all those who feel the urgency of stopping the rush of Canadian thought downward to utter degradation to do likewise.*
Pierre Elliott Trudeau, April 1963

Every now and then in the life of a government, something happens that reveals the inner workings of the administration with startling clarity; the corner of the blanket is not merely lifted, it is thrown back, and we see the squirming bodies beneath. It happened in Diefenbaker's time with a cabinet revolt, in Pearson's time with a long, sordid series of scandals, in Trudeau's time with the resignation of Communications Minister Eric Kierans. Kierans was not the first cabinet minister to go; as we have already seen, Paul Hellyer departed in early 1969 after his ambitious housing policy was lost at sea. But Hellyer went quietly; after the initial break, he kept his counsel, hugging his own views of the Trudeau administration to himself. By the time he unburdened himself of a stinging attack on the government's economic policies, in early 1971, it was too late; he had not been a member of the cabinet for two years — what did he know? His new political group, Action Canada, founded

in May 1971, looked like the American Know-Nothing party of
the last century.

Kierans was different; Kierans went out kicking and screaming — and talking. He was critical not only of the economic
policies that were the immediate cause of his departure, but of
almost everything about the way the Trudeau government is
run, from its timidity in dealing with the U.S. to the
overwhelming tendency to concentrate political power in the
hands of a small group in and around the Prime Minister's
Office. To move inside the cabinet chamber with Kierans is an
enlightening, but disheartening, experience.

Every Thursday morning, just before ten o'clock, members of
the federal cabinet emerge from their House of Commons
offices and head towards a long, dark room just off the Ro-
tunda Gallery on the third floor of Parliament's Centre Block
— Room 340S, the cabinet chamber. They come from every
corner of Parliament, scurrying through the tunnel from the
West Block, shoaling up from the lower reaches of the Centre
Block, where lesser lights are barracked, drifting down from
the lofty suites on the fourth and fifth floors, the dwelling-
places of the mighty. They are drawn like lemmings to the sea,
or migratory birds to the mating-ground; they answer a call as
imperative as any at nature's command, the call of power. At
ten o'clock, trading the small jokes and corridor gossip that is
Ottawa's real medium of exchange, they file into the cabinet
room and make for thirty straight-backed, leather-upholstered
armchairs set around the long oval table that dominates the
room. Each minister sidles into his own appointed place, its
boundaries marked by note pads, pencils and a pile of cabinet
documents, many bearing the impressive notation: Secret. A
moment later, the Prime Minister enters, having covered the
200 feet from his own third-floor office, 307S, in a few dozen
purposeful strides. He walks straight to his place half-way
down one side of the oval table. He is flanked, on his right,
by Senator Paul Martin, Government Leader in the Upper
House, and on his left by Public Works Minister Arthur Laing,
with the other ministers ranged down the table on either side in
order of seniority of service. The Prime Minister glances
quickly at the two agendas prepared in the Privy Council Office
the day before; one notes the four or five major items to be
discussed at this meeting; the other lists the twenty to thirty

decisions taken by the eight standing committees of cabinet during the past week. Beside the agenda items are listed the names of cabinet ministers who have told his office they wish to speak to specific points. The Prime Minister nods, "Well, gentlemen. . ." and the meeting begins. (When the House is not sitting, the ministers gather in a similar room in the East Block, but the procedure is the same.)

For two years, the man who sat directly opposite the Prime Minister was Eric Kierans, the Minister of Communications. He was sandwiched between Transport Minister Donald Jamieson and Minister Without Portfolio Robert Andras; low seniority brought them near the tail end of the line of precedence, which happened to be opposite Trudeau. Now he is gone. Frustrated, irritated and isolated inside a cabinet whose major economic policies he disputed in vain, he resigned on April 29, 1971. He left behind no broken hearts; Kierans was never popular with his cabinet colleagues; they thought he meddled too much in matters that were not his affair. Once, a minister whose decisions he was questioning snarled, "Well, you're the only one who takes that stand, Eric — as usual." Kierans had a disconcerting habit of butting into other departments, particularly those concerned with economics. (There are eight economic portfolios, none held by anyone with Kierans' qualifications — former director of McGill University's School of Commerce, former head of the Montreal and Canadian Stock Exchanges, former Revenue Minister for the Province of Quebec, and a self-made millionaire.) Worse, he did his homework, and often knew more than the minister involved. In one case, a colleague proposed offering a huge government contract to an American-owned company operating in Quebec. Without such a contract, company officials had argued, the firm would go bankrupt, throwing hundreds of Quebeckers out of work. Kierans investigated — nothing fancy, he simply looked up the company involved on data cards supplied by the *Financial Post* — and discovered that the U.S. firm owned stocks worth $46 million in another, and profitable, Canadian company. "That money came out of the Canadian economy," he said, "let them use that to keep the thing afloat." His colleague was not pleased to receive the information. His officials would check the details, he informed the cabinet stiffly, but for his own part he resented the fact that Kierans had raised such a matter in full cabinet, rather than coming to him privately. "There wasn't time," Kierans responded blandly, "I was in the Parliamentary Library at nine o'clock, where this information is readily available, and left to come straight to this meeting."

Kierans never learned to tailor his views or curb his tongue to meet the demands of politics; with his elbows up, his index finger stabbing, his blue eyes aglitter with the light of battle, he would lean across the cabinet table to worry an issue his colleagues regarded as safely settled. Just when all the necessary motions had been put and all the necessary memoes drafted, along would come Kierans, spouting facts and spraying doubt and gnawing at the smug assurances of the bureaucracy like a terrier at a bone.

He made a startling contrast with Trudeau. Kierans is of Irish-Canadian stock, the son of a foreman in a Montreal railway-car factory. He was brought up in Montreal's tough east end, established a brilliant academic career and, while he was director of the McGill School of Commerce, busied himself on the side making a personal fortune by rescuing and revitalizing two failing companies. A combination of hard work, native shrewdness and stubborn persistence brought him success; no one ever handed him anything. He is one of the most charming men in politics today, not, like Trudeau, because of grace and style, but because he is open, friendly, cheerful and astonishingly frank. He taught himself French when he was in his fifties, because, as chairman of the Montreal and Canadian Stock Exchanges, he thought it criminal that he could not speak with many of his own employees in their native tongue. It was tough sledding — lessons squeezed in after his long work-day often left him with blinding headaches — but he kept at it and today is, despite an atrocious accent, thoroughly fluent in French. Like the Prime Minister, he loves to debate, but goes at it in quite a different way; Trudeau argues in syllogisms, prefers the abstract to the concrete, and, except when he is discussing the opposition, employs elegant phrasing; Kierans says "lookit", and "yuh see" and "okay"; his sentences are often convoluted, always freighted with facts, and fired by an earnestness that (contrasted with the Prime Minister's cool and often sneering approach) makes him a formidable foe. Of course Kierans lost all the arguments between the two.

He found the Prime Minister to be a good chairman, an incisive summarizer of cabinet discussion, and a ready listener — but he seldom appears moved by what is said. Normally, after every minister who wants to speak on a given subject has had his say, the Prime Minister sums up the debate, adds his own remarks and gives a "consensus", which is not really a consensus at all, but the laying down of government policy. There are no votes taken and where there is a difference of opinion, Trudeau nearly always comes down on the side of the minister whose department is most directly involved. "That's as it should be," Kierans acknowledged, "although it can be awfully frustrating when you're sure the guy is wrong."

The Prime Minister's overriding interest has been the problem of Canadian unity, and Kierans' impression was that on many other issues he simply didn't much care how the decision went, and so deferred to the minister in charge. "His major concern has been to shake up the Ottawa Establishment in one area, to make them recognize that this is a bilingual, bicultural nation, so that they know 100 years later what this country is all about. Well, they know now and didn't have a clue before he became Prime Minister, so he's been operating mainly in that area."

Beyond that major, favourable impression, Kierans felt a profound sense of unease with the Prime Minister's performance.

For one thing, despite his reputation for awesome efficiency, Trudeau runs an office that is astonishingly slipshod. Kierans grew accustomed to receiving letters addressed to the Prime Minister and forwarded for action, which had been sitting on somebody's desk for two or three months. "They would get bogged down somewhere in the Prime Minister's Office, not even acknowledged. Well, I couldn't admit that, so I'd have to write and say the matter was under urgent consideration, even though it had been hanging around since God knows when."

For another thing, the decision-making process, as Kierans saw it, was not a controlled, efficient progression, but "*ad hoc*, scrambling, and almost always tuned to 'How will this look in June 1972? [the date then favoured for the next federal election].'"

"We would get pushed into a project because it would provide some jobs in time for '72, and that would make one riding safe, whether the project made sense or not, whether it was for the long-run benefit of the country or not. It all came down to creating lots of activity for '72."

For nearly two years Kierans argued against what he considered to be the over-hasty development of Canadian resources to serve American markets, but, "For Joe Greene a mine that comes in while he's Minister of Energy, Mines and Resources is a lot better than one that's delayed for three years." The net effect of the huge subsidies and tax kick-backs paid to foreign mining firms, Kierans argued, is to provide a handful of jobs at the mine-site, where the ore is extracted, and many more in the U.S., where it is turned into finished goods. He wanted secondary manufacturing developed in Canada parallel to resources exploitation. He was brushed aside. "The Prime Minister was always hearing from three or four people who said go ahead, and the only opposition would be from Kierans. . . . After a while you lose credibility with your colleagues; you're just bitching. . . ."

Kierans once went to see Trudeau to argue that it was foolish and short-sighted to attempt to gather votes by promoting schemes that would provide a few jobs in the near future at the cost of giving away Canada's long-term development prospects. "Pierre replied that, 'Well, it's better for the people to have us re-elected than to let those others in because they would do a worse job than we do. They don't know how to run the country.' The basis of the argument was that the Liberals could do more to keep the country together than the other parties, and of course I believe that is true."

On that basis, Trudeau erected the ancient Liberal rallying cry he had parodied in 1963: "Put us in power because we are best fitted to govern." A project like Karl Landegger's pulp mill in northern Saskatchewan might be a bad deal for Canada, but it would provide some jobs, swing some votes, and keep the wicked Tories at bay. Therefore it was justified, as all things are justified, by the need to keep Liberals in power. "It was what is behind many of the charges of arrogance," said Kierans, "and I have to say there is something in them."

Finally, many of the decisions the cabinet thought it was taking had, in fact, already been settled by the powerful group of ministers in Trudeau's inner circle, and by the senior bureaucrats in the Privy Council Office and the Prime Minister's Office — the Supergroup. On one occasion, when Kierans attacked a major economic proposal, the minister responsible said that, well, perhaps there was something in the argument he made, but it was too late, because the decision had already been communicated to the Canadian banks. "Then what in the

name of God," Kierans demanded, "are we debating here?" He
got no reply.

"You were always listened to with great respect, but nothing would ever happen. The ministers would hear you out and then go back to their departments and do what the Establishment boys had told them in the first place. . . . It was like a procession. You know, when the Pope gets down off the altar at St. Peter's and walks down the aisle the one thing you know is that he's going to get to the other end of the aisle. You can argue and argue and in the end the procession goes on its way."

Kierans found that, for a man who was going to take patronage out of politics, Trudeau runs an administration that is touchingly sensitive to the needs of his friends. Shortly after he was named Postmaster General (a job he lost in a subsequent cabinet shuffle), Kierans proposed to find a new advertising agency for the department. He asked for submissions from a number of agencies and, on the basis of these, selected one. It turned out to be owned by Harry "Red" Foster, a Toronto Tory.

"Well, boy, I was really into it. There is a committee of cabinet ministers, a formal committee, that looks after the doling out of government advertising, and they were mad as hell. The contract went into the Treasury Board and it just stayed there for months. I told Foster to go ahead, that he had the contract, and he said, 'Yeah, but will I get paid?'. . . . I was haled before the committee and they kept saying 'These people aren't even our friends!' So what I said was, 'Lookit, in a way I'm doing you guys a favour. We're always telling everybody that we keep patronage out of this business — it's just coincidence that every one of the twenty-two other major contracts has gone to a Liberal firm. Well, here's the living proof — a Tory outfit with the Post Office contract.' They weren't very pleased, but they bought it."

In theory, a cabinet minister who pulls against his colleagues may make his views felt in a number of ways: he may speak in the confidence of caucus, tackle other ministers head-on in a cabinet committee meeting or, as a last resort, appeal directly to the Prime Minister. In fact, Kierans found, none of these vehicles will bear the weight of serious disagreement with the revealed truths of the Supergroup.

"When you get to a caucus meeting, the cabinet all line up on one side and the MPs on the other and what it turns into, really, is a question-and-answer period. Well, if the Minister of Finance and the Prime Minister have just finished saying that inflation is the most serious problem the nation faces today, and you happen to think that's a lot of hogwash, you don't say so, do you? Or I guess you could — that would be one way of resigning."

There are eight cabinet committees: four are responsible for developing policy, and four for co-ordinating programmes. The policy committees are: External Affairs and Defence, Economics, Social Policy and Communications, Works and Urban Affairs. The four co-ordinating groups are: Priorities and Planning, Legislation, Treasury Board, and Federal-Provincial Relations. Each cabinet member belongs to four of them. Here, discussion is more open than in caucus because cabinet solidarity is not at stake. Each minister may bring two or three advisers with him and often, Kierans felt, it was their views rather than the ministers' that came up for debate.

One matter he raised repeatedly in committee was the encouragement Canada appeared to be giving the Americans to build a pipeline down the Mackenzie River Valley to carry natural gas from the Alaskan North Slope to the rich markets in the middle states. Even if the U.S. goes through with the plan that David Anderson got in trouble for opposing, to send oil by pipeline and tanker down the west coast, the natural gas associated with that oil will have to come overland. Canada appeared anxious to bring it down the Mackenzie; Energy Minister Greene spoke publicly of hopes to have such a pipeline under way in 1973, although environmental studies to determine the extent of the inevitable damage that would be done cannot be completed in time for that. Kierans was opposed. "I said 'What are we in such an all-fired hurry for? We've got enough oil and gas for our own needs, and if the Americans need it, that's their problem.' We kept hearing that the Americans would be coming to us for an answer next summer and I said 'Well, let them wait. Maybe we should draw up a list of things we want from them, and do a little trading.' I said, 'Stop running down to Washington saying that we're doing this and doing that and it's going to be ready soon . . . you're giving the bloody country away.' Well, the reply was that I was the only one who thought so, and that was that."

Decisions of the cabinet committees are circulated the day

before a full cabinet meeting, and a minister who objects to a proposed action, even if he is not on the committee involved, may register his protest with the Prime Minister's Office.

"Then when you get into the full cabinet the Prime Minister reads out the list and where there are no objections he will say so and it will just go through. But you can say, 'No, I don't like that,' and he'll say, 'Well, we don't have time to go into it here,' and it will go back to the cabinet committee. Then you go before the committee and raise your points there."

If there is still disagreement, the matter becomes an item for the full cabinet. Ministers are listened to fully — "That part of it is done very well." However, some of the most crucial decisions the government makes, those on economic policy, never go to a committee. They are incorporated in budget proposals, which are the exclusive concern of the Finance Minister and the Prime Minister. Other cabinet members don't know, any more than the general public, what is going into a budget until the cabinet meeting on budget day. By then it is too late; the policies are set and become a matter of cabinet solidarity; objections are simply shrugged away.

Debate in the full cabinet centres on four or five items each session. The sessions are intended to last from ten a.m. to one p.m., but often the ministers lunch on sandwiches and work through until the House of Commons convenes at two p.m. Trudeau is addressed as "Prime Minister", other colleagues by their first names. The debate is not formal, but is normally polite. Trudeau notes the names of ministers who want to speak — they signal by raising their hands — and calls them in order of the hand-raising. Kierans said, "There is not much interruption, the way there is in the cabinet committees. Once in a while you say 'Wait a minute, John, that's not right and you know it's not right,' but mostly you hold your peace and wait your turn.

"The trouble is you are debating really with a core group around the Prime Minister who already have their minds made up, and nothing is going to change them. They are still responding to the same old advice we've been getting in this country for decades. You hear a good deal about all the changes that were made by Trudeau in the civil service, but if you examine the really big ones you find that (Robert) Bryce went from being Deputy Minister of Finance over to the Prime Minister's Office as his economic adviser, and (Simon) Reisman, who had been Secretary of the Treasury Board, went over to being Deputy Minister of Finance, and Al Johnson, who had been economic adviser to the Prime Minister, went in as Secretary of the Treasury Board. That was not so much a reorganization as a game of musical chairs. The same people were still giving the same advice."

A minister who has blunted his sword on that advice in caucus, committee and the full cabinet can still appeal directly to the Prime Minister, although, Kierans noted, "It's not something you do too often, or you begin to get an itchy feeling."

He tried this tactic once late in 1969. On October 27, the German government had revalued the Mark upwards. "Within the following ten days I was in the Prime Minister's Office seeing him about something else and as I was about to leave I said 'Pierre, I know it's not my affair, but I want you to talk to the Bank of Canada and the Department of Finance. The Germans revalued the Mark last week and if the Americans can make two other countries follow suit, that is, us and the Japanese, they will have succeeded in changing the exchange rate for the three biggest trading countries. In effect, they will have revalued the American dollar and exported their own inflation. That's what they're up to and I think we'd better do something about our own dollar.' "

The "something" Kierans had in mind was to remove the Canadian dollar from its fixed rate of exchange and allow it to float upwards to meet the American pressure — in effect, to roll with the punch. "But the Prime Minister was getting contrary advice from everybody else, so nothing happened." By the time Canada *did* go to the floating rate, in May 1970, we had poured huge sums into buying U.S. currency to hold our own dollar down. Kierans went back to see the Prime Minister. "I said, 'When was the last time after I spoke to you that you heard anything about the flexible dollar?' He said he wasn't sure but he thought it was perhaps six months later. I said, 'No, it wasn't; it was one billion, two hundred million dollars later.' "

Kierans had been right, but it didn't matter, the Prime Minister wasn't listening. He had his eye on other matters — promoting jobs to catch votes.

"As Minister of Communications, I was making speeches that Canada should hold on to the communications industry. We own 85 per cent of it, and it's an area where we could easily expand. I said let's go after this, but what do I see happening? The Department of Regional Expansion gives $22 million to

Control Data [a U.S. firm] to set up a plant in Quebec City.
Then Regional Expansion gives $6 million to IBM to build a
plant in Drummondville. Who can compete with that? It just
doesn't add up. You may create a few jobs temporarily and destroy a whole Canadian industry."

It was on this economic issue that Kierans finally broke with
the government. The Benson budget of December 1970 provided for 115 per cent depreciation on new plant and equipment. "It was a bribe to build factories in a hell of a hurry, but
the effect was to discriminate against labour and in favour of
capital. If you're going to build a factory for $2 million that em-
ploys fifty people and this thing comes along, you figure that
maybe you can build a factory with more machinery in it for $3
million that employs only thirty-eight people. It may not be the
best way in the long run to manage the plant, but it gets you a
tax gift of $450,000, so you do it that way. People see the
thirty-eight new jobs; what they don't see is that there might
have been fifty new jobs and that economic decision-making
has been distorted. . . . What's more, it's the guys with money
that can build plant and equipment in a hurry and *ipso facto*
this is really the Americans. In a crash programme like this,
you're not building from scratch, you're pulling stuff off the
shelf. The Americans are the ones with the full shelves, so all
the long-term benefits go across the border."

Kierans attacked the budget proposals in cabinet, but it
was, of course, too late; they were already government policy.
"So I went away and brooded about it for a while."

He contacted a number of economists and, over the next
three months, prepared a final argument for the Prime Minister, although he had little real hope of having the policy reversed. By the end of April, he had marshalled all his facts and, on
April 27, went to lunch with the Prime Minister at 24 Sussex
Drive. "He listened very politely. I told him I was going to
make a speech on economic policy and exactly what I was going to say. He asked me if I couldn't modify my remarks — he
wasn't asking me not to make the speech — so that I could stay
in the cabinet. I said, no, I couldn't, so I went home and wrote
out my letter of resignation."

That night, Kierans telephoned his eighty-six-year-old
mother to say that he was resigning. "Are you doing the right
thing, Eric?" she asked. "Yes, Momma, I am." There was a
pause, and then, "Can you get another job?"

The real economic issues were not debated between Trudeau

and his renegade cabinet minister, only the political issue of how the differences could be smoothed out. Kierans was battering against smoke. "There are two kinds of conservative government. One is a government that considers issues carefully and then comes down on the conservative side. That is honest conservatism. The other is a government that just won't listen to anything it doesn't already know."

Ultimately, Kierans was dislodged from the cabinet by that unseen presence at every cabinet meeting — "a core group around the Prime Minister who already have their minds made up".

It is that core group that runs Canada today. The Supergroup.

# 11

## The Supergroup:
## The de Gaulle Fist
## in the Kennedy Glove

*You have a system where people who are neither elected nor appointed, not accountable to anyone but the Prime Minister, are making all the decisions. A policy comes across your desk, and you're asked to comment on it, but you know the final say is going to come from somebody in the Supergroup. . . . They are, essentially, wheelers and dealers, and you have to ask yourself, do we really want a group of decision-makers who are responsible only to the Prime Minister and who wield all this power?*
A Very Senior Civil Servant, August 1970

A senior civil servant appears before a cabinet committee to argue for a policy hammered out by the experts in his department. The policy is rejected out of hand. "I was heard, but not listened to," the bureaucrat complains later. "Supergroup had been there before me."[1]

The Prime Minister goes to Montreal to make a speech. His subject is to be the Company of Young Canadians, and he will attack it. Secretary of State Gérard Pelletier reports to Parliament for the CYC, but he is not shown the speech and doesn't know that Trudeau will also attack the CBC — another agency for which he reports — and threaten to close down *Radio Canada* for its alleged separatist bias. The evidence of bias on which the attack is based does not come from Pelletier's officials — in fact, they reject it; it is gathered by Trudeau's own staff. Pelletier is upset by the speech, and a vice-president of the CBC threatens to resign, but what can they do?[2]

Canada is contemplating withdrawal from NATO, but the nation is sharply divided on the issue. Feelers are put out. The Liberal party is polled, and opposes any change in our NATO status; the cabinet is polled, and, at the end of two days of hectic debate, the Prime Minister sums it up: "I see we are about evenly divided." Three official reports are called for, one from the External Affairs Department, one from an interdepartmental task force of civil servants, and one from a Parliamentary committee. All support the *status quo*. But two other, unofficial, reports appear: one is an anti-NATO stand circulated by Donald Macdonald, then President of the Privy Council and now Defence Minister; the other is prepared by the Prime Minister's own staff. The fifth report suggests a partial withdrawal of troops from Europe, with further consideration to be given to the whole problem of the NATO alliance later. Trudeau acts on the fifth report, which becomes government policy.

Jim Davey, the Prime Minister's programme secretary, appears before a group of political science students at Carleton University. He has promised to tell them how the Canadian government is operated, and he does, in great detail. He finishes and asks for questions. A graduate student rises at the back of the hall. "I've heard you describing how our country is run for an hour and forty minutes," he says, "and there are two words I have yet to hear you utter — Parliament and Cabinet. What happened to them?"

A Member of Parliament wants a favour. He is Philip Givens, former mayor of Toronto and now Liberal MP for York West. The favour he wants is a small one. A girl in his riding, a seventeen-year-old who worked hard on his election campaign, is dying of leukemia. She is an ardent admirer of Trudeau, and Givens wants him to send her a personal card. Such favours are common, but Givens is not popular in the Prime Minister's Office, and a secretary says it can't be done. It would establish a precedent. Givens is outraged; he threatens to make a major issue of the refusal. A few days later, a higher official in the PMO telephones and wants to know what message should go to the girl. Givens thinks he has won. "But then do you know what they do?" he says. "They send her a telegram. Christ, I could have faked a telegram myself. I wanted the Prime Minister involved, just to the extent of writing his name on a piece of paper."

The Prime Minister is travelling; he is tired, and has gone to bed for an afternoon nap when the telephone rings. An aide takes the call. At the other end of the line is an agitated cabinet minister; he wants the Prime Minister awakened at once; a security issue has come up and he must have an immediate decision at the highest level. The aide asks for details, refuses to wake Trudeau, and gives the decision himself. The minister is outraged, but the decision stands.

None of these five incidents is particularly sinister, but taken together they indicate the increasing and arbitrary power wielded by the Prime Minister and his immediate circle of advisers, resulting in the increasing isolation of Canada's most important elected official behind the barricades of his office.

To all intents and purposes, Canada is no longer run by Parliament, or the cabinet, or even the party in power; it is run by the Prime Minister and his own personal power bloc. The Supergroup is an informal, loosely organized ring of advisers, some of them on Trudeau's staff, some in the public service, some elected, some appointed, some conspicuous holders of high office, some minor officials unknown to the general public. These are the People Who Count, not because of age or experience, rank or title, but because they have the ear and respect of Pierre Elliott Trudeau.

Take the NATO decision — the correct decision, to my way of thinking, but arrived at in a startling manner. The policy finally adopted was opposed by every official body it was put to, and by the two cabinet ministers most directly involved — External Affairs Minister Mitchell Sharp and the then Defence Minister, Leo Cadieux; but because it was approved by the Supergroup, it was adopted.

The same may be said of the anti-inflation war, described in Chapter 5. It was not the Liberal caucus or the Liberal party that sounded the tocsin for that war — Liberal MPs were the first to hear the screams of outrage. Nor did the civil service call out the troops. (The Department of Finance was, and remains, bitterly divided on the issue; the Economic Council of Canada, the government's official policy adviser, warned against the course that was taken.) It was not the cabinet that wanted inflation put down at any cost — indeed, the issue was never discussed in cabinet until *after* it had been embodied in Benson's budget in 1969. The inflation war has been waged, almost from the beginning, by a tight circle of cabinet ministers — Treasury Board Chairman C. M. Drury, Finance Minister Benson, Trade Minister Jean-Luc Pépin are the key members — on advice laid down by a few top public servants — Bank of Canada President Louis Rasminsky, Robert Bryce, the Prime Minister's financial adviser, Al Johnson, who used to be the Prime Minister's financial adviser and is now Secretary of the Treasury Board, and Sol Simon Reisman, who used to be Secretary of the Treasury Board and is now Deputy Minister of Finance. It is not the soundness of their advice that counts, but their closeness to Trudeau. (Remember how Kierans advised the Prime Minister, correctly, about the coming change in the dollar; remember how the ECC advised him, correctly, that the tight-money policies he was being urged to follow would backfire.)

In the Trudeau government, proximity is the key to power; if I had a policy to push, I would rather have the ears of half a dozen of the Supergroup — men who see him often, speak on his wavelength, call him *tu* instead of *vous* in French — than the mouths of half his cabinet. Consider Paul Hellyer and Jean Marchand. Hellyer, as the minister responsible for housing, proposed reforms that the Prime Minister could not accept, he said, because they would invade provincial jurisdiction. But Marchand, in establishing the Department of Regional Economic Expansion, set up a body which, almost by definition, invades provincial jurisdiction regularly and with impunity. Marchand flourished, Hellyer withered; Marchand is of the Supergroup, and Hellyer was not.

The men who surround a prime minister have always been important — witness Tom Kent in the Pearson years or Alvin Hamilton during the Diefenbaker interlude — but they have never been as powerful as they are today. Pearson tended to accept advice from all comers, which is why so many of his policies seemed confused and contradictory. ("It wasn't so much what you said," one of his former confidants noted, "as when you said it. Last in line was a good place to be.") Diefenbaker would accept only reinforcement of his own views. Trudeau tends to look for advice from a single group of like-minded men, and he will accept views that run counter to his own if they are well-argued and put forward by people he trusts.

His own work habits reinforce the power of his advisers. The Prime Minister is not a patient, steady worker; he operates in bursts of furious intellectual energy. He burns brightly, but he burns out fast; he needs a great deal of sleep — including, frequently, an afternoon nap — and a lot of privacy, a span of time every day to be himself and not The Prime Minister. (His most furious outbursts have stemmed from what he considered to be an invasion of his privacy.) Therefore, the way advice comes to him is important. A concise, well-organized, short report will carry more weight with him than one that contains more information but is not so easily grasped. His aides are, primarily, communicators, masters of the short memo, the pithy speech, the telling graph. Jim Davey, his programme secretary, loves to draw up time-flow charts and multi-coloured graphs that appear to let the eye take in a great deal of information at a glance. He gets a lot of kidding about his graphs, but he is listened to with great respect. Over-simplification has become a technique of government.

It is because he works in bursts that the Prime Minister finds it necessary to delegate authority, and naturally he does so to those he feels he can trust. Thus, in the midst of the Biafran war, he sent Ivan Head, his legislative assistant, to Lagos to negotiate with the Nigerian government. A much more normal course would have been to send an official from the External Affairs Department; but Head was not sent as the representative of Her Majesty's Government in Canada; he was the Prime Minister's personal representative, the equivalent of an American president's private emissary.

It is also a habit of the Prime Minister's to hold brainstorming sessions on matters of import. These are the free-wheeling discussions he learned to love as an academic, and in which he excels. In these rough-and-tumble debates held, not in cabinet, but with his own circle of aides, the Socratic query, the quick, witty thrust, the programmed language — Input, Output, Feedback, Counter-productive, all the non-words of machine-talk — carry more weight than an arm-load of research. Trudeau is a talker and listener, rather than a reader and digester, and this is why those people immediately around him wield so much more influence than the distant, toiling, memo-writing mandarins, MPs and ordinary experts out there who may know much more about the subject under discussion than his advisers, but sing to an empty hall.

At the heart of the new power structure are the Prime Minister's Office and the Privy Council Office. The distinction between the two is that the PMO is, in theory, the Prime Minister's personal staff, while the PCO is the staff of the cabinet secretariat, plus the Prime Minister's special staff for federal-provincial relations. PMO members are normally paid through the cabinet, by order-in-council; PCO members are normally paid through the civil service. In fact, the distinction between the two bodies is becoming blurred; they have been welded together into something like the White House corps of unelected experts, trouble-shooters, public relations agents and fixers. When the Prime Minister had decided where to place Quebec's new airport, he fired off his regional adviser, Pierre Levasseur, to Quebec to break the news; when he couldn't decide whether to accept an honourary degree at the University of Moncton in the spring of 1969 (the students were restless), he dispatched Jean-Eudes Haché, another personal aide, to scout the scene. The first was a task that would normally have gone to a cabinet minister, the second to a party official.

Senior officers in the PCO have become part of this personal team. Take Michael Pitfield, for example. Technically he is deputy secretary to the cabinet, but in fact he is a friend and personal adviser to the Prime Minister. A young, bright, attractive Montreal lawyer (most of the close advisers seem to be young, bright, attractive Montreal lawyers), Pitfield has influence far beyond anything envisioned in the Civil Service Act under which he was hired. On the night of Trudeau's Liberal leadership victory, when the new Prime Minister disappeared to the apartment of a friend for a steak and champagne supper, that friend was Pitfield.

A former government aide — I can say only that he is a man who worked at the highest level — once told me that Pitfield was responsible for a change in the Liberal party programme during the 1968 election. The party was preparing to endorse a campaign plank that opposed universal welfare schemes on principle; the programme passed the party hierarchy and the cabinet, but Pitfield pointed out that Medicare, to cite the most obvious example, was a universal welfare scheme, and the Liberals had introduced it. He won his point, and the paragraph was changed. This seemed so extraordinary that I telephoned Pitfield to ask him if it was true. It was not, he said; he was "flattered and flabbergasted" by the suggestion that he

wielded such power, but in fact he was only a normal civil servant performing a normal civil servant's duties, which did not
include messing with party programmes. I was impressed by
the forceful sincerity with which he spoke. Very shortly there-
after, the Prime Minister left on a holiday cruise, accompanied
by one member of his staff — Michael Pitfield. Well, hell, even
a normal civil servant has to have a holiday.

The welding together of the PMO and the PCO has been accompanied by an enormous jump in their growth, a jump unaf-
fected by any of the freezes, cut-backs or austerity programmes
applied to the rest of the government service. In 1967, the last
Pearson year, the Prime Minister's personal staff numbered
twelve; today it numbers sixty (if it hasn't gone up since I began writing);[3] the Privy Council staff went from 156 to 181
members in Trudeau's first year, and in his next, 1969, the year
of the freeze for every other department of government, the
combined staffs went from 211 to 288 members, a jump of more
than one-third in that single, austerity year. Next year, 1972, it
will reach a combined total of 384, ninety-two of them in the
PMO.[4]

With the new growth has come new organization; the PMO
has been pinned to paper with an organization chart exactly
like those used to delineate responsibility in the civil service. At
the top is the Prime Minister, and in separate little boxes to the
sides, his private secretary, executive assistant and appointments secretary. Directly below the Prime Minister is his principal secretary, with his own clutch of side-boxes (legislative
assistant, special assistant, administrative assistant, senior correspondence secretary, correspondence secretary) and, directly
below the principal secretary, a line of four linked boxes (press
secretary, special assistant, regional adviser, programme secretary), each in turn with its own dependent links. The heads of
department — all those who get a separate box to themselves
— meet once a week to discuss administrative problems. The
Prime Minister has not, as often claimed, by-passed the bureaucracy. He has simply set up his own counter-bureaucracy.

In all this new organization, perhaps the most important
innovation in the PMO has been the creation of regional desks,
manned by a small flotilla of regional desk officers, one for each
major region of the country.

The original idea, when the regional desks were established
in late 1968, was that they would serve as listening posts for the

Prime Minister across the land. There was to be a network of contacts — people in the universities, in business, in the professions — who would be consulted regularly, and would feed opinions, ideas and complaints to the desk officers, for processing through the rungs of power to the Prime Minister. The MPs resented the desks intensely; they saw them — and rightly so — as the usurpation of one of the Member's key roles, which is to serve as a link between his riding and the centre of power. In caucus meetings, the Liberal MPs kicked like mules. They were told they had nothing to worry about; the whole scheme had been misconstrued; the press, as usual, had got it wrong. The desks were not listening posts, merely organizing points, so that when, for instance, the Prime Minister was to make a foray across the land, the way would be prepared for him. In fact, one of the jobs of the desk officers is to prepare a little black book for sojourns into the countryside, to make sure the Prime Minister doesn't shake any wrong hands. But that is only the smallest part of the desk job; its main role is to expedite problems, to feed information to the Prime Minister on the one hand, and to fend off inquiries — including those of MPs — on the other. The desks do, in large measure, replace the communications role of the MP. (Much was made of the fact that the Prime Minister invited the Liberal MPs, four at a time, to lunch with him at 24 Sussex Drive. But the ground-rules forbade the Members from bringing up local problems; the talk was always on a lofty, national plane. "It was all bull-shit and bird-food," said one disgruntled MP.)

The first desks were established for Quebec, the Maritimes and the west. The Ontario MPs dug in their heels hard enough to fend off a desk for over a year, but it came to them, as it must to all, and now every section of the nation has its own desk officer in the PMO. The ordinary citizen who has a complaint to raise with his government can now safely ignore his MP. As Phil Givens put it, "If I was John Doe Public and I wanted something done, I wouldn't waste my time contacting my MP. I'd send a telegram to the Prime Minister's Office, with a copy to the Leader of the Opposition." That telegram would be taken up, and dealt with, by the appropriate regional desk.

All these changes haven't really simplified government; instead of one bureaucracy, there are now two, one scattered across Ottawa, the other stashed in the numerous nooks and crannies of the East Block, home of the PMO and the PCO.

Among the babble of advising voices, it is, of course, not possible for the Prime Minister to listen to everyone; there are perhaps thirty to thirty-five men — no, ladies, there is not a woman among them — to whom he pays special attention. This is the Supergroup.

Describing the Supergroup is not easy.[5] It is not a club, there are no membership dues, no badges of office; the only distinguishing characteristic is that these are the people whose influence counts when crucial decisions are made. The personnel of the group is constantly shifting, not only with time (some of the young, bright lawyers go back to Montreal, some get tired of the grinding pace, some simply don't fit in), but with the subject under discussion. On economic matters, the Prime Minister turns to one clutch of advisers, on foreign affairs, to a second, on the constitution, to a third. Nor is it easy to find out about the Supergroupers; they prefer to keep what Jim Davey calls "a low profile of visibility". Just the same, it is possible to build up a picture of the group, and the first fact that emerges is that it is not a monolithic mass, but a series of concentric rings of power, fanning out from the PMO.

Let us call those rings, for purposes of convenience, The Inner Circle, The Operators, and The Task Force.

The Inner Circle is, of course, the most important. It consists, as I see it, of only four men: Marc Lalonde, the Prime Minister's Principal Secretary and chief of staff; Jean Marchand, Minister of Regional Economic Expansion; Gérard Pelletier, Secretary of State; and Gordon Robertson, Secretary to the Cabinet and chief of the PCO.

These are the men who see the Prime Minister every day (Lalonde and Robertson meet with him for half an hour every morning as a matter of routine). They are the men whose advice is sought on all the great issues; it is not always taken, but is always sought.

Of the four, Lalonde is the most powerful, simply because his job amounts to being Assistant Prime Minister, while Pelletier and Marchand have ministries to run. Lalonde is a large, balding, shrewd, quick, tough man, the undisputed boss of the PMO. ("When he chews you out," said one man who has survived the ordeal, "there is no shouting and screaming, but, man, you know you've been chewed out.")

In many ways he is like the Prime Minister, the product of a superior education, a Quebecker who opposed Duplessis, a lawyer and law teacher who drifted into politics. Unlike Trudeau, he has not born to wealth; his father was a farmer at Ile Perrot, just outside Montreal, and he scrambled to success mainly by dint of hard work and superior brains. Like most of the Prime Minister's confidants, he is an old friend, having met Trudeau in the early 1950s. He taught law at the University of Montreal after completing his MA in political science at Oxford, then, in 1959, went to Ottawa as special assistant to E. Davie Fulton, then Minister of Justice in the Diefenbaker government. (Like Trudeau, he is a pragmatist; party labels don't count; power does.) He returned to Quebec to campaign in the 1960 election, the one that brought a Liberal government and a Quiet Revolution, and for the next few years shuttled between Quebec and Ottawa, where he worked on three royal commissions. In 1966 he caught the eye of Prime Minister Pearson, whose own chief adviser, Tom Kent, had become far too visible, and had to be found a niche in the civil service (he is now Marchand's deputy). Lalonde was hired on contract as a special adviser, and it was from that perch that he helped launch the Trudeau leadership campaign. Trudeau made it a condition of his accepting the nomination that if he won, Lalonde would become his principal secretary. Lalonde accepted.

The move was a shrewd one, because while the two men are alike in many respects — they share the same strong belief in federalism, the same pragmatism, the same political outlook (both signed the May 1964 manifesto, *"Pour une Politique fonctionelle"*, which reads, to me, like a technocrat's dream) — Lalonde possesses endless stamina and an apparently insatiable appetite for work. Five years after his base of operations became Ottawa, he had not moved his family from Montreal; he worked such long hours that there was no point in it. Essentially, he is a technocrat. He once told a *Time* magazine reporter, "Technology means the systematic application of scientific or other organized knowledge to practical tasks. That's what we are trying to achieve: the ability to apply reason to broad social and economic problems."

It is Lalonde, more than any other man, who guides the Prime Minister, decides whom he will see and who can safely be ignored, what policy papers should be discussed and what put off. In any serious disagreement between the two men, Lalonde would lose, of course; but the two men are so alike in

their basic approach as to make real disagreement unlikely. Lalonde has been called the second most powerful man in Canada
and he is.

Gérard Pelletier and Jean Marchand are, like Lalonde, old
friends of Trudeau and each other. As described in Chapter 1,
Pelletier and Trudeau met at college, and the two met March-
and during the bitter 1949 strike at Asbestos, Quebec. March-
and was the hero of the strike as an organizer for the Confederation of Catholic Workers; Pelletier was a $35-a-week re-
porter for *Le Devoir*, covering the action, and Trudeau drove
down from Montreal with Pelletier as a kind of freelance
rabble-rouser. The three men have been linked ever since.

When the Liberals asked Marchand to join the party in 1965,
he said he would come only on condition that his two friends be
found ridings, too. The Liberal hierarchy were happy to have
Pelletier, less certain about Trudeau, who was an unknown
quantity at that time, but eventually accepted all three. When
they arrived in Ottawa, they were promptly dubbed "The
Three Wise Men from Quebec". (In Quebec they were "*les
trois colombes*" — the three doves.) They served their Ottawa
apprenticeship together, and when the time came for Pearson
to step down in 1968, it seemed inevitable that one of them
would run for the leadership with the backing of the other two.
Pelletier is not a notable campaigner, and Marchand was
hampered by health problems, so the choice went, almost by
elimination, to Trudeau.

As Prime Minister he has naturally stepped out ahead of his
old friends, but they remain close confidants and constant advisers. It was Pelletier who was given the task of forming and
carrying out the programme to advance bilingualism, a task the
Prime Minister rightly considers his government's most impressive accomplishment to date. Pelletier is also consulted on
virtually every major decision, although he is sometimes over-
ridden, as he was on the *Radio Canada* issue. He is an austere,
complex, difficult man, and those who know him well say of
him mostly that they do not know him well.

Marchand is, if anything, more powerful than Pelletier. It is
Marchand who controls the Quebec wing of the Liberal party;
he is more experienced than either of the others in the day-to-
day thumb-twisting that makes up politics. During the 1968
election, it was he who took on the task of parachuting candidates into the Quebec ridings where the local association had

mulishly picked the wrong man. Marchand simply brushed aside the undesirables and inserted new candidates, without the tedious formality of calling another nomination meeting. Like Trudeau, he believes in dynamic leadership.

Marchand's department, Regional and Economic Expansion, is one of the most powerful in government, and he runs it, unlike any other cabinet minister, as his own personal fiefdom. But his influence, like Pelletier's, extends far beyond his department. During the kidnapping crisis in Quebec it was, as much as anything else, Marchand's shrill cries of alarm ("There is an organization which has thousands of guns, rifles, machine-guns, bombs and more than enough dynamite to blow up the core of downtown Montreal") that tipped the scales towards the War Measures Act. Marchand is a principal source of information and advice about Quebec, and that is a pity, because, like Trudeau, Pelletier and Lalonde, he seems to hold separatism in such hatred and contempt that he cannot believe it is a major political force. The Trudeau regime has consistently and grossly underestimated the drawing-power of the Parti Québécois because the Prime Minister's closest advisers persist in seeing bombs and guns that are not there and ignoring votes that are.

The fourth member of The Inner Circle is Gordon Robertson, a tall, slim, handsome man with steel-grey hair and an unobtrusive manner, who can be seen at every constitutional conference sitting just behind the Prime Minister's right shoulder, ready for instant consultation. Robertson has a clutch of titles — Clerk of the Privy Council, Chairman of the Continuing Committee on the Constitution, Secretary to the Cabinet — and enormous influence with the civil service, who regard him as a kind of lay pope of the memo set. He has been in the civil service since the days of Mackenzie King, and is everything a mandarin should be: discreet, intelligent and honest. He sees the Prime Minister every morning and, while he is not a creator of policy, he has a good deal to say about how policies will be carried out. If politics is the art of the possible, Robertson is the man who says what is possible and what is not. He exerts a strong conservative influence inside the administration; he has always, as Peter Newman wrote of him, "revered the state of the unrocked boat".

An argument could be made for including Michael Pitfield in The Inner Circle, but my personal view is that he lacks the political clout, as yet, to be admitted to the elect. He belongs to the second ring of power, The Operators. These are the men who, while not involved in all decisions of policy, are involved in many of them, because they are the ones whom the Prime Minister leans on for information and who are charged with carrying out the legwork of administration. Most of them work in the PMO or the PCO.

I have already mentioned some of them — Ivan Head, Jim Davey, Michael Pitfield. There are others: Marshall Crowe, Deputy Secretary to the Cabinet; Gordon Gibson, the Prime Minister's executive assistant; Peter Roberts, a press secretary; Roger Rolland, a special assistant and speechwriter; Tim Porteous, who was hired as a speechwriter, but works more as an appointments secretary; David Thomson, the chief regional desk officer; and Jean-Eudes Haché, a desk officer. They are a remarkably similar group: young, bright, self-assured, pragmatic. They are the ones with the jobs to do, the errands to run, the information to gather. Ivan Head, for example, sees the Prime Minister every day, just before Question Period, to brief him on the questions most likely to be asked, and to suggest plausible replies. Marshall Crowe is, with Pitfield, a key link to the Privy Council, and an expert consultant on matters of finance.

Beyond the circle of Operators runs the circle I have called The Task Force, whose members the Prime Minister calls on for help with specific problems. Some are cabinet ministers, some are members of the PMO or PCO, some are party figures and some have no official connection with the government beyond the fact that they have earned the Prime Minister's respect. In this last class I would put men like Jean Beetz, Dean of Law at the University of Montreal, who is a special adviser on constitutional matters, and Carl Goldenberg, the Montreal lawyer, whose quiet voice and puffing pipe have been *de rigueur* at constitutional meetings for twenty years. I have already mentioned some of the other Task Force members — the financial whiz-kids behind the inflation fight: Robert Bryce (who is soon to move to Washington as chief of our International Monetary Fund delegation), Albert Johnson, Louis Rasminsky, Simon Reisman. These men are not consulted on a wide range of problems, but are likely to be listened to carefully in their own areas of specialization. The same may be said of such top civil servants as Allan Gotlieb, Deputy Minister of Communications, who happens to be an authority on both constitutional and international law, and of top party figures such as the Liberal Federation President, Senator Richard Stanbury, who sees the Prime Minister regularly about party problems.

As for the federal cabinet, it is sharply divided into two groups — the Ins, and everybody else. The Ins are members of the Task Force; their views carry far more weight than their portfolios warrant. Jean-Pierre Goyer, the Solicitor-General, for instance, is a low-ranking cabinet minister who is much more influential than, say, Public Works Minister Arthur Laing.

The In ministers, besides Marchand and Pelletier, are Defence Minister Donald Macdonald, Finance Minister E. J. Benson, Goyer, External Affairs Minister Mitchell Sharp, Treasury Board President Charles Drury, Trade Minister Jean-Luc Pépin, Labour Minister Bryce Mackasey and Transport Minister Donald Jamieson. Other ministers, from Justice Minister John Turner to Northern Affairs Minister Jean Chrétien, may hold sway in their own departments, but the Supergroup ministers — who are distinguished by the happy coincidence that all of them but one, Jamieson, were active in Trudeau's leadership campaign — have an influence that extends far beyond the bounds of their own ministries.

One incident may show what I mean. Some time ago, a Toronto firm was hired to perform a consultative service for one of the departments whose minister did not belong to the In group. The deputy minister of the department, who had dealt with the firm on another matter, felt it was not up to the task and managed to have the funds for the job dried up — in effect, he fired the firm. The Toronto company, however, had a direct political connection with one of the In ministers, and took its case up with him. Not long after, the deputy minister was removed from his post, on the order of the Prime Minister, and not long after that, the consulting firm was busily back at work. Its president told me gleefully, "That so-and-so fired us, so we fired him."

The most astonishing thing about the Supergroup is its homogeneity. Its members are drawn from the law, business, politics and communications. Of the thirty Supergroupers I have mentioned by name, no less than eleven are lawyers, as is the Prime Minister. There are no farmers among them, no plumbers, only one, Bryce Mackasey, who was ever an ordinary

worker. They have seldom known hunger or felt cold. Housing
is no problem for them, because they have never lacked a roof;
social issues, from the problems of Indians to the wrench of unemployment, are less attractive than the fascination of power
and the fine legalisms to be drawn from constitutional debate.

They are not party men, in the old sense; few of them were
active politically before Trudeau came along, and many of
those who were, like Lalonde, could work as easily for a Tory as
a Liberal, or, like Marchand and Pelletier, as easily support the
NDP as anybody else. They are pragmatists all.

Confident, tough and aggressive, the Supergroupers move
through their tight agendas with ease, but their ability to grasp
the great raw mass of Canadian problems is limited by their
own narrow compass. They want neat problems to which technology can provide solutions, and we are in short supply of
those; our real problems, from increasing regionalism to continental absorption, from too much wheat to too few jobs, demand solutions that are often messy and opposed to much that
they hold dear. For example, Canada cannot free itself of the
American embrace without embracing, in turn, some sort of
economic nationalism; since that is unthinkable, there is
nothing to be done.

The emergence of the Supergroup has had wide-ranging effects in Canada, not the least of which, as we have seen in the
last chapter, is a decline in efficiency; there are simply too
many things to be done to leave the decision-making to such a
small body. In most nations (and formerly in Canada) decision-
making is divided among party leaders, bureaucrats, professional advisers and politicians. Even in the U.S., where power is
centralized to an alarming degree, decisions are shared with
science councils, economic advisory commissions, the White
House corps, congressional leaders and the federal cabinet. In
Ottawa, there is an increasing tendency to buck all decisions
through to the Supergroup, which gets around to them in its
own good time. But there are two other, longer-range implications that need examination: the first is the effect on Canada's
civil service, the second the effect on the Canadian political system itself.

The Prime Minister's counter-bureaucracy is playing hell
with the real bureaucracy. One mandarin, whose job would not
last five minutes if he were identified, put it this way:

"What we see happening is the development of this little

group of lieutenants in the PMO and the PCO that are really the Prime Minister's people. The lines of loyalty flow directly to him. They are not responsible to anyone else and they are more or less hatchet men who go around shooting down other people's ideas. . . . You develop a kind of government by terror, where the civil servants are no longer giving the best advice they can and letting the chips fall where they may. They are continually looking back over their shoulders. With everything you do, you don't think What's the best policy?, but What's that S.O.B. in the PMO going to do with this?"

Canada's civil service has been, by and large, a good one, firmly rooted in the notion of responsible government. Civil servants have certainly made policy decisions — despite what the political-science textbooks say, they always have; even the way in which various alternatives are put forward by the bureaucracy amounts to decision-making — but there has always been a visible chain of command, from the lowliest pen-pusher up through the deputy minister to the minister, and a chain of responsibility, which could be pulled, sharply, by a single question in the House of Commons. All that is changed; there is no longer any accountability for major government decisions, except the general accountability borne by the Prime Minister at an election to be held when he sees fit. Not surprisingly, the bureaucrats have begun to withdraw. In one instance, a group of senior civil servants who held regular meetings to co-ordinate the policies of several departments on transport issues has stopped meeting. All the policy decisions, they felt, were going to be made further up the line anyway.

This is how it was put by a bureaucrat who is now looking around for another job: "You get this feeling of why should you knock yourself out on this or that subject, because somebody else will make the decision anyway. It's a soul-destroying kind of thing. You didn't come to Ottawa for this. It's not just the job, the feeling you get is not that we're developing a bad government, but a tough, hard, ruthless, heartless government that doesn't seem to be weakened by any streak of humanity. . . . It's the de Gaulle fist in the Kennedy glove."

The alienation of the civil service is more important than a nation used to scoffing at it may imagine. Our civil service is the envy of most nations, and in particular of the United States; there the spoils system, under which most of the major jobs change with every election, has fostered an *ad hoc*, patchwork,

ever-ballooning bureaucracy that in some instances — *viz.* the
Pentagon — has moved almost beyond political control.

The civil servants are demoralized today because they can see, as anyone can, that Canada is moving towards a presidential system in everything but name.[6] I don't mean that the Prime Minister is about to opt for a U.S.-style division of powers among the legislative, executive and judicial branches of government. He prefers, as he has said, to have the supportive arm of the legislature, so that he can put through his programmes free of the harassment and vetoes imposed by various levels of the U.S. Congress. But he has already appropriated to himself many of the powers of a president, and such trappings of office as his own bureaucracy, without any of the checks and balances of the American system. He sets economic policy, foreign policy, constitutional policy, within his own small group of advisers; he rules over Parliament, his cabinet and his party without any kind of check except a straight Yes or No from the electors once every four or five years. The crucial point about invoking War Measures was that it was done in the middle of the night on the say-so of a small group of advisers, that it suspended all the normal practices of Canadian law, and that Parliament was then presented with a *fait accompli* and a series of lame explanations. No American president would have dared such a move; in fact, not long after the Act was imposed, an admiring official in the U.S. Defence Department told me, "You guys sure know how to keep the punks in line; we'd never dare try that."

In short, the significance of the Supergroup lies not only in the havoc it has wrought so far, but in the danger it portends. The power so assiduously won away from cabinet, Parliament, the party and the bureaucracy will not be readily returned; the trend towards centralizing power in the PMO will not be easily reversed. Trudeau has constructed, in the bowels of the East Block, a huge, powerful decision-making machine. Even if you think the products of that machine have been perfection itself so far, you must pause to wonder: what happens if it falls into the hands of a real incompetent or a megalomaniac?

Or, as the mandarin with whose quote I began this chapter asked, "What if we get, God save us, a Canadian Nixon?"

1. I am in some difficulty substantiating many of my stories about the Supergroup, for two reasons. The first is that my sources are, in the main, those people whose jobs would be forfeit if I named them. The second is that it is hard, almost impossible, to trace the responsibility of various members of the Supergroup for various acts of legislation — indeed, the lack of accountability is one of my chief complaints about the Supergroup. I can say only that I have attempted to confirm everything that can be confirmed, and that I have used some of this material in print before, where it has been resented, but not denied.

2. Reported by Claude Henault in the Toronto *Telegram*, November 3, 1969.

3. They are listed in a return to the Clerk of the House of Commons tabled May 31, 1971, in response to a question from Robert M. Coates, a Conservative MP. (His question, incidentally, was asked on November 25, 1970.)

4. Canada, *Estimates of Government Spending* 1971-72, p. 20:6.

5. Because the Supergroup is an arbitrarily-defined organization, anyone can quarrel with the members I have put in or left out. I tried this list out on two cabinet ministers, Liberal party officials, fellow journalists and a number of senior civil servants. A different version appeared in *Maclean's*, October 1969; I have amended it to bring it up to date.

6. Not, I grant, an original thesis. Professor Denis Smith, Chairman of the Department of Politics, Trent University, made the same observation in a paper delivered to the Tory Thinkers' Conference in Niagara Falls, Ontario, in November 1969.

# 12

## The Opposition:
## The Feeble Foes

*The House meets, and in march the Opposition, and sit there ready to attack Ministers and their measures; never, if possible, to make a concession by word or vote to official shrewdness or skill. For the time being they are Her Majesty's loyal sappers and miners, not to be very particular if only they can hack and hew their way to the treasury benches.*
W. G. Moncrieff, 1871

*Well, if the government brings in a reasonable measure, something we think is for the good of the country, why, naturally, we are going to support them.*
Robert Stanfield, 1971

Well, life was simpler back in W. G. Moncrieff's day, and Parliament was more of a game — brutally played, sometimes, but not so serious in its consequences. Or, if it was serious, the general public did not know it, and the Commons could continue in droning debate for weeks without drawing down the wrath of the voters. That is no longer true; an educated public wants and demands action to tackle the problems of a complex society; there is no time for gamesmanship in Parliament; an opposition can lose support by blockading too vigorously or too successfully a programme advanced by a government.

But it is the function of the opposition to oppose, both in the sense of seeking out the chinks in the administrative armour and in the sense of providing a realistic, acceptable alternative to the ruling party and thus presenting to it a constant threat, in Parliament and out. Since the election of Trudeau at the head of a majority government in June 1968, Canada's opposition has failed to perform that role adequately; and some of the blame for the difficulties Parliament and the nation find themselves in today must fall on the opposition.

The most crucial issues of our time — national unity, the preservation of Canadian independence, the War Measures Act, even the emasculation of Parliament — have found the opposition parties not only divided among themselves, which is reasonable and natural, but internally divided. While the government phalanxes march and wheel, turning right, turning left, advancing, retreating, all to the beat of the Prime Ministerial drum, the opposition parties tug and pull, lurching from issue to issue, out of step, out of time, out of sorts. The genius of the Liberal party has always lain in her promiscuity; she can accept, absorb, almost any person, almost any doctrine, ingest, ruminate and regurgitate a compromise which then becomes official fodder. The genius of the New Democratic and Progressive Conservative parties has always lain in the fact that their internal battles are fought with more vigour than ever they carry against the enemy, and that the doctrines that emerge from policy conventions often meet their most bitter opposition within the party itself.

This is not a new development, but the finest flowering of a long historical process. When the NDP was first being formed from the old CCF and the Canadian Labour Congress, the fledgling party split into two bitterly opposed factions on the issue of whether anyone should be allowed to run against the executive's choice for leader, Tommy Douglas, then the Premier of Saskatchewan. A typical debate took place in the livingroom of a prominent Toronto party stalwart, with David Lewis (now party leader and then president of the disappearing CCF) and a member of the Ontario provincial executive screaming at each other. Lewis wanted to block Hazen Argue, who has since gone to his reward as a Liberal senator, from opposing Douglas; the executive member argued that Lewis was trying to stifle debate and the right of delegates to a free choice; as they hurled arguments and epithets at each other, the wife of an MP chanted in the background, over and over, "Hazen Argue is a sonofabitch, Hazen Argue is a sonofabitch." A Labour Party MP, visiting from England, was visibly appalled.

"What's the matter," someone asked him, "don't you people ever have disagreements?" "Quite so," the dazed Labourite replied, "quite so. But nothing like this."

The same internal dissension is the most firmly held tradition of that tradition-minded party, the Progressive Conservatives. The stampings and bellowings of Lester Pearson and John Diefenbaker could never match, for pure vituperation, the snarlings that emanated from the forces of party president Dalton Camp and Diefenbaker during the long, painful deposing of the Chief, and today nothing Robert Stanfield says in public or private about the Prime Minister carries the freight of bitterness his own western followers unload on him at every possible occasion. Camp, no longer the party's national president but still a powerful Tory figure, took note of this in a speech in Toronto on March 12, 1971. The Conservatives could be destroyed, he said, "Not by artful design, but . . . by personal pique and folly. . . . What stands in the way of a stronger party is the deliberate intent of a few to see the party destroyed." Camp's remarks, of course, were much applauded by one wing of the party, bitterly resented by another.

Besides the preoccupation with personal rivalries, the two major opposition parties (I am unable to take the Ralliement Créditiste seriously any more than its own members do; it was born a splinter of Quebec rural discontent, and has grown longer and sharper, but no broader) labour under the handicap of internal policy disputes.

The Conservatives, for instance, cannot agree on an approach to Quebec. At the leadership convention in August 1967, which dumped Diefenbaker and elevated Stanfield, a policy committee on the constitution approved a "two nations" approach to Quebec. That approach grew out of the Montmorency Falls thinkers conference earlier that year, dominated by such weighty Quebec personages as Marcel Faribault, president of the *Trust Général du Canada*. In his acceptance speech, Stanfield tried to move away from that resolution, which was not, in any event, binding on him. He spent the next four years painstakingly explaining that *"deux nations"* did not mean "two nations" at all— although anyone with a French dictionary could see that it did — but referred to the "two founding peoples" that came together at the time of Confederation. That was both bad history and bad politics, and it was made more embarrassing by the fact that western Tories repudiated the phrase however translated. In the 1968 election, Diefenbaker campaigned under the slogan, "One nation, one Canada, indivisible." The issue remains unresolved, and the split became even wider in early 1971 when a group of Quebec Tories moved to set up a separate wing of the party in that province, with only loose ties to the national body. The voter who marks his ballot for a Conservative hasn't the foggiest notion whether he is supporting a concept of "two nations", "one Canada, indivisible", or something in between.

The NDP is caught in the same cleft. The party leader, David Lewis, is a strong federalist, and, while he supports a "special status" approach to Quebec (the phrase is offensive to many Canadians for reasons that remain a mystery to me; Quebec's status has been special since Confederation, inevitably so), he insists on Ottawa's primacy in the crucial area of economic development. His campaign for the federal leadership of the NDP looked like a waltz to power until he clashed head-on with the party's far-left Waffle wing, which was flirting openly with the Parti Québecois. Lewis repudiated a proposal made by Waffle candidate James Laxer that the PQ and the NDP come to an understanding in Quebec elections, but he was not able to exercise much control over a Quebec wing whose real thrust comes from the radical left, most of whom are separatists. A number of delegates to the Quebec NDP meeting in March 1971 simply moved a few blocks away to attend a PQ meeting a week later, where they looked equally at home.

The Waffle also forced an open party split on the issue of economic nationalism. The NDP Establishment has always taken a strong stand on the need to preserve Canadian ownership, but seems uncertain exactly how to go about the task. The Waffle, led by academics like Laxer and Mel Watkins, harbour no uncertainties; indeed, this is one of their least attractive political attributes. Nationalism — and their socialist corollary, nationalization of industry — is their speciality. Nationalism brought the Waffle into being.

The party Establishment, including both David Lewis and his son Stephen, NDP leader in Ontario, argue that the Waffle is self-righteous, doctrinaire and anti-democratic. It will not accept any decisions of the party that fail to fit its notions, and it advances radical programmes with all the conviction of academics who are never likely to face the problems of implementing them. There is justice in the accusation. I once attended a meeting of the Brantford, Ontario, NDP association where the Waffle was busy ramming through a resolution on housing, which said, among other things, that when houses were expropriated for massive new urban schemes, fair prices would be paid to the owners but "This, of course, does not include landlords." After the meeting a man came up to question Watkins. He had built a couple of houses that he was renting until he could sell them. "Doesn't this resolution mean the government could take away my places and pay me nothing?" Watkins had to admit that it did. "Do you think that's fair?" the man asked. Watkins allowed that, no, when you came to think about it, it wasn't. The man went on, "How about a guy who's moved by his company and rents his house until he can sell. He's a landlord, too, isn't he?" Well, yes, he is, and no, he wouldn't get any compensation either. But the resolution stood, and is still the model resolution for the Waffle.[1]

But it is not merely a question of thoughtlessness, or ruthlessness; the real division between the Waffle and the rest of the NDP is a fundamental difference on the use of nationalization. The Waffle considers it the essential first step, while the rest of the party regards it as only a last resort. In fact the Waffle is not a wing of the NDP, but a separate party warring within the old party's bosom; if the Waffle were ever to win the party control it so desperately seeks, much of the rank and file would simply opt out and vote Liberal.

The doctrinal differences within the major opposition parties would be important in any circumstances. But both parties are hampered by another weakness; both have leaders who, however commendable and intelligent they are individually, are not taken seriously by the public as prime ministerial candidates.

With Lewis, the problem is not so visible, at least not in Parliament. In the House of Commons, Lewis is the single most effective spokesman across from the Treasury Benches. (Donald Macdonald, when he was Liberal House Leader, said, "If there were a dozen David Lewises over there, things might be different.") A firm and eloquent speaker, he is always listened to in the House. While occasionally sharp of tongue — he once said of Trudeau, "There, but for the grace of Pierre Elliott Trudeau, sits God" — his speeches are normally moderate, persuasive and free of personal spite.

But Lewis has a fatal flaw, one he can do nothing about. He put it himself with brutal frankness: "I've been around too long; I've been around since the 30s." It is not merely a question of age — he is sixty-two — but of image; no one will believe in the vigorous new approach of a party led by a man whose eloquent denunciations were rolling across the land before most Canadian voters were born. Lewis is a caretaker leader; he would not have run if party vice-president Charles Taylor had offered himself; he will step down as soon as a suitable replacement can be found. As a caretaker, he is more than adequate; as a real alternative to the present Prime Minister, he is hard to take seriously.

Robert Stanfield has a different flaw. Sweet reasonableness is his strong suit, and unfortunately sweet reasonableness is not always necessary or even useful to an opposition leader. When Stanfield became Conservative leader in September 1968, he looked a very plausible prime minister indeed, cool, tough, intelligent. He had a dry humour, a quiet self-assurance that was an immense relief after the struttings and growlings of John Diefenbaker, and even if he was a slow and hesitant speaker, he sounded impressive. As he himself explained, "The way I make a speech, people know I'm not out to impress them, so I must be telling the truth." He refused to be glamourized, or to swallow any of the image-building gimmicks his advisers wanted to thrust on him. "They will accept me as I am," he said, "or not at all."

In short, he still looks a plausible prime minister. But he lacks that cutting edge, the instinct for the jugular and the passion for power that go with the job. It has become conventional wisdom to say that Stanfield was eclipsed by the arrival of Trudeau on the Canadian political scene, but there is more to it than that. Stanfield made his first monumental blunder (and it was, characteristically, a blunder born of innate decency and a sense of responsibility) long before Trudeau became Liberal leader.

On February 19, 1968, three days before Trudeau entered the leadership race, the Liberal government stubbed its toe. In the House of Commons, Finance Minister Mitchell Sharp's budget resolutions were up for debate, but many Liberal MPs were away — among them, a clutch of leadership candidates beating the bushes for delegate support, and Prime Minister Pearson himself, taking the sun in Jamaica. During the late afternoon an important section of the bill carried on a voice vote by the narrow margin of sixty-five to sixty-two. That should have been a danger signal, but it was ignored by the party leaders, including Sharp. That evening, at 8:10 p.m., when Deputy Speaker Herman Batten called out, "When shall the said bill be read a third time?" a few Liberals called out "At the next sitting" — which was in accord with normal practice, since bills do not usually pass more than one stage at a sitting. But Batten did not hear them, assumed the government was ready to go ahead, and called for third reading at once. The House was committed to a vote, which the government could easily lose. The division bells were kept ringing for seventy-eight minutes while the government whips, now frantically aware of the danger, tried to round up members. (A couple were rounded up in a bar and taken, willing but comatose, to the House.) With forty-eight Liberals absent and the opposition voting *en bloc* against a tax hike, the government was defeated, eighty-four to eighty-two.

The elated opposition contended that defeat on a major money measure could mean only one thing — an immediate election. Prime Minister Pearson cut short his vacation at once and flew back to Ottawa, where he asked Stanfield to consent to a twenty-four-hour adjournment. Stanfield agreed. Pearson then went on national television to argue that the vote had been "a mishap of minority government" and did not constitute a true defeat. Stanfield replied that defeat on such a measure was, by definition, a vote of want of confidence in the government, which no longer had the right even to meet the House of Commons, much less lead it.

A number of the more militant Tories refused to attend committee meetings, on the ground that Parliament no longer existed, and Stanfield was pressed either to boycott the House or to blockade any legislation until the government was forced to go to the country. But then the Conservative leader had a private meeting with Bank of Canada Governor Louis Rasminsky. Rasminsky convinced him that the Canadian dollar was under pressure, and that defeat of the budget resolutions, if it stood up, would lead to economic disaster, because international confidence in Canada would be shaken. (This strikes me as an extraordinary argument; foreign financiers are as capable as anyone else of realizing that political scrimmages do not mean Canada is headed straight for hell; but Stanfield was persuaded.) Stanfield also felt, and it was a reasonable position to take, that the defeat in the House *was* something of a fluke, and that the nation might not be grateful to the Conservatives for having to face another election—the fourth in six years.

So Stanfield went back to the House and beat his followers into line to follow him there. On February 21, Prime Minister Pearson introduced a motion to the effect that the earlier defeat had not constituted a vote of non-confidence, and that resolution was sustained a week later by a vote of 138 to 119. Stanfield had shown himself to be a reasonable man, but a bad tactician. As it turned out, he did not save the country an election—we got it in the following June, but on the government's terms, with the Liberals sporting a brand new leader instead of being in a state of disarray. All Stanfield had done was to alienate many of his own followers. One Tory MP, who had supported Stanfield in the leadership race, told me bitterly, "Diefenbaker wouldn't have behaved like that. Diefenbaker would have said to hell with the formalities, we've got the bastards on the run; he'd have pushed and pushed until we got an election, and with the Liberals looking so damn stupid, we might have won. Not Bob. Well, I voted for Bob because I thought he was a winner. Hell, he doesn't even *want* to win."

Much of Stanfield's subsequent trouble has stemmed from that early, reasonable decision.

There is a tendency among the public to assume that Trudeau and Stanfield stand, essentially, for the same political approach, and that the choice between them is really one of public personalities, an area where Trudeau has a distinct edge. In fact, although they sounded much alike on many issues during the 1968 election campaign — both were for Motherhood and against Pollution — since that time it has become clear that Stanfield is much more progressive that the Prime Minister. His strategy has been to portray the government as preoccupied with legal and procedural reforms, and to carve out a new area of ideology, concentrating on the social and economic problems of urban Canada. His difficulty has been that his divided party will not follow where he leads. Take, for example, the matter of a guaranteed annual income. Trudeau has consistently blocked any such scheme; the furthest he ever went was a proposal made just before the June 1971 constitutional conference, and later dropped, that the federal government would finance half of such a project for any province foolhardy enough to take it on. Stanfield has been, just as consistently, in favour.

On August 22, 1969, at Kingston, Ontario, he outlined the objectives of a good welfare programme: "First, it must try to see that every Canadian will have the opportunity of a decent standard of living. Second, it must make sure that public welfare funds are not given away to people who don't need help. Third, it must incorporate a system of incentives, a plan that positively encourages a man to get out and work as much as possible."

Points two and three were the conventional bow to Conservative suspicions that most welfare funds are gobbled up by the shiftless, but the first point indicated a guaranteed-income scheme of some sort. Although he cautioned "It is not the final word and it is not the official policy of the party," Stanfield was shifting noticeably left. That same night, in Ottawa, the party's research bureau released a study undertaken at the leader's behest. It outlined a minimum-income plan that would guarantee $2,030 a year for every Canadian family of four. Not much, but a beginning. "A minimum annual income plan," the study said, "cannot be dismissed casually as a nice idea but much too expensive for the present. Debate on minimum annual income plans should not focus solely on cost. Canadians must grapple with the fundamental welfare issues involved and decide whether such a plan represents a significant improvement over our present attempts to assist the poor and underprivileged."

The first party reaction to this proposal came at a Tory policy conference in Niagara Falls, Ontario, in October. The conference brought together 400 delegates, including academics, MPs, party workers and organizers, to advise the national caucus on priorities. Stanfield managed to keep the ticklish question of national unity off the agenda; policy in this area, he told the baffled reporters, was "quite clearly defined" and "a settled matter". But he did not dodge, or seek to dodge, the welfare issue. In this keynote speech he said, "We now know that it costs our economy more to put up with poverty than it would cost to stop poverty. Thus, economics confirm what our sense of decency suggests — we must break the back of poverty and we can."

He was clobbered. Party old-liners like George Hees, the former Trade Minister, wanted to settle the poverty issue by rais-

ing the federal minimum wage and letting it go at that. Daniel
Cappon, a psychiatrist, sneered, "All that money for the poor
would do would be to increase the price of pot." The conference settled for a compromise resolution to provide assistance
for people who were unemployed by reason of age or dis-
abilities, and to provide incentives to get off welfare for the rest.
Stanfield rolled over this flat rejection of his progressive approach and blandly announced that the resolution was a
mandate for the development of a scheme that would "include
provision for the working poor as well as for the non-working
poor".

But the party leader was damaged, and so was the party. He
had not succeeded in establishing himself as its leader. That
became painfully clear in August 1970, when thirty western
Tory MPs gathered in Saskatoon for a bitch-in behind closed
doors. They discussed the party's sinking fortunes in light of
recent Gallup poll figures that showed the Conservatives had
sunk to 27 per cent of popular support, a drop of five percentage
points since the 1968 election. Diefenbaker attended the two-
day meeting, but Stanfield, who was in the west when it began,
was not invited. His subsequent assurances that all was well
had a hollow ring. All was not well. The Tories were not in
much better shape than during earlier party splits in the Diefenbaker years.

Stanfield has been on the defensive during much of the
Trudeau reign, reacting to government moves rather than proposing his own. This is not merely a matter of his own style,
which is low-keyed and loose; it is a reflection of the quality of
his front benches, which are no match, man for man, for the
Liberals opposite. The Tory shadow cabinet, composed of such
luminaries as Wallace Nesbitt, Stan Korchinsky and Angus
MacLean, is more shadow than cabinet, as any visitor to the
House can see at a glance. During debates it is the NDP, led by
David Lewis, Stanley Knowles, Ed Broadbent and Max Salts-
man, that carries the attack. In part, the Tories are victims of
fate; key candidates like E. Davie Fulton, Dalton Camp, Marcel Faribault and Duff Roblin were defeated in 1968, while
some who are no more than an embarrassment to the Tories,
like George Hees, swept noisily back in. Hees, as chairman of
the caucus, lays down the daily approach to Question Period,
and since he himself has difficulty putting a question that is
within the rules of order, the process is not an edifying one.

The outstanding Tory members — men like House Leader Gerald Baldwin and foreign affairs spokesman Gordon Fairweather — are required to carry a load that would normally be shouldered by twenty or thirty members. They cannot do it.

And always, always in the background, is John Diefenbaker. He is a special personage in the House, bossy, cantankerous, witty, sometimes well-nigh incomprehensible, but never dull. When the House breaks up and reporters crowd around the politicians for the statements that will fill their columns and their television cameras, they always, after a ritual word with the party leader, turn to Diefenbaker for a colourful quote. He usually obliges, and the effect is to keep him before the public in constant and often invidious comparison with the titular head of the opposition. Even the Ancient Mariner was able to shake his albatross faster than Stanfield.

All these factors — the splits within the opposition parties, the personal handicaps of the opposition leaders, the weakness of the Conservative front benches — help the government. When a vital issue comes before the House, such as the War Measures Act and its successor, the Public Order Act, the opposition parties do not wheel and fire, they break and run. The vote to approve War Measures was 190 to sixteen. The sixteen opposed were NDP members, but the party was not solid; four members voted with the government. When the Public Order bill was introduced, the NDP voted for a motion to send it to committee, wiping out whatever public kudos the party might have reaped for a stand against it. David Lewis explained, "We wanted to get the matter into committee, because we knew the Public Order bill, however reprehensible, was an improvement over War Measures, and we wanted to get it where we could put amendments to it. Later on, of course, we voted against it when our amendments were not accepted." The logic was flawless but the net effect was to convince most of the public that the NDP simply couldn't make up its mind.

Any government always has at least one enormous advantage over the opposition, in Parliament and in the country as a whole. After all, it is proposing, while the other parties are merely opposing. It is offering the solutions to problems — or, more likely, busily denying that problems exist — and it is left to the others to carp and criticize, often on the basis of incomplete information. With the advent of television, the government lead has lengthened; for every goodie to be dropped into the public craw there is a friendly government spokesman waving his wand at the camera, followed in due course by three opposition spokesmen who have, apparently, nothing good to say about anything.

In all these circumstances, it is inevitable, perhaps, that the Trudeau regime should come off looking so much better than it deserves; but to this equation must be added another factor — the weakness of our national press.

## Note

1. *For a Socialist Ontario in an Independent Socialist Canada*, a pamphlet of the Waffle group, p. 23.

# 13

## The Press:
## The Flattering Friends

*Question:*
*Mr. Trudeau, could you give us a general outline of*
*the matters discussed by Cabinet this morning.*
*The Prime Minister:*
*No.*
Ottawa, July 31, 1968

The Parliamentary Press Gallery is a long, bright room on the
second floor of the House of Commons Centre Block. It's an un-
inspiring place, where solid rows of desks — each wearing a
typewriter and a miscellaneous pile of junk — march beneath
windows that provide an edifying view of the Ottawa River and
the paper mill opposite. At the back of the room is the door to
the Press Gallery lounge, dark, dull, and private, the home of
desultory political discussion and endless games of Hearts. At
the front is a message desk, and the entry to Canada's most-
publicized blind pig, where MPs and reporters may buy drinks,
and often do. Along the wall, between the windows, are por-
traits of former Press Gallery members, sombre, sober-look-
ing men; it's hard to believe so many of them were rogues.

Over this room, most of the time, drifts a constant clatter of
assaulted typewriters, ringing phones, tape-recorders regurgi-
tating interviews, reporters exchanging notes and gossip. You
get the feeling, standing in the welter of sound, that something
important is happening here, which is true, and that Canada's
top newsmen are furiously engaged in their duty as watchdogs
on the government, which is laughable.

More and more, the Press Gallery is becoming the handmaiden of government rather than its critic; more and more, reporters regard themselves as personalities, rather than ferrets; more and more, electronic journalists, whose job is to reduce the most important, complex and difficult story to sixty seconds of tape, are setting the tone, and tough, thoughtful, investigative reporting is disappearing. I was a member of the Press Gallery for more than seven years, and, frankly, we do a lousy job.

When I was posted to Ottawa, one of my first assignments was a profile on Judy LaMarsh, then Minister of Health. I went into Question Period every afternoon to watch her under fire. One day, she was asked a series of biting questions about the proposed — as it then was — Canada Pension Plan; she answered civilly, and at some length. I was surprised, because I had heard that she was normally blunt and aggressive (and so, on many occasions, she was). After Question Period, I wandered back to the Gallery, where my colleagues were discussing her performance. She had been, I learned, snappish, biting, frumpish; what I had deemed to be a full and clear reply to one question was simple sarcasm, a small joke became a shaft of wit. By the time we had finished gossiping, Miss LaMarsh was due for another send-up in the next day's papers, a send-up that had little to do with her actual performance, much to do with our preconceived notions of how she *should* have behaved.

As I say, we do a lousy job.

The job gets lousier, I think. Perhaps that's not quite fair; what I really mean is that, as our politics become more complex, and the task of interpretation more difficult, the gap between what we should be doing and what we actually do widens. We're not necessarily worse at our job, but the job has become more unmanageable and more important, and we have not kept pace, so that what was once merely an inadequate performance has become stunningly bad.

This has become particularly obvious since Trudeau came on the scene. From the first, we followed this man around like so many moon-struck lovers, just as we had, in turn, fallen for John Diefenbaker and Lester Pearson. (Where do people get the notion that reporters are cynical? We're hopeless romantics, always looking for a saviour, often certain we have found him.) We whined after him, strewing his path with adjectives, pouring bile on his enemies and scorn on his competitors. He rejected us, of course; he told us he didn't read our wild ramblings. We loved him for it. We begged him to kick us again, to tell us once more to mind our own damn business. We were sure this was no fly-by-night affair; we were enduringly entranced.

The day Trudeau announced that he was running for the Liberal leadership, he called us all to the conference room in the Norlite Building on Wellington Street, just across the road from Parliament's West Block. We went, eagerly. He told us of his decision, and let us know that we were part of it:

If I try to assess what happened in the past two months, I have a suspicion you people had a lot to do with it. . . . I think it started out like a practical joke on the Liberal Party. I mean that, because, in some sense, the decision that I made this morning and last night is in some ways similar to that I arrived at when I entered the Liberal Party. It seemed to me, reading the press in the early stages a couple of months ago, it seemed to me as though many of you were saying, you know, "We dare the Liberal Party to choose a guy like Trudeau."

We wriggled with joy at that; it was rich. We were so pleased that none of us thought to ask how come, if he had made his decision "this morning", how come aides were even now circulating among us, handing out printed biographies, complete with a picture of the new candidate? How the hell was that little miracle pulled off between the time when Trudeau wrestled his soul to the ground in the Ottawa dawn and we gathered to learn his decision? If Paul Martin had tried that one on us, we'd have hooted him out of the hall; for Trudeau, we were silently content.

The leadership campaign was a joy; we revelled in it. We dashed around the country asking people whom *they* would back for the Liberal leadership, and if they weren't sure, we told them. At the *Star Weekly*, where I was working then, we conducted a coast-to-coast survey for the leadership favourite at Canadian universities. After weeks of research, the survey produced a result any literate Canadian could have predicted without leaving his shower-stall, and we sprang the results, in three massive articles, on a waiting world. On the daily papers, Trudeau-watchers blossomed; as the campaign wore on, his step became springier, his wit wittier, his smile more glowing, his athletic prowess more dazzling. That wasn't him, it was us. He was good copy, and we made him better.

Then it was over and, in Ottawa's Civic Centre, on the afternoon of April 6, 1968, while 8,000 voices assaulted the stale air and placards bannered their banalities over our heads, Trudeau rose in his place to acknowledge the acclaim of his party, his nation — and the press. We were jammed about his box, at his feet, watching his every move, recording his every word, blotting out his privacy and our own critical faculties. Some reporters were shouting as loudly as any Trudeau partisan. I remember, in that swelling crush, a colleague pounding me on the arm. "Jesus Christ!" he said. "Did you ever see anything like this?"

"Yes," I replied, "every time a political party changes leaders."

He eyed me coldly.

"You're a sour bastard," he said.

Perhaps I was, and am, but it seemed to me we were losing our sense of perspective, that knack once referred to by historian Frank Underhill as the capacity to emit a few rousing "Oh yeahs" from the back of the hall, that calculating streak that must be our saving grace. Ever since the Great Pipeline Debate of 1956, when the Press Gallery mingled joyously and openly into politics, when journalists took sides — and rightly so — against a government swollen with arrogance, we had been longing to play once more the role of shapers, rather than reporters, of history. The Pipeline Debate was our finest hour; we never forgot it; we always wanted to go back to that feeling of excitement, of being at the centre, of making things happen. Trudeau gave us that chance, and we took it. When he won the leadership, we told ourselves that we had made him. Later we denied this, of course; we said we were only doing our reporting job; but at the time we believed it, and it made us proud. The claim was, to put it gently, piffle. We didn't make Trudeau. Television made him, organization made him, moxie made him, his own particular brand of charisma made him. We only transmitted him; but our belief that we were part of the manufacturing process gave us a warm glow. At the centre of that glow, we were ripe for news management.

News management is as old as politics. It means, in brief, manipulating the media to present the kindest possible description of government. Generally it occurs with the co-operation of the press; reporters are seldom raped — they seduce easily. Cabinet ministers' secrets are safe with them; they can be counted on to sort out what is safe for the people to know, and what should be locked away, what should be trumpeted to the winds, and what should be leaked out, syllable by syllable, in decent discretion. This process suggests a staggering arrogance. When I ask for an appointment with a cabinet minister (or, in vain, as it now happens, with the Prime Minister), he doesn't grant it to *me*; he doesn't really give a damn what I think, but he does care what my readers think. He talks for them, not me. I am in his office on behalf of perhaps two million people, and I have no right, on their behalf, to make a pact to protect him from their legitimate queries.

The Pearson years were marked by heavy-handed news management. When the Prime Minister wanted to try out a design for Canada's new flag, he called a small group of reporters over to 24 Sussex Drive to leak out the news. It was a kite-flying expedition; we were supposed to attribute everything to "a highly placed source". I blabbed, and got in trouble not only with the Prime Minister, which was natural enough, but with my colleagues. But I had made it clear before attending the meeting that I would not regard it as off the record, so I felt no pangs.

When Trudeau swept to power, we all thought that such tricks were at an end. Participatory democracy was in — secret huddles were out; sidewalk debate was in — cabinet leaks were out. (During Pearson's tenure, cabinet leaks got so bad that when the Prime Minister complained about them to his colleagues, the news made the Ottawa evening papers.) We were all going to be on a professional, business-like basis. Oh yeah.

Trudeau was sworn in as Canada's fifteenth Prime Minister on Saturday, April 20, 1968. At first, the handing over of power was to have taken place on April 22, a date that would have allowed Pearson to complete five years in office. But the ceremony was moved up, and the papers carried small stories explaining that the change was made with the knowledge and consent of the retiring Prime Minister. George Bain of *The Globe and Mail* was not satisfied with the official story; he investigated, and printed an item indicating that Pearson had, in fact, been startled and upset when a note informing him of the advanced date was handed to him during a television interview.

The Bain story struck a sour note; it made the hurry-up take-over seem petty. After it appeared, Romeo LeBlanc, Trudeau's press aide, arrived in the Press Gallery lounge to talk about the Prime Minister's travel plans and, as the meeting was breaking up, raised the matter of the change-over. Without ever naming the author, LeBlanc regretted the appearance of the account, and gave us a little "friendly advice" — to ignore it. What was truly sad was that the reporter — still unnamed — could have known the truth by simply checking with LeBlanc, who would have set him straight.

Well sir, that made us all feel pretty good. We all knew who had written the story, and we were all a little jealous of Bain; his goof was a comfort. Later that day, I ran into Bain — who had missed the lounge meeting — and asked him about the incident. In fact, he explained, he *had* checked his story with LeBlanc, as any seasoned reporter would, and LeBlanc had denied its truth. He had then gone back to his sources, verified the story, and decided that LeBlanc either didn't know the real facts or wasn't prepared to admit them. His story was true, and he was going to write it — as he did. In short, his sin was not in neglecting to check his story, but in refusing to believe its denial. No matter, the Gallery believed — still believes — that Bain had been caught in a simple error of fact, because the Prime Minister's press aide, in an off-the-record, not-for-attribution-or-even-checking statement, had told them so.

The very day of the LeBlanc-Bain affair, the Gallery went on to invite more news management. Pearson had been begged by the Gallery executive to attend a farewell dinner with the press, and was asked to make a speech outlining his behind-the-scenes handling of events during his term of office. The invitation specified that the event would be off the record. He was not asked if he wanted it that way; we applied our own gag. That is, a major newsmaker was asked to unburden himself before the nation's top reporters, who would go agreeably deaf, dumb and blind for the occasion. The rationale, apparently, was that this was to be a social occasion; we were just having the PM over to dinner, the way any private person would, and you wouldn't report the dinner conversation of a friend. Nor would you ask a friend to make an hour-long speech at your place. Nor would you consider as "a friend" a man you met only under the most rigid and formal occasions and towards whom your attitude was supposed to be coldly objective. The last time the Gallery had held one of these farewell dinners was to bid a premature adieu to John Diefenbaker in September 1967. He said a number of things at that dinner that subsequently appeared in print (among them, that he wouldn't be running again), and the two reporters responsible were haled before the Gallery executive, rebuked, and suspended for three weeks from their appointed places in Parliament.

Charles Lynch of Southam News Services, one of the chastised reporters at that time, decided to fight the censorship battle early in the Pearson case, and asked for a special meeting of the Gallery to reverse the gag-rule. It took about a week to collect the necessary five signatures to force the meeting, which turned out to be an exercise in futility. Those of us who fought the muzzle (and the debate was, of course, off the record) were listened to fully and fairly, then swamped by a better than three-to-one vote. The Gallery membership, in fact, went further than the executive, and insisted that tickets for the dinner should be sold only to those who would pledge themselves in advance to secrecy. (We weren't to have any repetition of the shameful Diefenbaker affair.) I didn't get to go to the dinner, under the circumstances, and when I asked some of those who did go whether they paid the $15 tab themselves or billed it to their papers, I was told it was none of my damn business. Which is true, I guess, it being a social occasion and all. I hear Pearson made a fine, witty, informative speech, and maybe someday we'll learn what he said.


News management in Canada is not the same as it is in the United States, where correspondents are not merely misled but lied to as a matter of government policy. Arthur Silvester, a Defence Department spokesman in Washington, repeatedly defended the government's right to tell whoppers to the press and people in the name of the national interest; and as I write, the Pentagon is doing its damnedest to make sure the *New York Times* is blocked from printing the truth about the beginnings of U.S. involvement in Vietnam. Our government isn't quite that crude. It is pretty crude, though. Reporters are subject to the continual pressure that they will be denied interviews if they get out of line, and the reporter who can't get the interviews his editor wants will not last long in Ottawa. Crude, too, is the way the Prime Minister throws threats around. It was

Trudeau who, in a Montreal speech in October 1969, told *Radio Canada* (the French-language CBC network) that he would shut it down if it didn't drop its alleged pro-separatist line. It was also Trudeau who informed the English-language CBC that it was overplaying the Cross kidnapping during the early days of that crisis, and who told one of the nation's top political observers that if he began printing cabinet secrets, the RCMP would be called in to investigate, not the reporter, but cabinet ministers who talked out of turn. That kind of blatant interference was fiercely resented when Spiro Agnew tried it in the U.S., but the Canadian press corps is less sensitive. *Radio Canada* went through a convulsive house-cleaning after Trudeau's speech, the English CBC reacted in such panic to his rumblings during the Cross kidnapping that it cancelled a documentary on Lenin, apparently on the grounds that it would fan revolutionary fervour. The political observer, I am happy to say, paid no attention.

Besides hints and threats, Trudeau keeps the press under control by refusing reporters access, wherever possible, to what is going on. Christina Newman, in a *Maclean's* article on his May 1971 Russian tour, described the technique:

> Since he took office, Trudeau has attempted rigorously to curb press activities, but his means of achieving news control on this Russian journey were ingenious in the extreme. He, or more particularly his aides in collaboration with the Russian press office, managed to turn the forty-person press corps into two busloads of croaking tourists who caught glimpses of the official party only on occasion. . . . The press was housed in different quarters from the official party, transported in different airplanes as the group junketted around the country, and kept away from official talks and social functions.

It is also part of the Prime Minister's policy not to release the reports of commissions and task forces, paid for by the people of Canada, unless absolutely necessary. The report of the Gray Task Force on Foreign Ownership, already referred to in Chapter 8, is a prime example. The task force wasn't working for Trudeau, but for us; we paid for it, our shrill nationalist cries inspired it, and we have a right to know what it said. We will not know, except in the Prime Minister's good time and in whatever truncated version he chooses to release.

One of the problems in combatting this policy of concealment is the interlocking nature of the Press Gallery. It is not a collection of 140-odd fearless reporters striving to outdo each other, but a society within the government, whose principal occupation appears to be drinking its own bath water.

Like everything else in Ottawa, the Press Gallery has a hierarchy, although its lines are becoming a little confused of late by the rise of the electronic media. The print reporters still hold sway in the matter of status, because they have been around longer; but because they reach fewer people, they are far less influential than their plugged-in brethren.

At the top of the hierarchy are the members of the Toronto *Globe and Mail's* Ottawa bureau, regardless of ability, experience or byline, simply because the *Globe* is the most seriously read newspaper in the nation's capital. Happily, the *Globe* deserves its distinction. The paper's Ottawa columnist, George Bain, probably causes more early-morning dyspepsia than any other man in Canada; he is witty, shrewd, a good reporter who can write, an experienced journalist who manages to use his Ottawa contacts without being used by them — no mean feat. The rest of the *Globe* bureau is also a cut above other bureaus, although its material is so often badly edited, and subject to so many misleading headlines, as to undo much of its good work. Murray Goldblatt, the bureau chief, is one of the best-informed and hardest-working members of the Gallery.

The other large newspaper bureaus, those manned by the Montreal *Star* and *Gazette* and the Toronto *Star* and *Telegram*, are not taken so seriously by the politicians, and therefore rank behind the *Globe* in the Gallery pecking order. Though competently manned, these bureaus are often mis-managed by their home offices. The Toronto *Star* and *Telegram* are particularly bad in this respect; both feel that every major story must carry a staff by-line, which means that bureau members spend most of their time covering debates already adequately reported by Canadian Press, and almost no time digging up original stories. In my years with the *Star Weekly*, then wholly owned by the Toronto *Star*, I watched some of the most gifted reporters I have known turn in mediocre copy week after week on the orders of a memo-prone crew of Toronto editors who never learned that the way to develop a digging reporter is to let him dig. Both the Montreal *Star* and *Gazette* tend to leave their men so long in Ottawa that they become indistinguishable from the surrounding landscape.

The two Ottawa newspapers also mount considerable bureaus on Parliament Hill, but the chief hands — Norman Campbell, Greg Connelly, Dick Jackson, Peter Jackman — have become experts on the trivia of Parliament rather than its significance. The best political reporting in the Ottawa *Citizen*, for example, is always written by its editor, Christopher Young, who seldom appears on the Hill.

Canadian Press covers everything that moves, and much that doesn't, in Parliament, with a large staff distinguished mainly by its capacity to embalm the most momentous development in numbing prose. The outstanding CP reporters — like Dave MacIntosh, who specializes in defence matters — become so entangled in the flatulent phraseology demanded by CP editors that their best stories wind up among the truss ads. Nonetheless, CP staffers have longevity, and tend to occupy many of the top positions on the Press Gallery executive, which brings glory of a sort.

Southam News Services, CP's rival, draws more attention because of the superior writing skill of its members (bureau chief John Walker is usually a pleasure to read) and because of the presence on its roster of one of the Gallery's superstars, Charles Lynch. Lynch is an excellent television moderator, whose weakness as a political reporter helps to underline the difference between the print and electronic media. Lynch is charming, quick, and, as an interviewer, has the happy knack of questioning his subject rather than grilling or haranguing him. Since television is primarily an entertainment medium, in which only small bits of information can be conveyed at any one time, he is ideally suited to the camera. He is not, however, much of an investigator, and has no political philosophy to buttress his observations; his most memorable columns often turn out to be about "Momma" — his charming wife — their children, dogs and horses, or about Lynch's adventures as a harmonica player, all subjects that appear to stir him more than, say, the plight of the farmer. To Lynch, politics is a series of anecdotes told about friends. He is, nonetheless, much ad-

mired, and his conservative judgements are slavishly aped by
his fellows.

Another name to be reckoned with, although he is not nearly as admired, is the *Telegram's* Douglas Fisher. Fisher's success, as I see it, comes not so much from his shrewd analyses (as a former MP and major figure in the CCF, he knows much more than most of us about how politics work), as from the refreshing fact that he has something to say and says it well. Most of the Gallery rejoices in the notion of "objectivity", which comes down, in the main, to covering all contacts or possible future contacts with fulsome praise, and not overturning any unpleasant-looking rocks. Fisher, because his politics are clearly identified, writes with much more freedom than his colleagues, and the *Tely* balances him off on its political pages with Lubor J. Zink, the Press Gallery's only radical. I find it fascinating that the Gallery's one radical should be on the right wing (Fisher is no further left than many Liberals), but Zink's wild outbursts at anything he conceives to be a piece of communist-inspired skullduggery (and that turns out to cover an amazing range) make him at least an original commentator.

The same cannot be said for most of the rest of the Gallery, which seems to be divided between time-servers on their way down and nonentities who may, or may not be, on their way up. Many Press Gallery members do nothing but ape their brethren; one writer from western Canada spends most of his time re-writing *Globe* stories from the early edition to file to his paper, another from eastern Canada covered the entire 1968 election from Ottawa, re-writing CP stories and appending faraway datelines. There is also a good deal of cross-interviewing; after Question Period, to save all the bother of having to round up outside opinion on the day's activities, the reporters question each other. I was fascinated and flattered the first time I turned up in a story as "Parliament Hill observers say. . . .", and the quibble that I didn't know one damn thing about the subject under discussion (children's allowances) struck me as not worth raising. Some of these time-servers, by dint of many years on the job, attain a certain status in Ottawa; they work hard at it, attending all the right functions, buttering up the right contacts and never, by word or deed, compromising their right to conceal information from the world. Early in my Press Gallery career, I wrote a story indicating that one of Prime Minister Pearson's aides was receiving income from an outside source. I thought I had scooped my colleagues; not at all, they had known about this unwise arrangement for two years, but had concealed it. I was in disfavour again for blabbing.

The temptation to become a government spokesman is almost overwhelming for anyone who stays in Ottawa too long; the friendly phone call from a cabinet minister, the quiet corridor chat, the dropping of pearls of wisdom for your ear alone, are not to be lightly by-passed. Even very good reporters need to be wary: Anthony Westell, formerly of the *Globe*, later of the Toronto *Star*, and one of the coolest minds in the Gallery, wrote an astonishing column on Gérard Pelletier's self-serving book on the War Measures Act, *La Crise d'octobre*, which began with a spirited defence of the book and ended with the admission that Westell had not, in fact, read the work yet.

Not only do certain reporters become favourites, so do certain publications. I noticed this when I moved from the *Star Weekly*, a non-favoured publication, to *Maclean's*, and was suddenly treated with new respect not only by the politicians but by my colleagues. I was basking in the reputation of my predecessor, the late Blair Fraser. At first I received telephone calls from high places and invitations to intimate meetings with senators, diplomats and other lofty persons. Then I began to get telephone calls from the External Affairs Department asking me to squire foreign visitors around. That ended when I refused point-blank to entertain an Egyptian publisher, who was going on, the nice lady told me on the telephone, to Toronto, where he would be meeting *my* publisher. I said that whatever my sins, I was not a dating service for External. Soon I was again being treated with the bare civility that had been my lot at the *Star Weekly*.

*Time* magazine has always had a special status in Ottawa, in part because of the excellence of its reporters. (The *Time* Ottawa bureau is manned by uniformly competent reporters whose copy appears in the magazine as uniformly bad; the secret is that their stories are so doctored by editors as to be virtually unrecognizable. When Courtney Tower, now a special assistant to Robert Andras, was a *Time* reporter, he filed an excellent report on the CBC that was turned into a Timese story that began by locating CBC headquarters on the wrong side of Ottawa, a slip that somehow spoiled the authoritative ring of all that followed.) But *Time's* status results mainly from the frenetic lobbying techniques employed by the magazine. The politician who is kind to *Time* "strides" into rooms; he who offends "slouches". *Time* reporter Martin Sullivan carried the technique to its ultimate in his book on Trudeau, *Mandate '68*, which noted, in conformity with the nice-guy image being pedalled, that Trudeau's strongest swear-word "is a British 'bloody' ". Of course, this was before the Prime Minister had publicly invited unemployed postal truck drivers to "eat shit" on Parliament Hill, or emitted his famous "fuddle duddle". Why Sullivan felt it necessary to make his hero clean of tongue I do not know; I suspect it was the sheer reflex action of a *Time* staffer. I discovered some of the *cachet* of *Time* when, after I had been refused an interview with the Prime Minister on several occasions, on the ground that he was too busy to grant individual interviews, *Time* appointed a new Ottawa bureau chief — Dick Duncan, an excellent journalist — who was at once accorded the interview I sought.

Television journalists face the same ranking system as print journalists, but experience the additional complication of being regarded as second-class citizens by most of their Press Gallery colleagues, yet fawned on by most of the politicians. They must find it confusing. A print journalist knows, or soon learns, that the television man need not be much of a reporter, and often isn't. His task is to ask a few superficial questions of politicians who are just dying to answer. There is no time in TV newscasting for detailed analysis; you get less information in a fifteen-minute broadcast than you will pick up reading the first paragraph on the main stories in a daily newspaper. The broadcaster is, therefore, not so much a reporter as a performer; he doesn't have to *be* authoritative, only to *look* authoritative. What is important is getting in fast, getting your questions asked and getting out again. It is also important to stay on the right side of politicians — particularly members of the government — so that permission to ask questions will be granted. The politician who refuses a print reporter's queries will often rue the day; the reporter can get what he needs elsewhere and use it to lambaste the politician; for television, the rules are reversed; the producer doesn't want the reporter's face on his screen all the time, he wants the politician's, especially the Prime Minister's. TV reporters soon learn to ask only obvious questions, and the reporter who transcends the temptation to butter up politicians — two I can think of are Tim Ralfe of the CBC and Peter Reilly of CJOH in Ottawa — is a valuable exception indeed.

CBC reporters are a special case; their prestige is high, in one sense, because their audience is large and immediate. One of the most entertaining sights on Parliament Hill is to watch a print reporter dogging the CBC camera around so that, when the lights go on, the print man can manoeuvre behind the subject into camera range and show the folks back home, including his editor, that he is in the thick of things. At the same time, CBC's official brand of neutrality comes out, in the main, as pro-government propaganda, so there is a certain disdain felt for its practitioners in the Gallery, however well-known they become. Ron Collister, one of the more able members of the Ottawa bureau, has a tendency to use coloured words likely to tickle the ruling powers. In his comments on the June 1971 budget — the so-called tax-reform budget — he referred to the original Carter proposals as "puritanical", presumably on the theory that anyone who expected equity in taxation must be a fanatic, and Benson's eventual mish-mash as "almost human". Both descriptions were dumb but friendly, a comment that applies to all too much of CBC's parliamentary coverage. The Prime Minister has the network so cowed that on his Russian trip he was giving the cameramen orders as to what kind of backgrounds he wanted to be shot against — and they were accepting them.

One reason — apart from craven fear — that the Prime Minister gets such a sympathetic hearing in the press is that he is so easy to cover. People want to read about Trudeau, where he goes, how he looks. A major part of any parliamentary reporter's job has become Trudeau-watching, and that is a great deal easier than, say, covering meetings of the External Affairs committee, or ploughing through the Department of Agriculture estimates in search of chicanery. Trudeau's approach to most subjects is simple, clear, and rationally argued; when he has something to say, he blurts it right out, even if it is as brutally unfair as his question to western farmers, "Why should I sell your wheat?"

In short, he makes good copy, and this, as much as anything else, explains the personality cult that the media are said to have built up around him. We need to be a little wary of the "personality cult" label; often it is nothing more than the complaint of a party stuck with a bum candidate about the sympathetic coverage given to a good candidate. Personalities are important in politics. A Liberal government headed by Pierre Trudeau is, as we have seen, quite different from the same collection of men led by Lester Pearson; the Tories under John Diefenbaker were not what they are under Robert Stanfield; had James Laxer beaten David Lewis for the NDP leadership, that party would be radically different in aim and style. Reporters concentrate on the personal traits of leaders not only because they are interesting to readers, but because they are important clues to policy. (Where the hell were reporters in the good old days when Mackenzie King was consorting with spirits about important policy matters? We had a right to know about that.) However, the line between what is legitimate interest and what is illegitimate puffery is not an easy one to draw. When Trudeau married Margaret Sinclair, that was a major story, and quite properly appeared as such in the nation's press. Later, however, when the newlyweds had settled down and the Prime Minister had announced, firmly, that his wife would have no part in his political life, we might have been spared all the glamourizing prose about her. Gushing headlines from Russia — "They're In Love!" — or from Toronto — where she flew in unannounced to a dance to give her husband a loving kiss while the cameras clicked — were not only overdone, but a little sickening.

So let us say, as a working rule, that coverage of the important elements of a leader's personality is relevant and necessary, while endless dwelling on trivia makes for a personality cult. Under this definition, there can be no doubt that coverage of Trudeau has been of the personality-cult variety. Schoolchildren who don't know what the British North America Act is know that he wears a flower in his buttonhole; his sandals are more famous than his opinion of Parliament; and housewives whose grasp of regional disparity is minimal know where his wife buys her clothes, and how much she pays.

The Prime Minister has always complained about the invasion of his privacy, but he has always made shrewd use of opportunities to further his swinging image. Sometimes his attempts fall flat — in Russia, when he leapt onto an anti-aircraft gun at a war memorial and pretended to fire it, he was greeted with the stony silence he so richly deserved — but more often his peacock displays are put down to boyish high spirits, and win applause.

Covering such stuntsmanship presents the reporter with a dilemma; if the Prime Minister leaps onto a motorcycle and begins tooling around the official party — as he did in Russia — that is obviously of interest, and bound to be reported. But the air of awestruck joy such occasions promote baffles me. In a radio broadcast, Ab Douglas, the CBC's Moscow correspondent, mentioned with obvious approval how Trudeau's performance had unsettled the Russian security guards. Well, why wouldn't it? Who the hell would expect a presumably grown man on a presumably important foreign mission to hurl himself onto a motorcycle and take off like a drag racer? When President Lyndon Johnson behaved childishly, he was treated with thinly-veiled contempt by the U.S. press corps; the day our press corps follows suit, the Prime Ministerial stunts will cease.

Those stunts are usually performed for the benefit of television, the medium Trudeau understands and uses best. As a nation, we have been incredibly slow to adapt to television, and the Press Gallery has been at least as slow as the general public. We print reporters have fought against it, cursed its coiling cords, damned its reporters and cheered the steps that have so far blocked it from its rightful place in the House of Commons. That damned usurper, television. Well, television is here to stay, has been here for decades. Most people get their first, often their only, information about political affairs from the television screen. What that means, as things now stand, is that they get Trudeau. Not only do they get Trudeau, they get him under the conditions he selects, on the subjects he cares to talk about, and nothing more. The Question Period, which should be a harrowing time for the government, has lost most of its meaning because television isn't there. Instead, when Question Period ends, the Prime Minister files out into the lobby outside the Commons, and the press closes in. An aide goes to him, tells him what the press wants to ask about, and he says Yes or No. If he says No, that's that, and the issue, however important, will receive routine treatment. If he says Yes, he goes out into the corridor and answers — without the debate he would be subjected to in the House — questions that are a re-run of those he has already faced. What the viewer sees is the Prime

Minister answering, fully and openly, the questions put to him;
what he doesn't see are the issues he declines to discuss, the debates he loses to the opposition, the arrogant shrugs with which he meets so much of the criticism directed at him inside the House.

Even if the Press Gallery were inimical to the Prime Minister — and I'm not suggesting it should be — the influence of television would give him a tremendous advantage in putting his point of view before the public. Even if we were objective, the Prime Minister's importance would be enormously swollen by the fact that television producers and reporters want him on camera, answering their questions, so that he becomes almost the sole government spokesman on key issues. But we are not objective, we are dependent, and we become more so every day.

Part of the reason for this dependence is the dominance, already referred to, of the Supergroup. The reporter who doesn't have at least one contact among the Supergroup is in trouble; he cannot know what is really happening within Ottawa's circles of power. But if the reporter sets forth views or findings that do not coincide with the truth as revealed to the Supergroup, he may not have his contact long. There has always been an uneasy balance for journalists between the need to protect their sources within any government and the duty to pass on essential information to the public. Too often, the scales have come down on the side of withholding information. The late Ralph Allen, editor of *Maclean's* magazine, once remarked that "Some of the best-informed reporters on Parliament Hill are the worst."

In the past, there have always been a number of alleyways to the same information — cabinet ministers, MPs, aides to important ministers, senior bureaucrats. Many of these sources have dried up since Trudeau made it clear that he will not tolerate leaks from cabinet or caucus. At the same time, the decision-making process has drained into fewer and fewer hands; there are fewer people to talk out of turn, and stronger reasons for those few not to do so. The result is that we of the press know a great deal less about what is going on inside our government than we ever did, and what we know we carefully screen before letting it out to the public.

Just in case the press doesn't process its quotient of news carefully enough, Trudeau has now given us Information Canada.

The Ministry of Truth came into being as a result of a task-force study of government information services. In a report published in 1969, the task force argued that the federal government and the people were not coming into meaningful contact, and that more should be done to keep each informed of the tastes and intentions of the other. It was suggested that a co-ordinating body was needed to eliminate much of the duplication among the vast array of government information services. It was felt that people who wanted to find out about their government's activities should be able to do so, easily and quickly. It was argued that a policy of openness should be encouraged, and that recalcitrant bureaucrats should be jiggled, if necessary, to make them cough up information. No one could quarrel with any of that.

But what happened? The task force made seventeen recommendations, and the government acted on all of them but two. One would have set up an Information Ombudsman, who could step between an aggrieved citizen and the government to get information that was being withheld; the other would have established Citizens' Advisory Bureaus, where people could go not merely to get information but to lodge their views and complaints. The government decided we could do without the tools that might have made Information Canada into a two-way street. Knowledge is a double-edged sword, and it seemed wise to sharpen only one edge.

The Ministry of Truth became yet another bureaucracy to co-ordinate all the other information bureaucracies. The departmental information departments have not withered; they prosper; they put forth and multiply, scattering glowing press releases across the fruitful land. According to a government return tabled on February 7, 1971, departmental information staffs more than doubled in the first year of Information Canada's existence, from 900 to 1,992 persons. We haven't saved any money with the Information Canada budget, we have merely spent another $7 million annually to support a propaganda arm of government, an arm whose chief accomplishments to date have been to call meetings without number and to unify the headings on departmental press releases. (Information Canada didn't actually design the new letterheads, but it did oversee the letting of the $24,000 contract.)

We are no closer today than we ever were to finding out what is in the confidential reports prepared for government, for which we pay, and which often affect key spending decisions. (In 1967, Judge Walter Robinson reported on Canada's Air Traffic Control system; he said, in brief, that it was in a dangerous mess. The first volume of his report, which was non-controversial, was released; the second, which attacked the government head-on, was suppressed. It is still suppressed. The government says the major recommendations have been adopted, but we are to take its word for that, and in fact, at least two key recommendations are still in limbo, although we are not supposed to know it.)

Information Canada has not played, and does not intend to play, any role in prying loose these hidden reports. They are, in the view of Robert Stanbury, the Minister responsible, not his concern, although he personally favours the widest possible disclosure. He's not going to fight for it, he just favours it.

It is surely some indication of the role Information Canada is to fill that its first chief, Jean-Louis Gagnon, is not only a personal friend of Trudeau's, but a pillar of the Quebec wing of the federal Liberal party. Gagnon is a first-rate journalist, and an upright man, but his objectivity must be open to question. If, in the Diefenbaker days, the Prime Minister had put up, say, his friend Joel Aldred to head such a body, and then argued that the body was simply a co-ordinating device, snorts of derision would have rolled across the land. On Gagnon's appointment, the issue was raised by the opposition, but never pursued by the press.

To put Information Canada into perspective, it must be viewed in the context of a Press Gallery not notable for its fierceness, a political scene dominated by a single figure, and a government run by a small group bound to secrecy both by its own instincts and the Prime Minister's orders. In such a milieu, an independent information-seeking body might prove useful, but a service that is simply a louder and more elegant horn in the government band must be regarded with grave suspicion.

In short, one reason the Trudeau government has been so well received lies in the fact that we have not been well informed by the press; there is no sign that the performance will get better in the near future.

# 14

## Conclusion:
## Where Have All
## The Flowers Gone?

*What is important about the next federal election is not so much who wins, but how it is won, the degree to which there remains some balance between the political forces in the country, the degree to which government is tempered by the presence of an opposition of quality and united purpose, representing itself as a minority opinion of a national character.*
Dalton Camp, March 12, 1971

I have come to the part in this book which in a magazine article is called the tailpiece. That is where, after tearing someone or something to pieces for a great many columns, the author suddenly puts it all back together again and tells the reader, not just what was done wrong in the past, but what *should* have been done, what he himself would do. With the Trudeau regime, putting it all together is simple enough, and requires no more than a quick glance back through these pages. Such a glance will show that, measured either by his own objectives when he ran for office, or by the standard of accomplishment of his predecessor — no very high mark — Trudeau has not done well. His handling of the economy has been disastrous, and his treatment of Parliament degrading. His record in foreign policy has been patchy, and his defence of the independence of his country has been nonexistent. Such social legislation as has been produced has been grudging and incomplete; he is more conservative than the opposition parties and, I believe, than the nation as a whole. His technique of government-by-confrontation has aggravated the problems of Canadian unity and undone much of the positive effect of legislation to reduce regional disparities. He has not, despite all the fanfare, opened politics to the people; quite the reverse, in fact. His real accomplishments — improvements in Canada's stance on some external-affairs issues, extension of unemployment insurance benefits, a strong push towards bilingualism— have been more than offset by a dangerous re-structuring of government and the concentration of power into fewer and fewer hands.

While it is easy to say what has gone wrong, it is harder to say what I would have done in the Prime Minister's place. Nor is that my task. The music critic who goes to the opera is not expected to sing better than Jan Peerce before he dares criticize him; he is trained to recognize sour notes, not strike sweet ones. For some reason, political critics feel they must go further than music critics and lay down, on the basis of inexperience and incomplete knowledge, a plan for the Almost Perfect State. I have no such plan up my sleeve, but I can say many of the things I would like to see done.

I would like to see Prime Minister Trudeau replaced, Parliament restored, television admitted to the House of Commons. I would like to see Information Canada abolished and the Press Gallery take up its ancient role of comforting the afflicted and afflicting the comfortable. I would like to see strong new social legislation, meaningful tax reform, new and more vigorous policies on housing and urban development. I would like Canada to adopt a much stronger nationalist stance, to end the Defence-Production Sharing Agreement with the U.S., and to tell our good neighbour firmly and forever that we are not interested in continental resource development. I would welcome the disbanding of the Supergroup. I wish an end to the politics of confrontation and a return to civilized bickering between the provinces and Ottawa over the division of power and dollars. I have no very high hope that any of these things will happen.

In the coming election, Trudeau will be re-elected. His action during the Quebec crisis of last October, so unpopular with those of us he calls "bleeding hearts", was immensely popular with a general public more willing than we are to take him at his word. His destruction of the ancient powers of Parliament appears, in many eyes, as simply the updating of a crumbling institution, and every stripe laid on a bureaucrat's back brings him more votes. Curious and sad, but true. His marriage to a delectable and eminently acceptable daughter of a noted Liberal family had just the right combination of romantic dash and pious respectability to enrapture a whole new generation of Canadian females. They are older than the teeny-boppers he once sent shrieking, but they have the vote. (I am not, just to be clear, suggesting that the Prime Minister's marriage had anything to do with politics, but it will certainly help him at the polls.) His non-reform of the taxation system will bring him support not only from the business community, who were terrified of the White Paper (what a relief, when you think you are going to be beaten and robbed, merely to be asked for a capital-gains contribution), but from many in the lower- and middle-income brackets who, dazzled by the higher exemptions and other marginal improvements, fail to see that they are still paying enormously more in taxes than the rich, and that the last chance to bring real reform for at least a decade has been stomped to death by the Prime Minister's advisers.

True, the Prime Minister is in trouble on some fronts. The academics are cooling off on him; those who, like Stephen Clarkson, John Saywell and William Kilbourn, carolled his praises in 1968, have grown either silent or snide. The press, too, is somewhat less slavish in its devotion — even Charles Lynch, who once wrote "That man Trudeau doesn't miss a thing," has been known to raise an occasional quibble. Then, too, some of the Canadians who were hurled out of work during the anti-inflation drive may show pique at election time. But against these negative points must be raised the positive one that, for most Canadians, the Liberals are the only game in town. In 1935 Mackenzie King ran on a platform of "King or Chaos", and Trudeau, who resembles that slippery little autocrat more with every passing day, embodies the same general principle, joined to an immensely greater personal appeal. (George Bain, who has been as consistently critical of Trudeau as any observer in Canada, still describes him as "an immensely attractive political leader".)

So, it seems to me, Trudeau will be re-elected, and the programmes and policies he has installed, from Information Canada to the Supergroup, will remain in place. Accordingly, it would not make much sense to end this book by predicting that

Canadians will rush out and defeat Trudeau at the polls, because that will not happen.

Just the same, it is possible to lean on a government, even this government, without turning it out of office; it is possible to sound warning notes on the major issues by supporting those MPs who, regardless of party, appear to be on the side of the angels, and by punishing those who are not. What follows, then, is a personal guide as to how I would vote to restore some sense of balance to our political system if I were (a) a Liberal, (b) a Conservative, or (c) a New Democrat. (I have tried to imagine myself as a Créditiste, but I can't get either my voice or arms up high enough to make the grade. Sorry.) Because we live in a nation fractionized by geography, the pattern I would follow varies from region to region.

*As a Liberal*, I would back the party candidate only if he were a maverick, or a man thoughtful enough to be a moderating influence in the inner councils (or woman, ladies, or woman; though there will be precious few Liberal women allowed to run in ridings where they have a chance of election). The general, run-of-the-mill, desk-thumping, back-slapping Liberal candidate I would pass on by; he will be just another voice and vote for a government already swollen with power.

In the Atlantic area, unless I happened to live in Allan MacEachen's riding (the thoughtful, moderate Liberal House Leader is not only an immense improvement over Donald Macdonald in that position, but an ornament to any cabinet), I would give serious thought to voting Tory. Stanfield needs all the help he can get, and much of it has to come from the east. If that is too much to ask — Atlantic-area Liberals take their party politics seriously — I would just stay home. That is contrary to everything the civics texts teach, I know, but politicians don't read civics texts, they read riding returns, and a drop in the Liberal vote will receive as much attention as a rise in the Tory one.

In Quebec, a Liberal has little room to manoeuvre; a vote for a Tory or NDP candidate is wasted in most of the province, and for a Liberal, a Créditiste vote is simply bizarre. The choice is between staying home or following the party ticket, but trying to find a candidate who is not simply a member of the claque. The litmus test might be to find anyone whose name sets Jean

Marchand's teeth on edge, but of course such a one may have a tough time getting the nomination. If I lived in Bryce Mac-kasey's Verdun riding, I would vote for him (he is the only member of the Supergroup I would support) because he is, down deep, a reformer, and a necessary voice in the cabinet.

In Ontario, I would give serious thought to jumping the party line and voting NDP, because that party is bound to do well in urban Ontario. The exception would be that if I lived in the riding of one of the young, thoughtful Liberal MPs — Robert Kaplan in Toronto Eglinton, John Roberts in York Simcoe, for instance — I would stay with the party for one more round.

If I lived in western Canada, I would not vote Liberal unless the candidate promised to be a maverick, like Hu Harries in Edmonton-Strathcona, or David Anderson in Esquimalt-Saanich.

Finally, as a Liberal anywhere, I would be much more interested in candidates than parties, and I would resolutely reject the inevitable pleas to vote the party line no matter how I felt on specific issues, because we must not have a minority government. Minority governments have worked well in Canada; they are noisy, but they demand a salutary humility from the governors, and it is simply horsefeathers to say they can't pass legislation. As we saw in Chapter 2, Pearson's minority government did far better, in terms of significant legislation, than Trudeau's majority.

*As a Conservative,* I would devote my energies to rounding up a team of supporters for Robert Stanfield, a man whose chief difficulty is that he is too good for his party. What he needs, since he cannot compete with the Prime Minister on an image-for-image basis (and why should he?), is a group of bright, progressive benchmates to replace the geritol ginger-group he is lumbered with today. If Dalton Camp is serious about the need, expressed at the beginning of this chapter, for a stronger opposition, let him run again, and try to persuade other reform-minded Tories to do likewise.

Anywhere in the Atlantic area I would, as a Conservative, back the party candidate, since that is the one region that Stanfield can claim as a power base. In Quebec, I would be more wary; the election of a bloc of strongly nationalist Quebeckers might do Stanfield more harm than good; they make such easy pot-shots for the Prime Minister on the unity issue. The wise course for a Quebec Conservative is to find a pro-Stanfield candidate to back — one possibility is Heward

Grafftey, the former member for Brome-Missisquoi, (the riding is now called, simply, Missisquoi, and held by a Liberal), and an ornament to the House — or to sit this one out.

Ontario Tories should concentrate on improving the quality of candidates offered, since the party has a good chance to pick up seats on the basis of urban discontent. Longevity is not the only requirement for political office, and so, as a conscientious Conservative, I would work against the re-nomination of some of the sitting candidates, notably George Hees in Prince Edward-Hastings, Waldo Monteith in Perth, Wallace Nesbitt in Oxford, Douglas Alkenbrack in Frontenac, Lennox and Addington, Harold Danforth in Kent-Essex and Lee Grills in Hastings. In a few ridings, I would back the party choice cheerfully — Lincoln Alexander in Hamilton West, Gordon Aiken in Parry Sound-Muskoka, Alfred Hales in Wellington. In new nominees I would be looking for the two qualities now most lacking in the party, loyalty to Stanfield, and vigour.

In western Canada, I would cast my vote resolutely against the caucus cowboys whose presence is so damaging to Stanfield, starting with Jack Horner in Crowfoot and finishing — regretfully, but firmly — with John Diefenbaker in Prince Albert. I would cross party lines, if necessary, to get rid of the rebels; a Liberal in, say, Crowfoot, would strike me as preferable to a Tory maverick. (To those who quibble that I am urging loyalty on the Tories and disloyalty on the Liberals I can only respond that I am after equity, not consistency.)

In British Columbia, unless E. Davie Fulton runs again, I would seriously consider jumping the party to back an independent Liberal like David Anderson, or the NDP — unless, of course, my party rounded up some plausible candidate who looked capable of breaking the NDP-Liberal stranglehold on the province.

*As a New Democrat*, I would be heavily influenced by where I lived. In the Atlantic region, an NDP vote is, in most ridings, simply a wasted vote (again, I know the civics texts say there is no such thing, but we're not writing an exam, we're picking a Parliament), so I would look around for a good Tory, like James McGrath in St. John's East or Gordon Fairweather in Fundy-Royal. In Quebec, I would either sit this one out or back a reform-minded Liberal, if any such get through the nomination screening process. In Ontario, I would vote the straight party ticket; the NDP could pick up as many as twenty seats in dis-

contented Ontario, enough to make a really impressive opposition block. If I lived on the Prairies, I would pick my candidate
by name and outlook, not party; where my party had a good
chance, I would vote for it, but in close Liberal-Conservative
contests, I would vote Liberal if it meant knocking off a yahoo,
Tory if it meant strengthening Stanfield. On the west coast, I
would again vote the party ticket, for the British Columbia
NDP is a strong and growing force for reform.

All the choices I have outlined are stop-gap votes, based on the
assumption that Trudeau is going to win again, and that the
real task, even for loyal Liberals, is to provide a strong opposition. All my choices are also, one way or another, anti-Trudeau
votes, and I make no apology for that. The Canadian political
system is badly out of balance; we are dangerously close to becoming a one-party state. The Liberals have been in power for
fifty out of the last seventy-one years, thirty out of the last
thirty-six years, usually by substantial majorities, and their
grip is as firm today as it has ever been. The results are devas-
tating for a political system built on the premise that control
will change hands from time to time. For one thing, the civil
service comes to regard anything but a Liberal administration
as an aberration, to be lived down, not with; for another, gifted
men who wish to enter politics almost inevitably gravitate to
the Liberal party and soon disappear, together with whatever
advanced ideas they may have held, into its all-engulfing maw.
Trudeau's own political career is a case in point; he backed the
NDP right up until the point when he wanted to get something
done, then joined the Liberals and took on a protective conservative colouration. In turn, his presence in the party attracted other able politicians who have become devoted, not to
promoting the reforms promised when they entered the fray,
but to keeping the party in power. The process grows by what it
feeds on: the longer the Liberals hold sway, the more powerful
the Prime Minister becomes; the more powerful he becomes,
the easier it is for him to control the political scene.

Among the first priorities for Canada, therefore, must come
the curbing of the Prime Minister's power through an electoral
rebuke; even if he is not defeated, a decline in the Liberal vote
and the election of a vigorous, numerous opposition will help to
crack the smug circle into which Canada has been driven. Unless that happens, the nation faces the prospect of another full

term of shrugs and smiles, of arrogance and autocracy, of a heartless, bloodless, cold administration that lacks even the self-claimed virtue of efficiency, and that threatens to twist the Canadian political system so out of shape that it may never be restored.

# Index